FEYNMAN

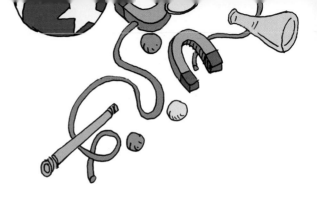

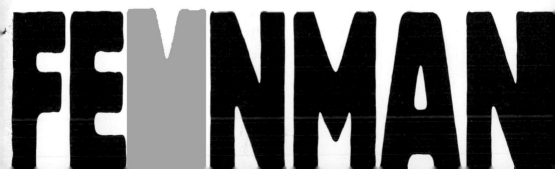

FEYNMAN

WRITTEN BY
JIM OTTAVIANI

ART BY
LELAND MYRICK

COLORING BY
HILARY SYCAMORE

:01

First Second

NEW YORK & LONDON

First Second

New York & London
www.firstsecondbooks.com

Text copyright © 2011 by Jim Ottaviani
Illustrations copyright © 2011 by Leland Myrick

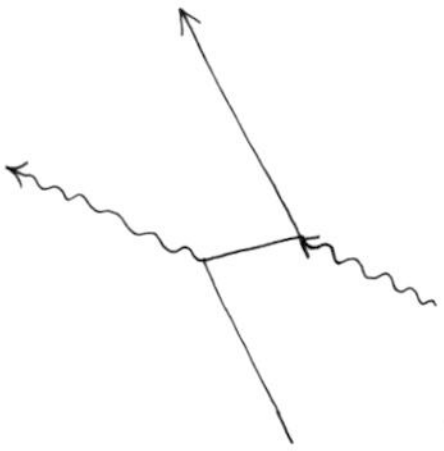

Published by First Second
First Second is an imprint of Roaring Brook Press,
a division of Holtzbrinck Publishing Holdings Limited Partnership
175 Fifth Avenue, New York, New York 10010
All rights reserved

Distributed in the United Kingdom by Macmillan Children's Books,
a division of Pan Macmillan.

Cataloging-in-Publication Data is on file with the Library of Congress
ISBN: 978-1-59643-259-8

First Second books are available for special promotions and premiums.
For details, contact: Director of Special Markets, Holtzbrinck Publishers.

Coloring by Hilary Sycamore and Sky Blue Ink with assistance from Marion Vitus

Book design by Marion Vitus
Printed in the United States of America

FIRST
EDITION

First Edition 2011

BY ART
WE LIVE

3 5 7 9 8 6 4

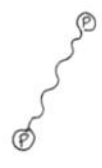

THANKS TO CARL FEYNMAN, MICHELLE FEYNMAN, AND RALPH LEIGHTON FOR THEIR GENEROSITY OVER THE YEARS. AND IF THE LAWS OF PHYSICS ALLOWED, I'D GO BACK TO THANK WHOEVER IT WAS THAT FIRST SHOWED ME "SURELY YOU'RE JOKING, MR. FEYNMAN!"
THEN I WOULD READ IT AGAIN, FOR THE FIRST TIME.
—J.O.

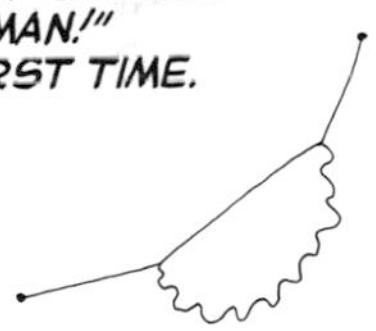

FOR MARIA.
—L.M.

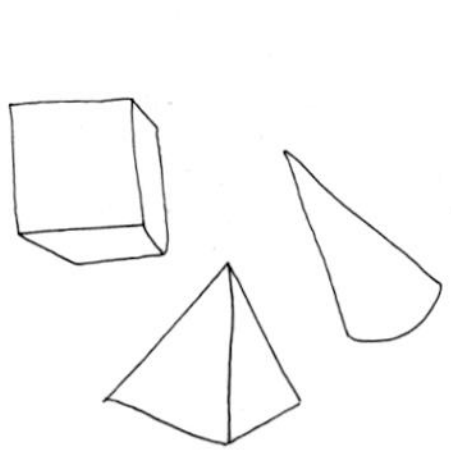

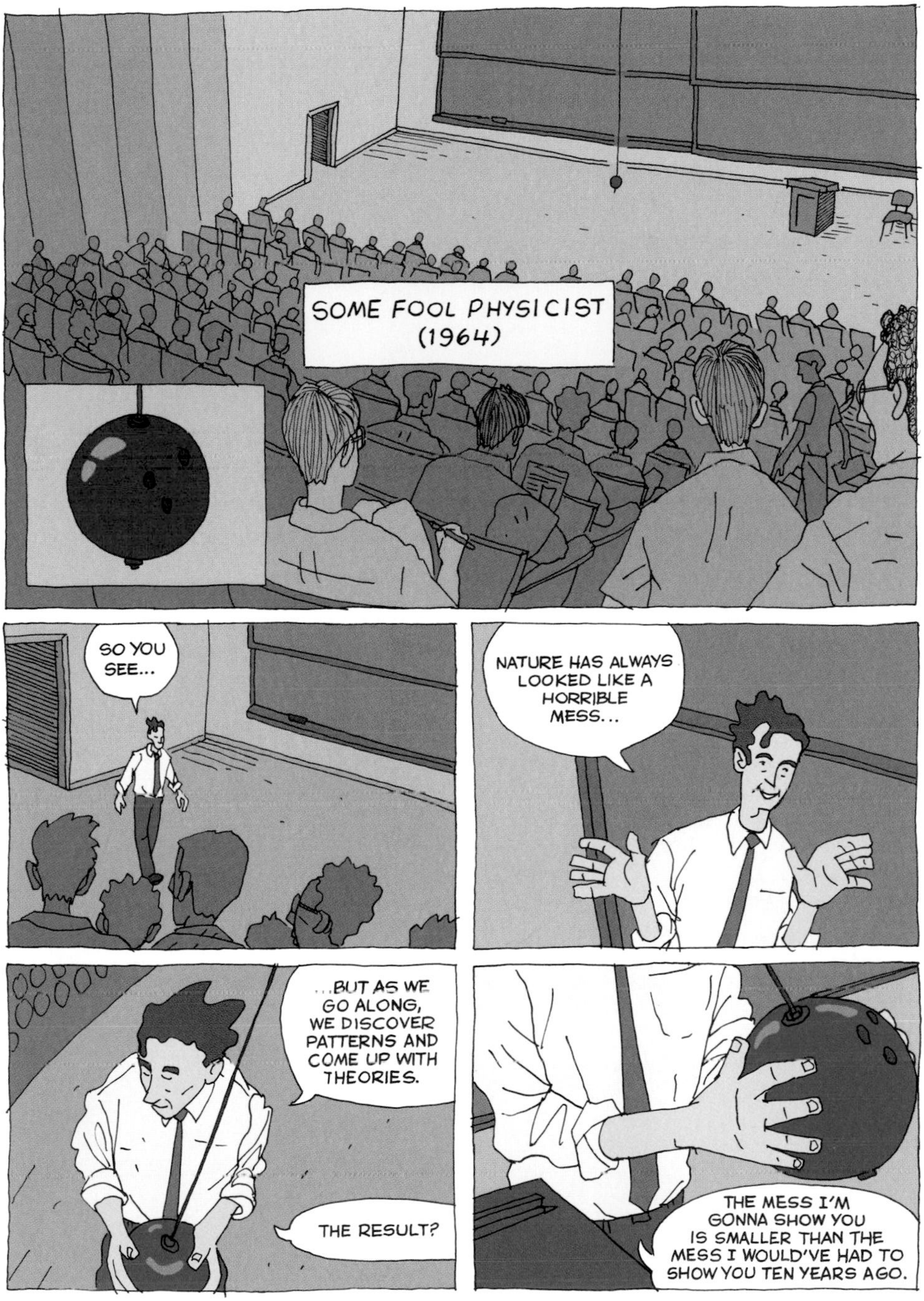
SOME FOOL PHYSICIST (1964)
SO YOU SEE...
NATURE HAS ALWAYS LOOKED LIKE A HORRIBLE MESS...
...BUT AS WE GO ALONG, WE DISCOVER PATTERNS AND COME UP WITH THEORIES.
THE RESULT?
THE MESS I'M GONNA SHOW YOU IS SMALLER THAN THE MESS I WOULD'VE HAD TO SHOW YOU TEN YEARS AGO.

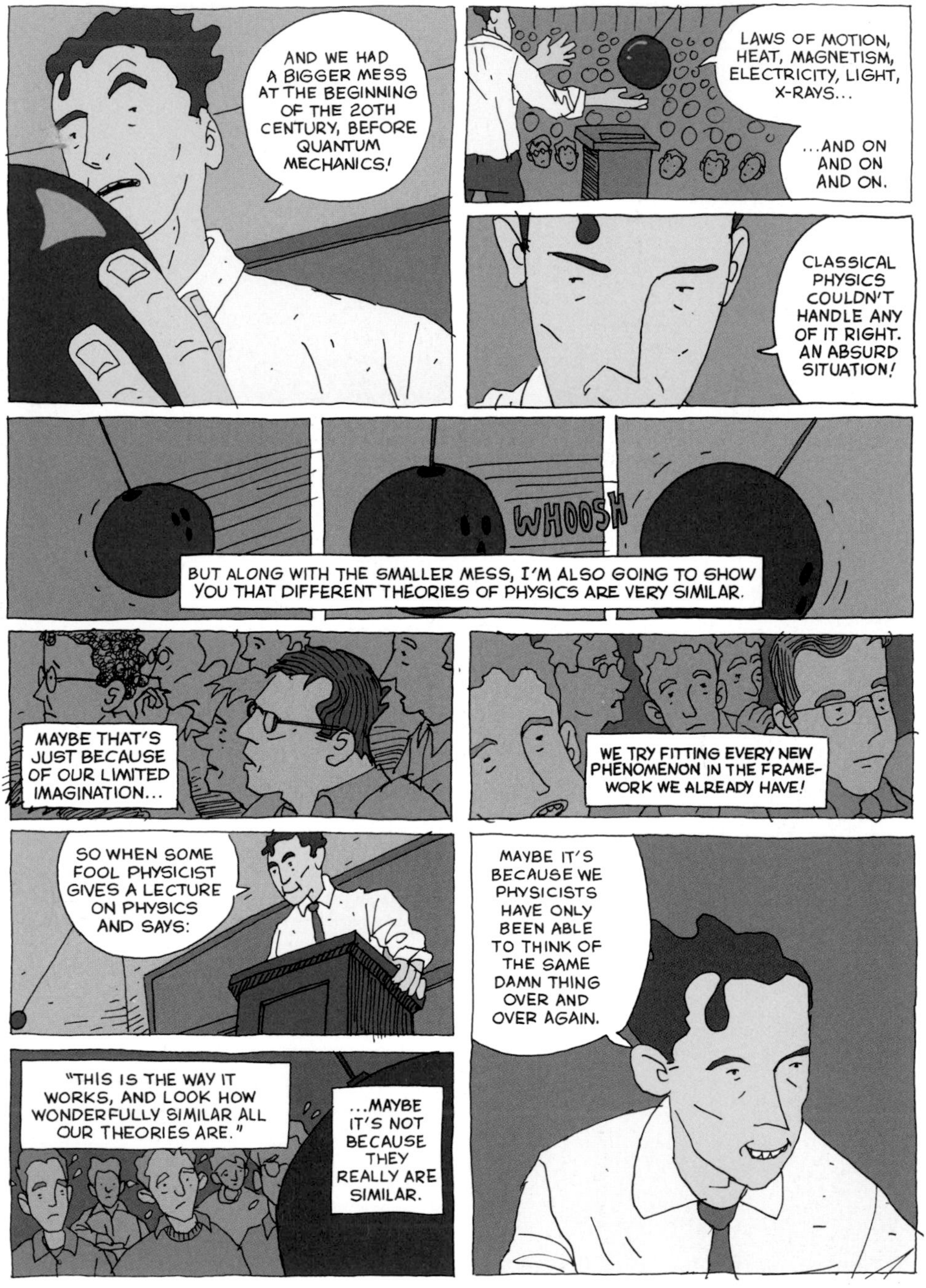
AND WE HAD A BIGGER MESS AT THE BEGINNING OF THE 20TH CENTURY, BEFORE QUANTUM MECHANICS!
LAWS OF MOTION, HEAT, MAGNETISM, ELECTRICITY, LIGHT, X-RAYS...
...AND ON AND ON AND ON.
CLASSICAL PHYSICS COULDN'T HANDLE ANY OF IT RIGHT. AN ABSURD SITUATION!
WHOOSH
BUT ALONG WITH THE SMALLER MESS, I'M ALSO GOING TO SHOW YOU THAT DIFFERENT THEORIES OF PHYSICS ARE VERY SIMILAR.
MAYBE THAT'S JUST BECAUSE OF OUR LIMITED IMAGINATION...
WE TRY FITTING EVERY NEW PHENOMENON IN THE FRAME-WORK WE ALREADY HAVE!
SO WHEN SOME FOOL PHYSICIST GIVES A LECTURE ON PHYSICS AND SAYS:
"THIS IS THE WAY IT WORKS, AND LOOK HOW WONDERFULLY SIMILAR ALL OUR THEORIES ARE."
...MAYBE IT'S NOT BECAUSE THEY REALLY ARE SIMILAR.
MAYBE IT'S BECAUSE WE PHYSICISTS HAVE ONLY BEEN ABLE TO THINK OF THE SAME DAMN THING OVER AND OVER AGAIN.

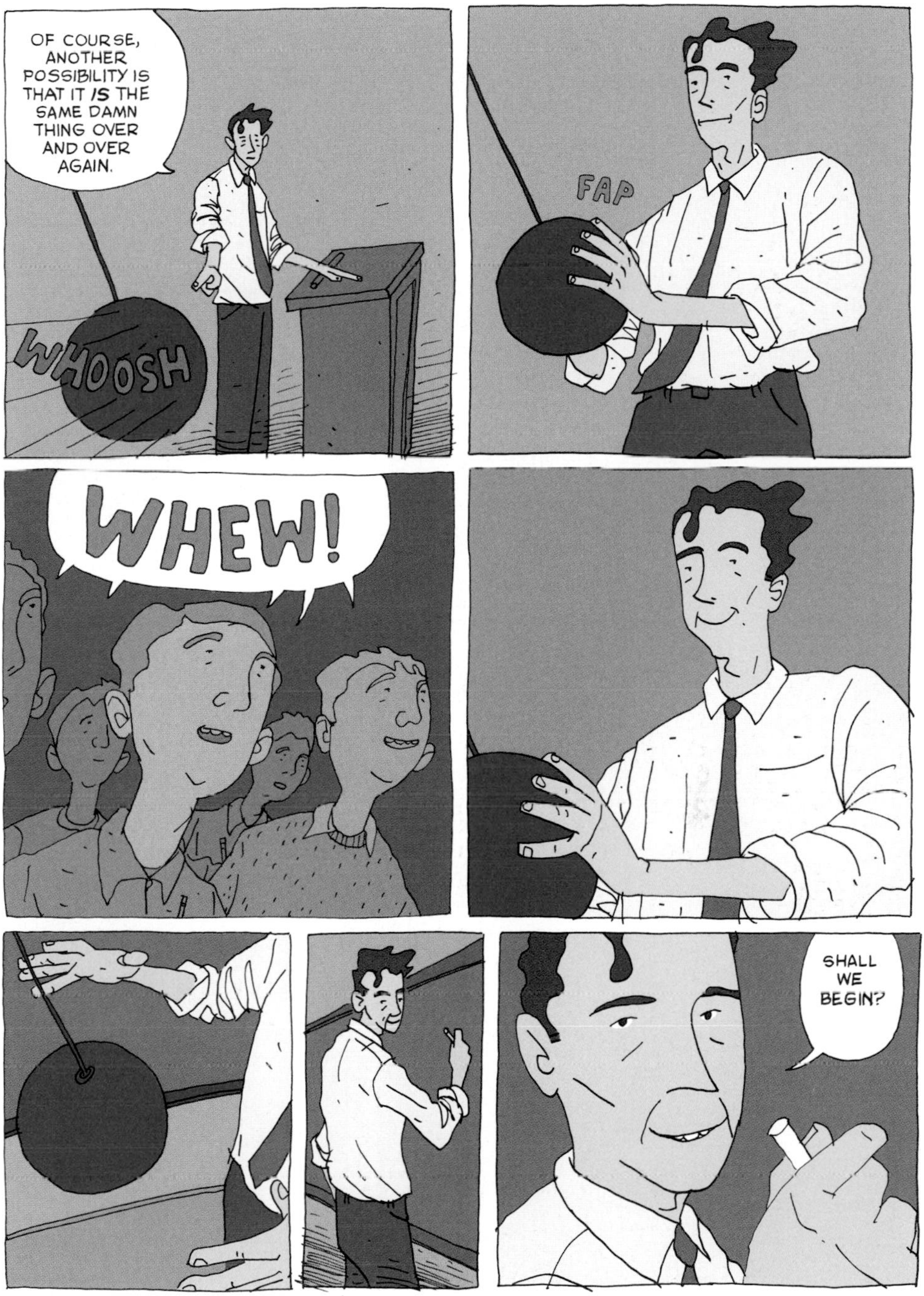

OF COURSE, ANOTHER POSSIBILITY IS THAT IT ***IS*** THE SAME DAMN THING OVER AND OVER AGAIN.
WHOOSH
FAP
WHEW!
SHALL WE BEGIN?

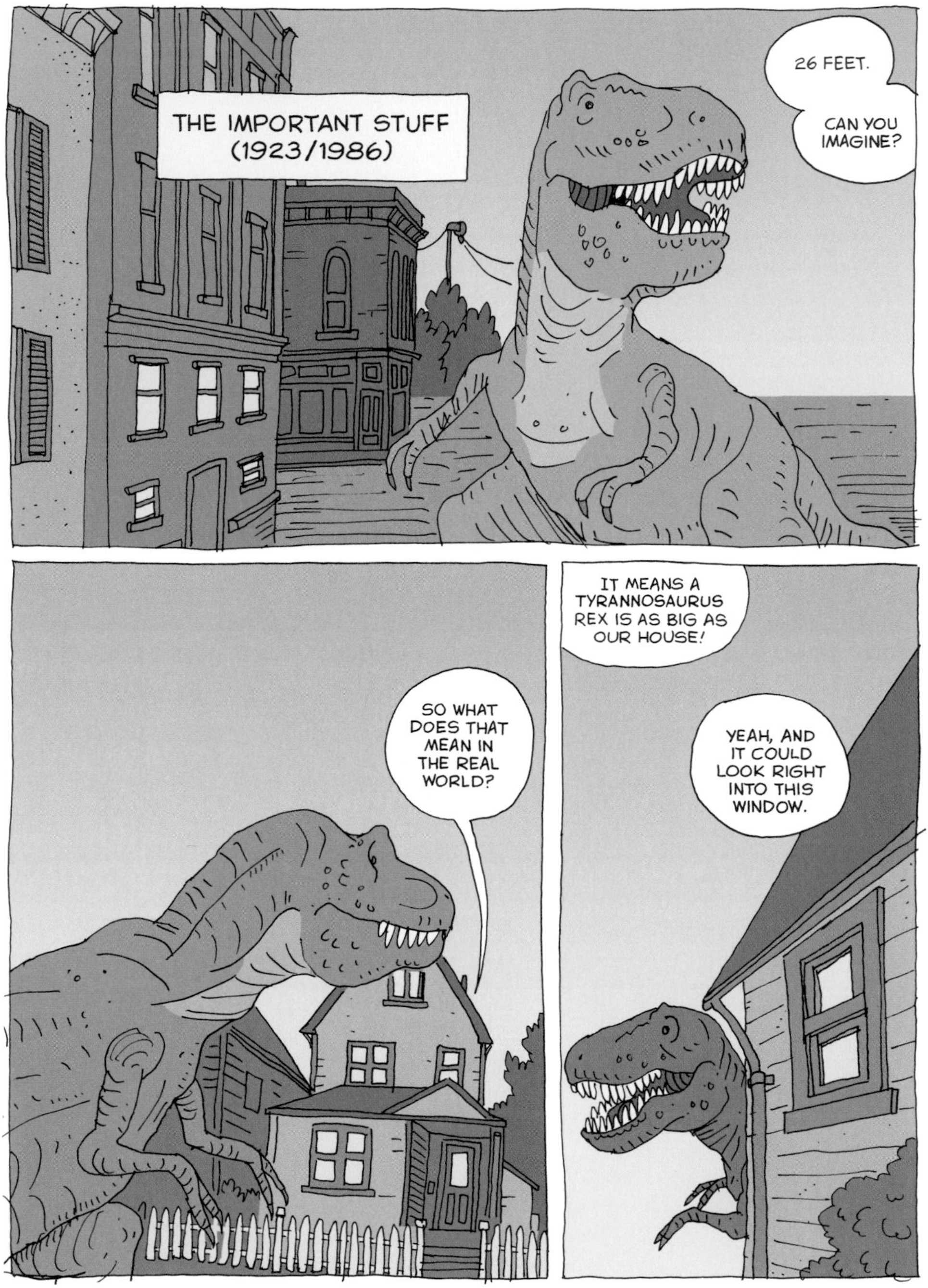
THE IMPORTANT STUFF (1923/1986)
26 FEET.
CAN YOU IMAGINE?
SO WHAT DOES THAT MEAN IN THE REAL WORLD?
IT MEANS A TYRANNOSAURUS REX IS AS BIG AS OUR HOUSE!
YEAH, AND IT COULD LOOK RIGHT INTO THIS WINDOW.

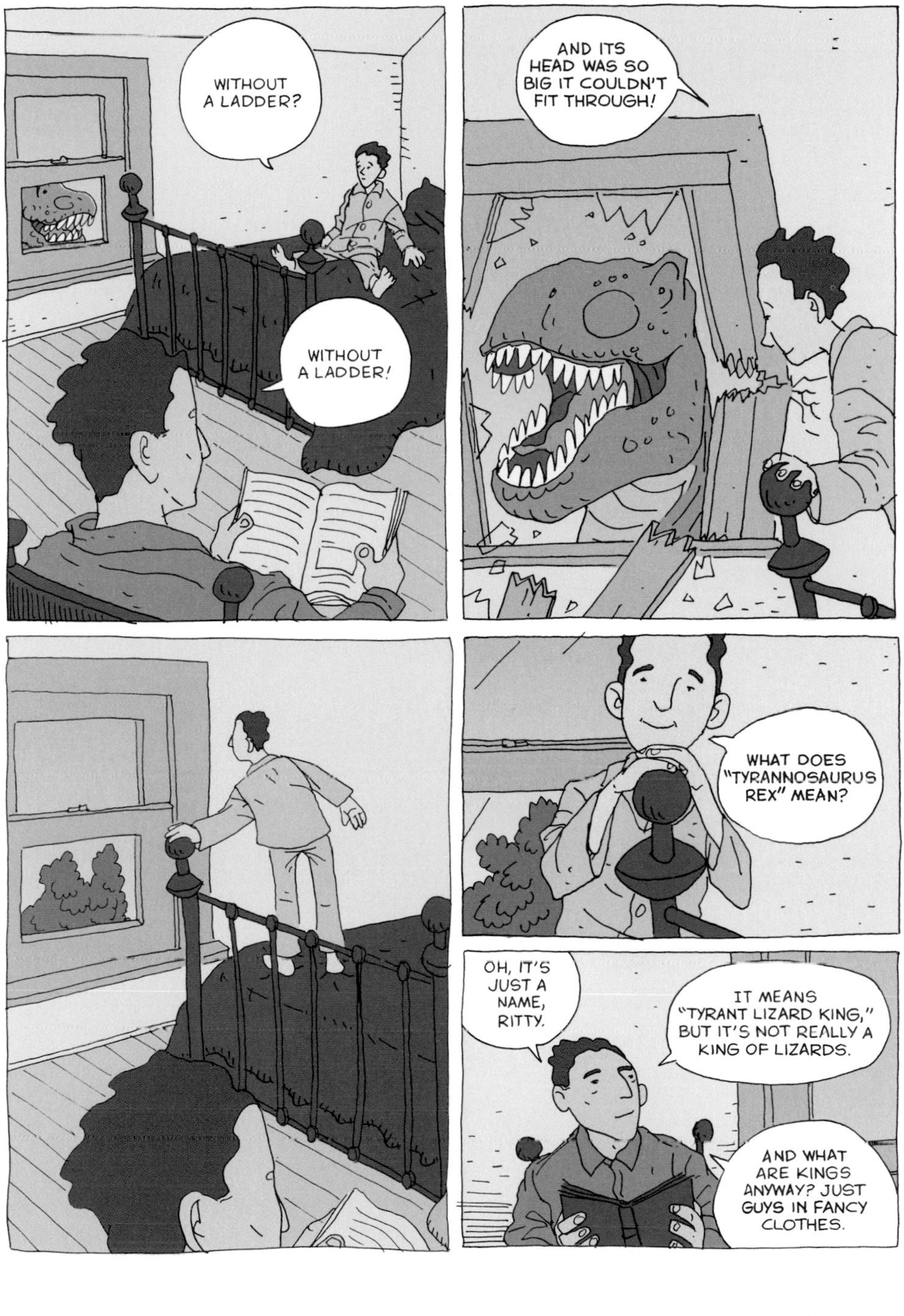
WITHOUT A LADDER?
WITHOUT A LADDER!
AND ITS HEAD WAS SO BIG IT COULDN'T FIT THROUGH!
WHAT DOES "TYRANNOSAURUS REX" MEAN?
OH, IT'S JUST A NAME, RITTY.
IT MEANS "TYRANT LIZARD KING," BUT IT'S NOT REALLY A KING OF LIZARDS.
AND WHAT ARE KINGS ANYWAY? JUST GUYS IN FANCY CLOTHES.

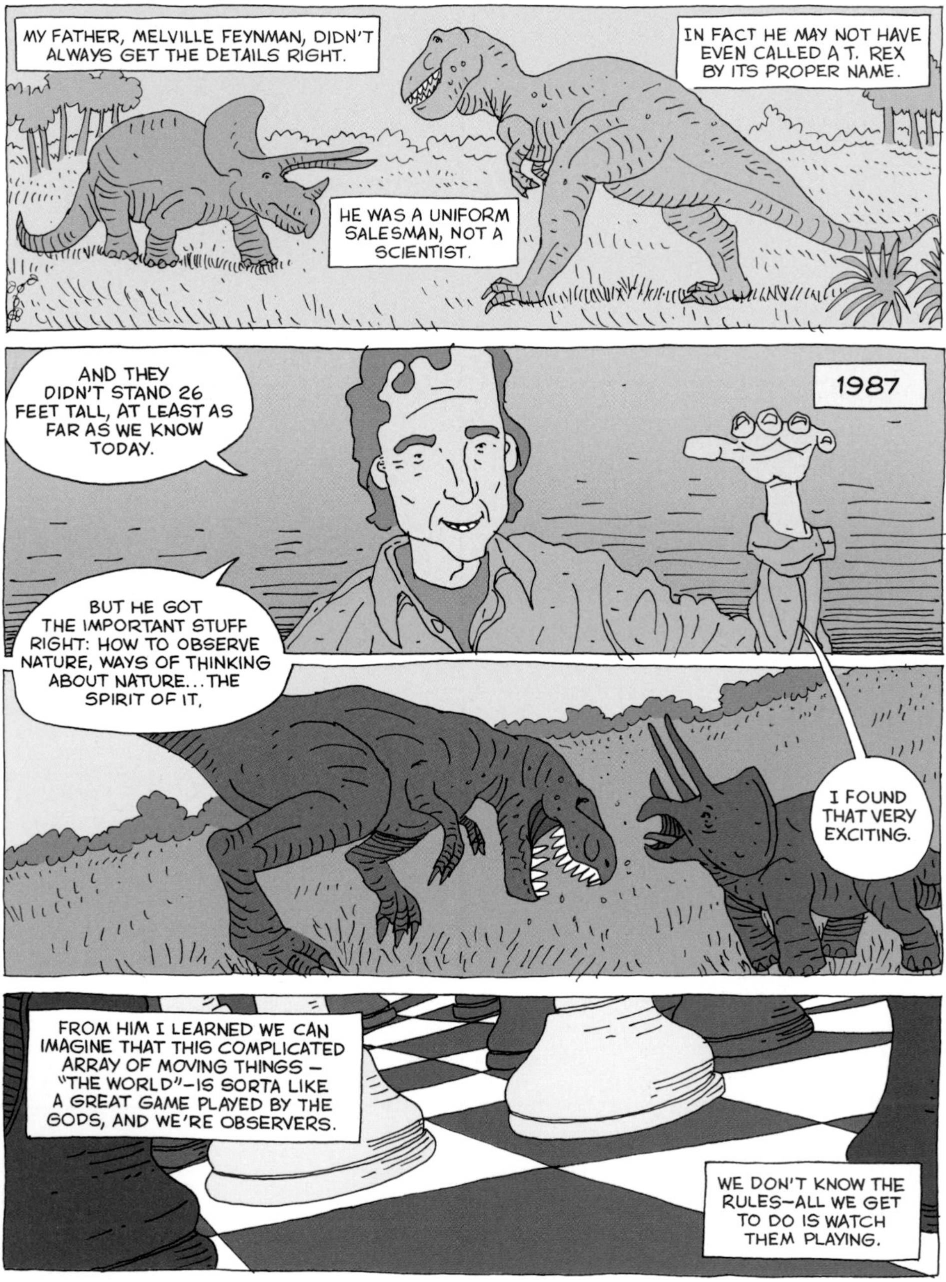

MY FATHER, MELVILLE FEYNMAN, DIDN'T ALWAYS GET THE DETAILS RIGHT.
HE WAS A UNIFORM SALESMAN, NOT A SCIENTIST.
IN FACT HE MAY NOT HAVE EVEN CALLED A T. REX BY ITS PROPER NAME.
1987
AND THEY DIDN'T STAND 26 FEET TALL, AT LEAST AS FAR AS WE KNOW TODAY.
BUT HE GOT THE IMPORTANT STUFF RIGHT: HOW TO OBSERVE NATURE, WAYS OF THINKING ABOUT NATURE... THE SPIRIT OF IT,
I FOUND THAT VERY EXCITING.
FROM HIM I LEARNED WE CAN IMAGINE THAT THIS COMPLICATED ARRAY OF MOVING THINGS — "THE WORLD"—IS SORTA LIKE A GREAT GAME PLAYED BY THE GODS, AND WE'RE OBSERVERS.
WE DON'T KNOW THE RULES—ALL WE GET TO DO IS WATCH THEM PLAYING.

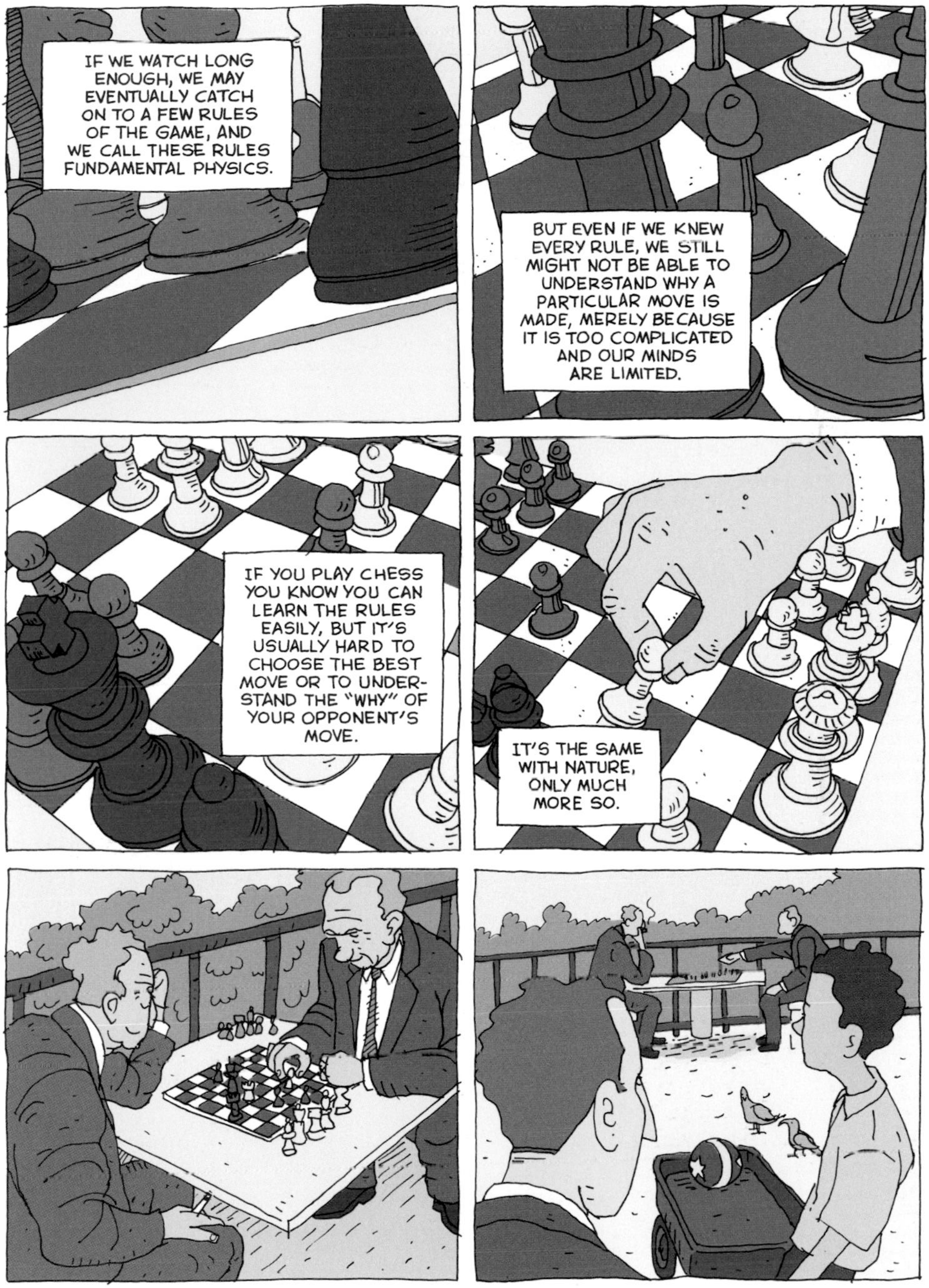
IF WE WATCH LONG ENOUGH, WE MAY EVENTUALLY CATCH ON TO A FEW RULES OF THE GAME, AND WE CALL THESE RULES FUNDAMENTAL PHYSICS.
BUT EVEN IF WE KNEW EVERY RULE, WE STILL MIGHT NOT BE ABLE TO UNDERSTAND WHY A PARTICULAR MOVE IS MADE, MERELY BECAUSE IT IS TOO COMPLICATED AND OUR MINDS ARE LIMITED.
IF YOU PLAY CHESS YOU KNOW YOU CAN LEARN THE RULES EASILY, BUT IT'S USUALLY HARD TO CHOOSE THE BEST MOVE OR TO UNDERSTAND THE "WHY" OF YOUR OPPONENT'S MOVE.
IT'S THE SAME WITH NATURE, ONLY MUCH MORE SO.

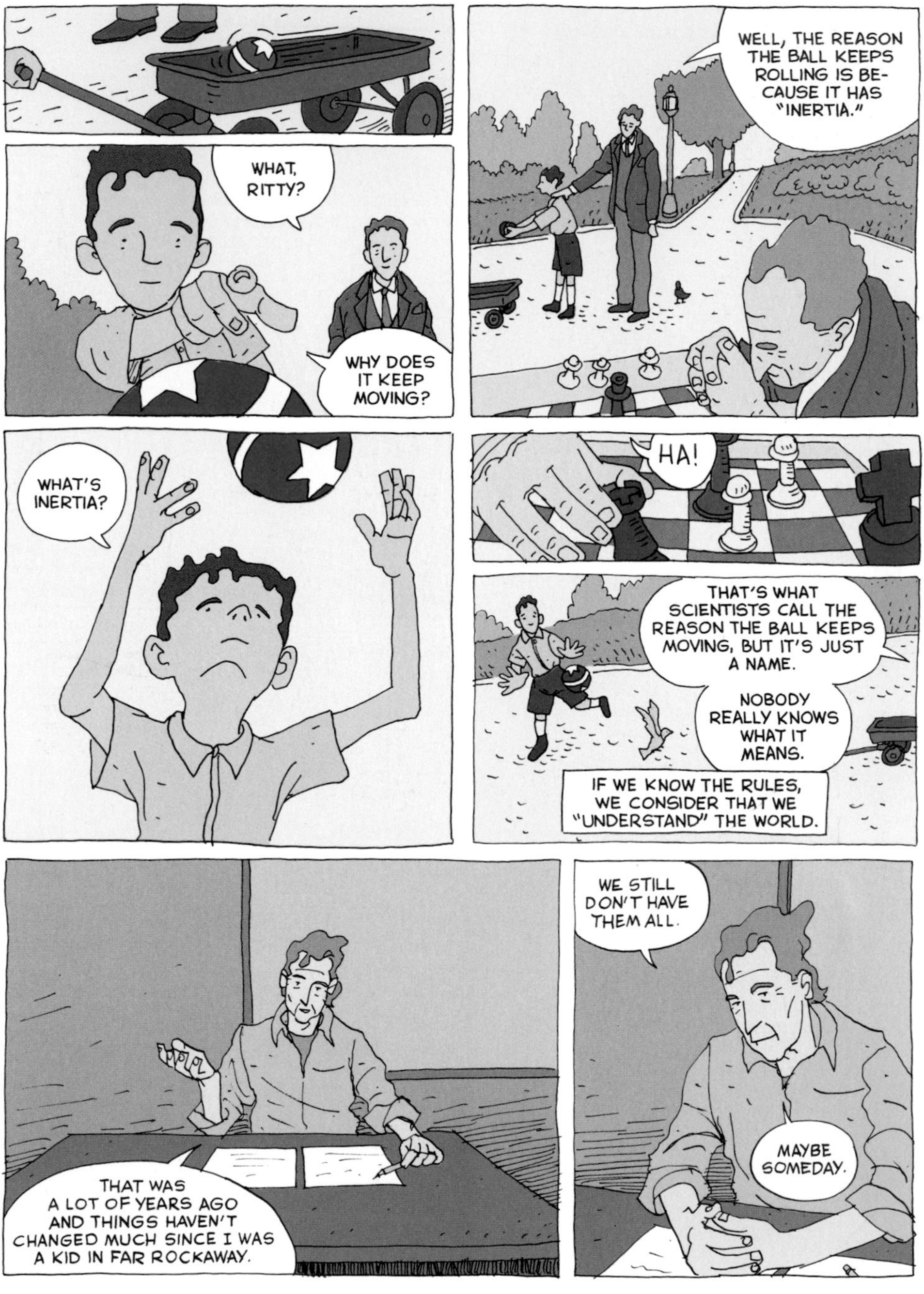
WHAT, RITTY?
WHY DOES IT KEEP MOVING?
WELL, THE REASON THE BALL KEEPS ROLLING IS BE- CAUSE IT HAS "INERTIA."
WHAT'S INERTIA?
HA!
THAT'S WHAT SCIENTISTS CALL THE REASON THE BALL KEEPS MOVING, BUT IT'S JUST A NAME.
NOBODY REALLY KNOWS WHAT IT MEANS.
IF WE KNOW THE RULES, WE CONSIDER THAT WE "UNDERSTAND" THE WORLD.
THAT WAS A LOT OF YEARS AGO AND THINGS HAVEN'T CHANGED MUCH SINCE I WAS A KID IN FAR ROCKAWAY.
WE STILL DON'T HAVE THEM ALL.
MAYBE SOMEDAY.

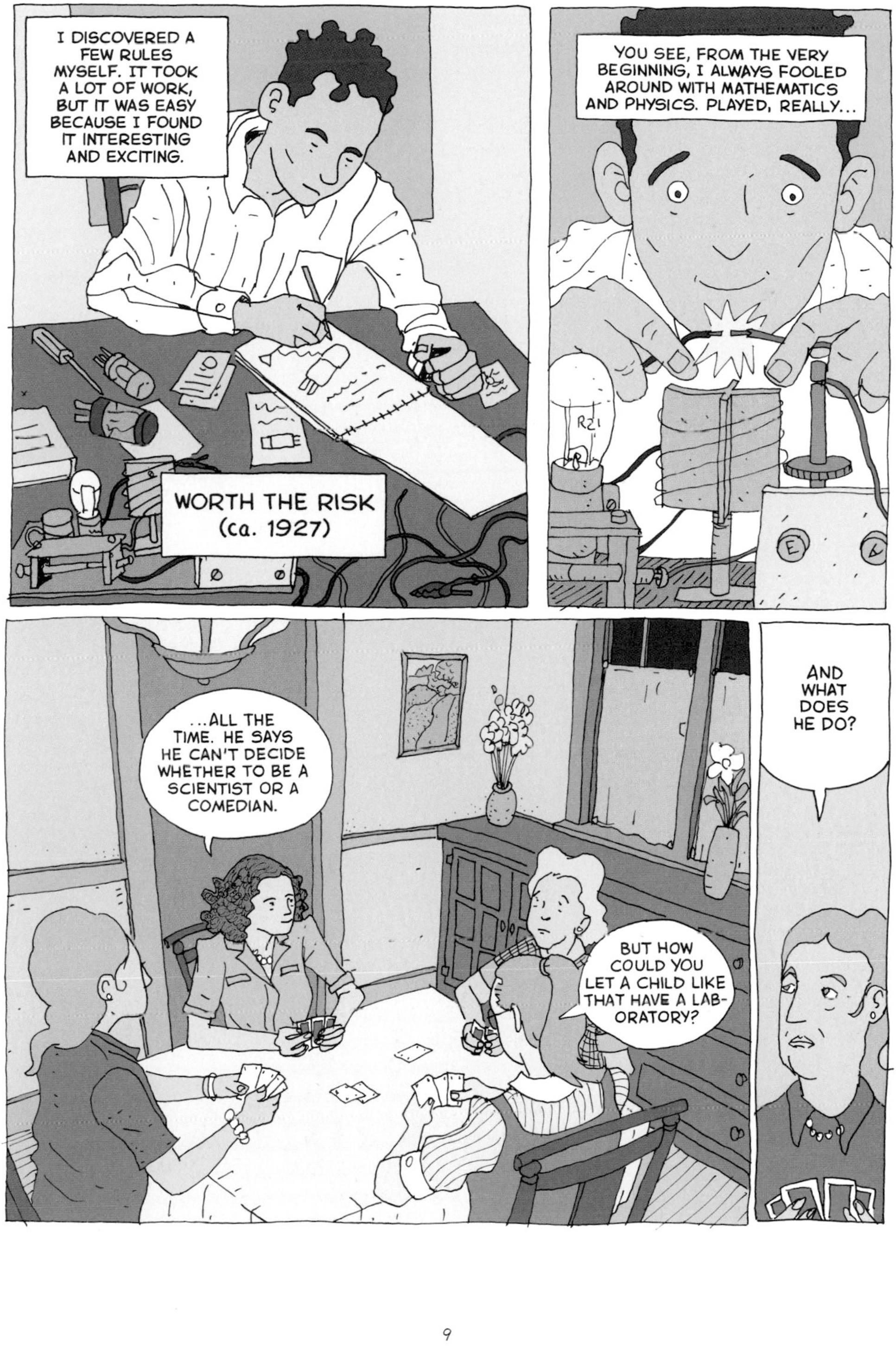
I DISCOVERED A FEW RULES MYSELF. IT TOOK A LOT OF WORK, BUT IT WAS EASY BECAUSE I FOUND IT INTERESTING AND EXCITING.
WORTH THE RISK (ca. 1927)
YOU SEE, FROM THE VERY BEGINNING, I ALWAYS FOOLED AROUND WITH MATHEMATICS AND PHYSICS. PLAYED, REALLY...
R21
E
...ALL THE TIME. HE SAYS HE CAN'T DECIDE WHETHER TO BE A SCIENTIST OR A COMEDIAN.
BUT HOW COULD YOU LET A CHILD LIKE THAT HAVE A LAB-ORATORY?
AND WHAT DOES HE DO?

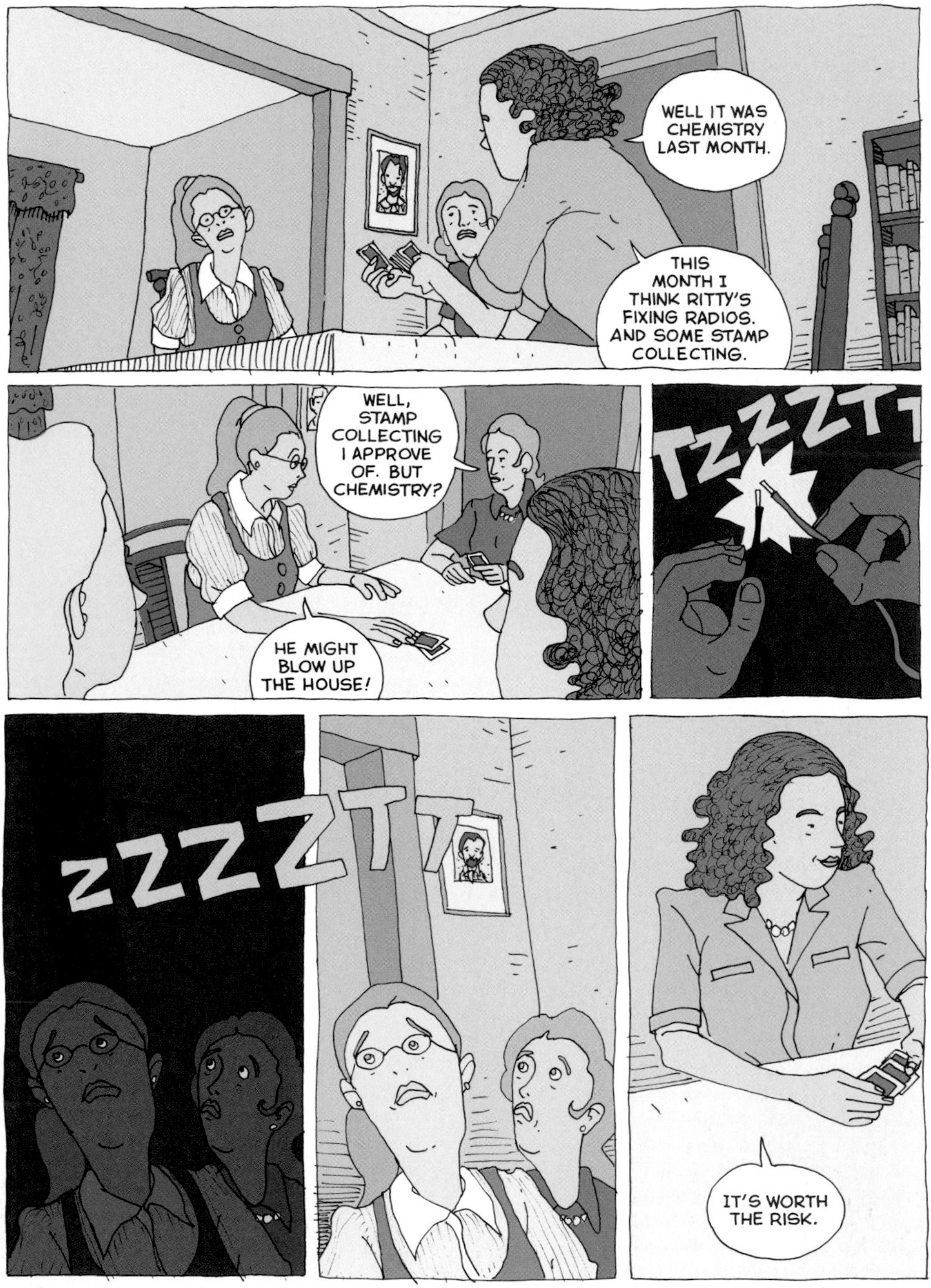
WELL IT WAS CHEMISTRY LAST MONTH.
THIS MONTH I THINK RITTY'S FIXING RADIOS. AND SOME STAMP COLLECTING.
WELL, STAMP COLLECTING I APPROVE OF. BUT CHEMISTRY?
HE MIGHT BLOW UP THE HOUSE!
TZZZTT
ZZZZTTT
IT'S WORTH THE RISK.

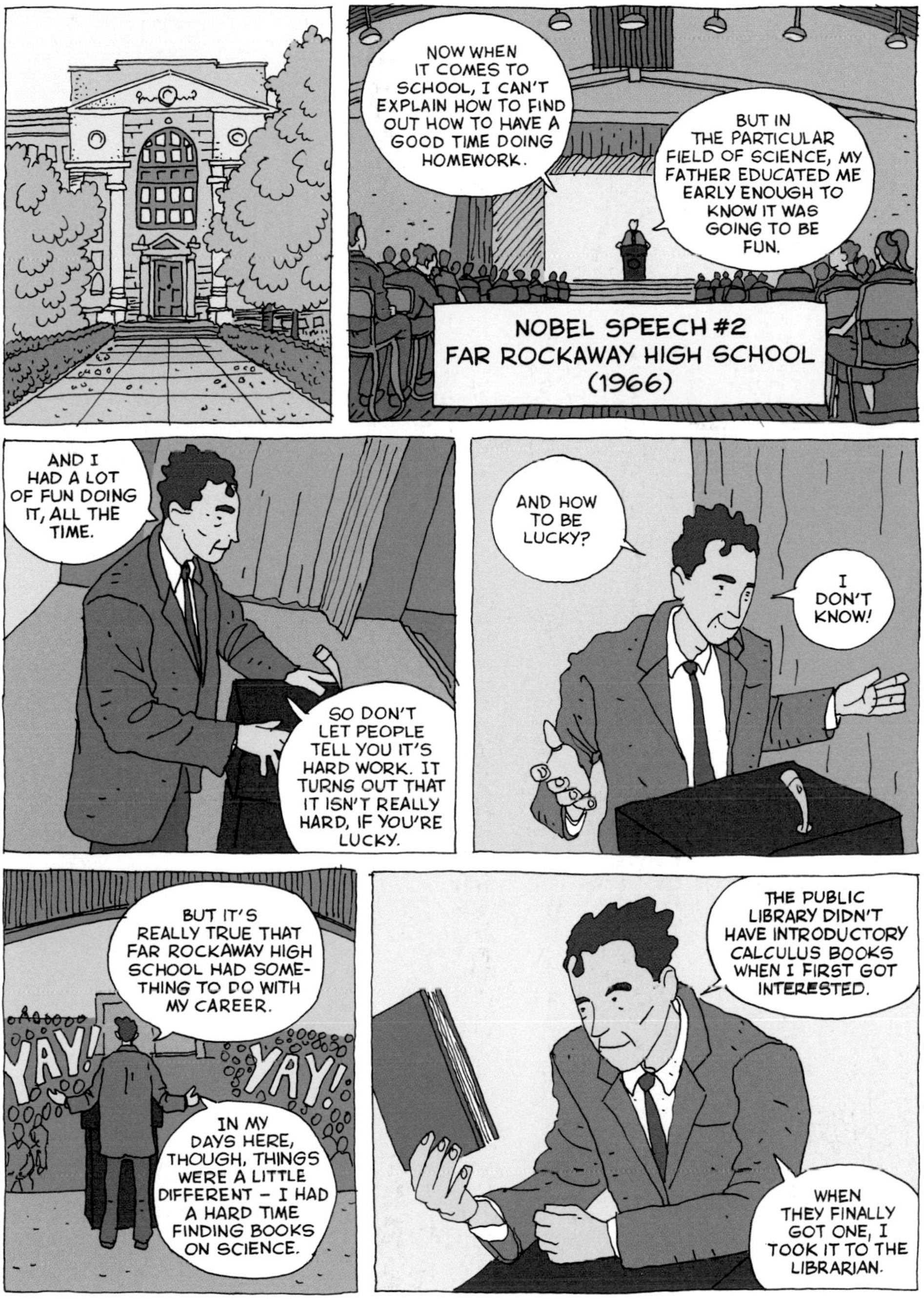
NOW WHEN IT COMES TO SCHOOL, I CAN'T EXPLAIN HOW TO FIND OUT HOW TO HAVE A GOOD TIME DOING HOMEWORK.
BUT IN THE PARTICULAR FIELD OF SCIENCE, MY FATHER EDUCATED ME EARLY ENOUGH TO KNOW IT WAS GOING TO BE FUN.
NOBEL SPEECH #2 FAR ROCKAWAY HIGH SCHOOL (1966)
AND I HAD A LOT OF FUN DOING IT, ALL THE TIME.
SO DON'T LET PEOPLE TELL YOU IT'S HARD WORK. IT TURNS OUT THAT IT ISN'T REALLY HARD, IF YOU'RE LUCKY.
AND HOW TO BE LUCKY?
I DON'T KNOW!
BUT IT'S REALLY TRUE THAT FAR ROCKAWAY HIGH SCHOOL HAD SOME-THING TO DO WITH MY CAREER.
YAY!
YAY!
IN MY DAYS HERE, THOUGH, THINGS WERE A LITTLE DIFFERENT – I HAD A HARD TIME FINDING BOOKS ON SCIENCE.
THE PUBLIC LIBRARY DIDN'T HAVE INTRODUCTORY CALCULUS BOOKS WHEN I FIRST GOT INTERESTED.
WHEN THEY FINALLY GOT ONE, I TOOK IT TO THE LIBRARIAN.

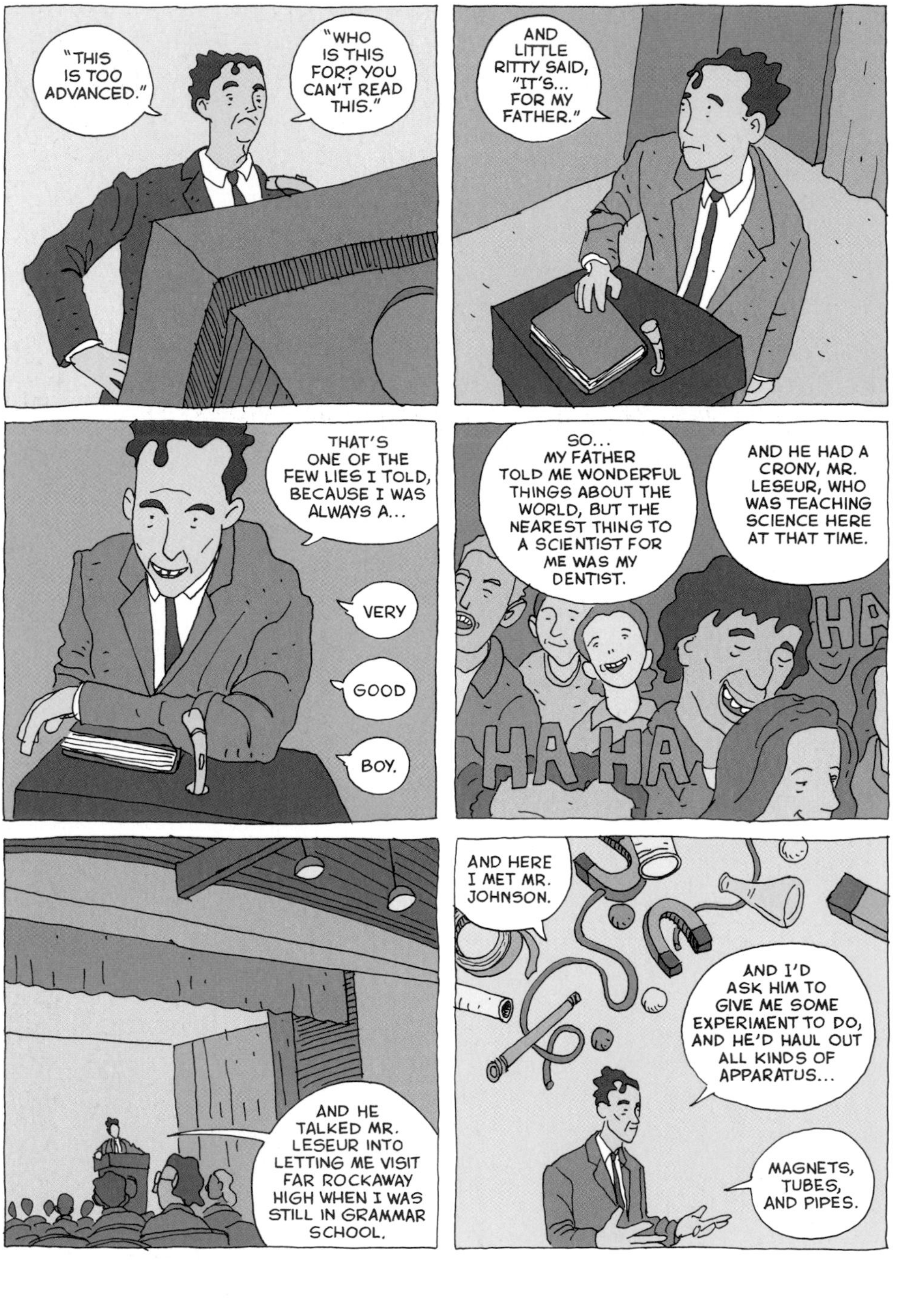
"THIS IS TOO ADVANCED."
"WHO IS THIS FOR? YOU CAN'T READ THIS."
AND LITTLE RITTY SAID, "IT'S... FOR MY FATHER."
THAT'S ONE OF THE FEW LIES I TOLD, BECAUSE I WAS ALWAYS A...
VERY
GOOD
BOY.
SO... MY FATHER TOLD ME WONDERFUL THINGS ABOUT THE WORLD, BUT THE NEAREST THING TO A SCIENTIST FOR ME WAS MY DENTIST.
AND HE HAD A CRONY, MR. LESEUR, WHO WAS TEACHING SCIENCE HERE AT THAT TIME.
HA HA HA
AND HE TALKED MR. LESEUR INTO LETTING ME VISIT FAR ROCKAWAY HIGH WHEN I WAS STILL IN GRAMMAR SCHOOL.
AND HERE I MET MR. JOHNSON.
AND I'D ASK HIM TO GIVE ME SOME EXPERIMENT TO DO, AND HE'D HAUL OUT ALL KINDS OF APPARATUS...
MAGNETS, TUBES, AND PIPES.

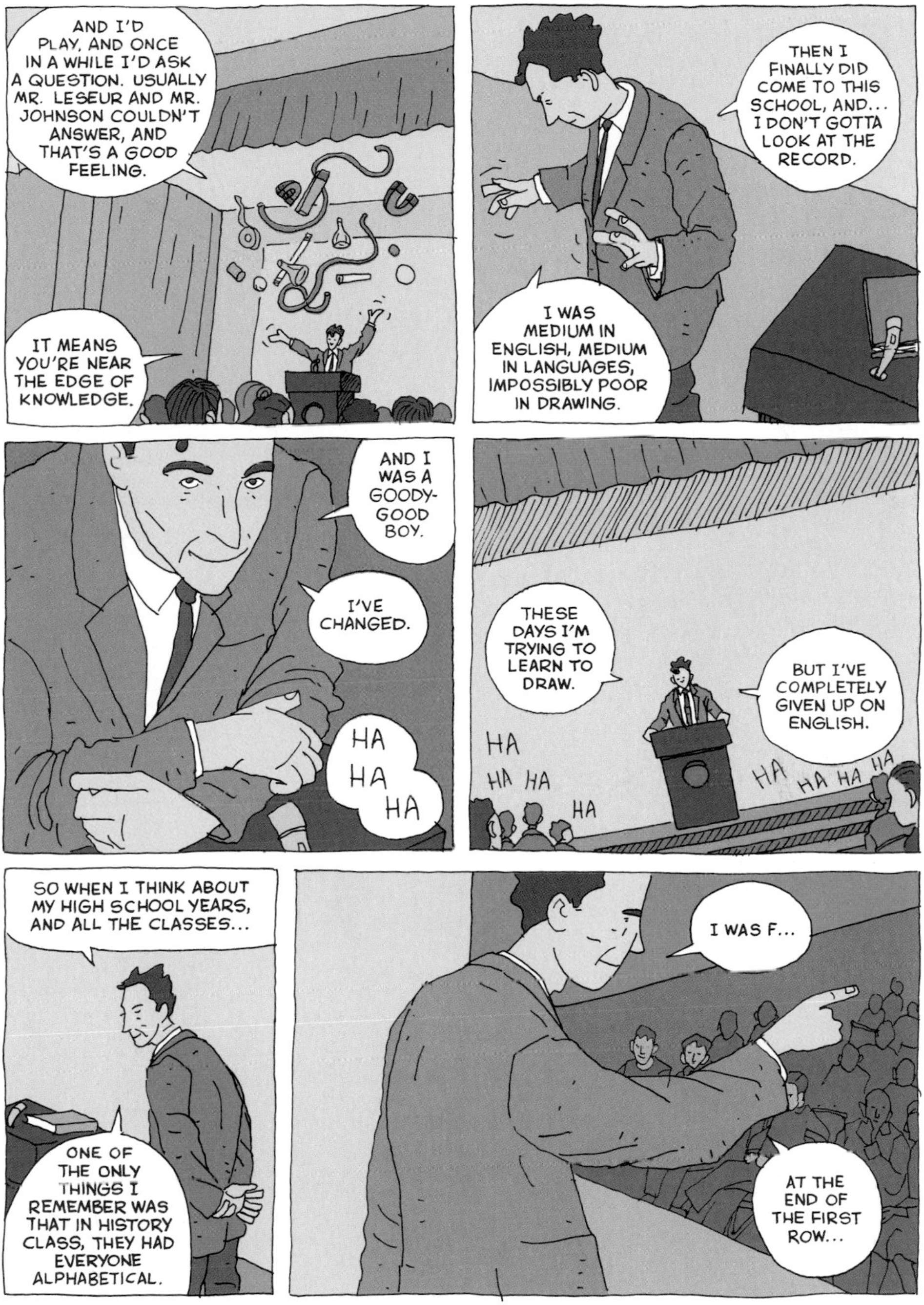
AND I'D PLAY, AND ONCE IN A WHILE I'D ASK A QUESTION. USUALLY MR. LESEUR AND MR. JOHNSON COULDN'T ANSWER, AND THAT'S A GOOD FEELING.
IT MEANS YOU'RE NEAR THE EDGE OF KNOWLEDGE.
THEN I FINALLY DID COME TO THIS SCHOOL, AND... I DON'T GOTTA LOOK AT THE RECORD.
I WAS MEDIUM IN ENGLISH, MEDIUM IN LANGUAGES, IMPOSSIBLY POOR IN DRAWING.
AND I WAS A GOODY-GOOD BOY.
I'VE CHANGED.
HA HA HA
THESE DAYS I'M TRYING TO LEARN TO DRAW.
BUT I'VE COMPLETELY GIVEN UP ON ENGLISH.
HA HA HA HA
HA HA HA HA
SO WHEN I THINK ABOUT MY HIGH SCHOOL YEARS, AND ALL THE CLASSES...
ONE OF THE ONLY THINGS I REMEMBER WAS THAT IN HISTORY CLASS, THEY HAD EVERYONE ALPHABETICAL.
I WAS F...
AT THE END OF THE FIRST ROW...

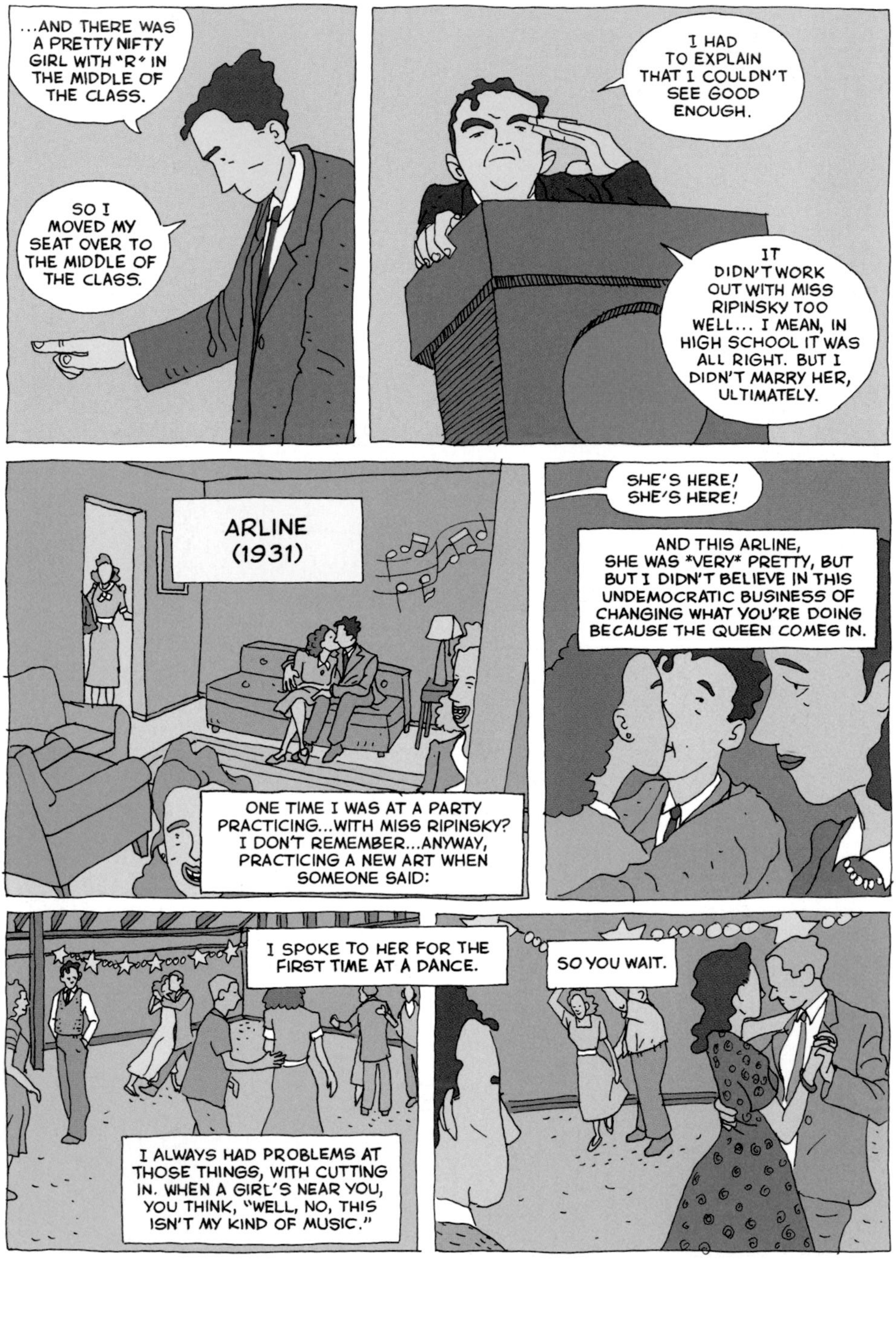
...AND THERE WAS A PRETTY NIFTY GIRL WITH "R" IN THE MIDDLE OF THE CLASS.
SO I MOVED MY SEAT OVER TO THE MIDDLE OF THE CLASS.
I HAD TO EXPLAIN THAT I COULDN'T SEE GOOD ENOUGH.
IT DIDN'T WORK OUT WITH MISS RIPINSKY TOO WELL... I MEAN, IN HIGH SCHOOL IT WAS ALL RIGHT. BUT I DIDN'T MARRY HER, ULTIMATELY.
ARLINE (1931)
ONE TIME I WAS AT A PARTY PRACTICING...WITH MISS RIPINSKY? I DON'T REMEMBER...ANYWAY, PRACTICING A NEW ART WHEN SOMEONE SAID:
SHE'S HERE! SHE'S HERE!
AND THIS ARLINE, SHE WAS *VERY* PRETTY, BUT BUT I DIDN'T BELIEVE IN THIS UNDEMOCRATIC BUSINESS OF CHANGING WHAT YOU'RE DOING BECAUSE THE QUEEN COMES IN.
I SPOKE TO HER FOR THE FIRST TIME AT A DANCE.
I ALWAYS HAD PROBLEMS AT THOSE THINGS, WITH CUTTING IN. WHEN A GIRL'S NEAR YOU, YOU THINK, "WELL, NO, THIS ISN'T MY KIND OF MUSIC."
SO YOU WAIT.

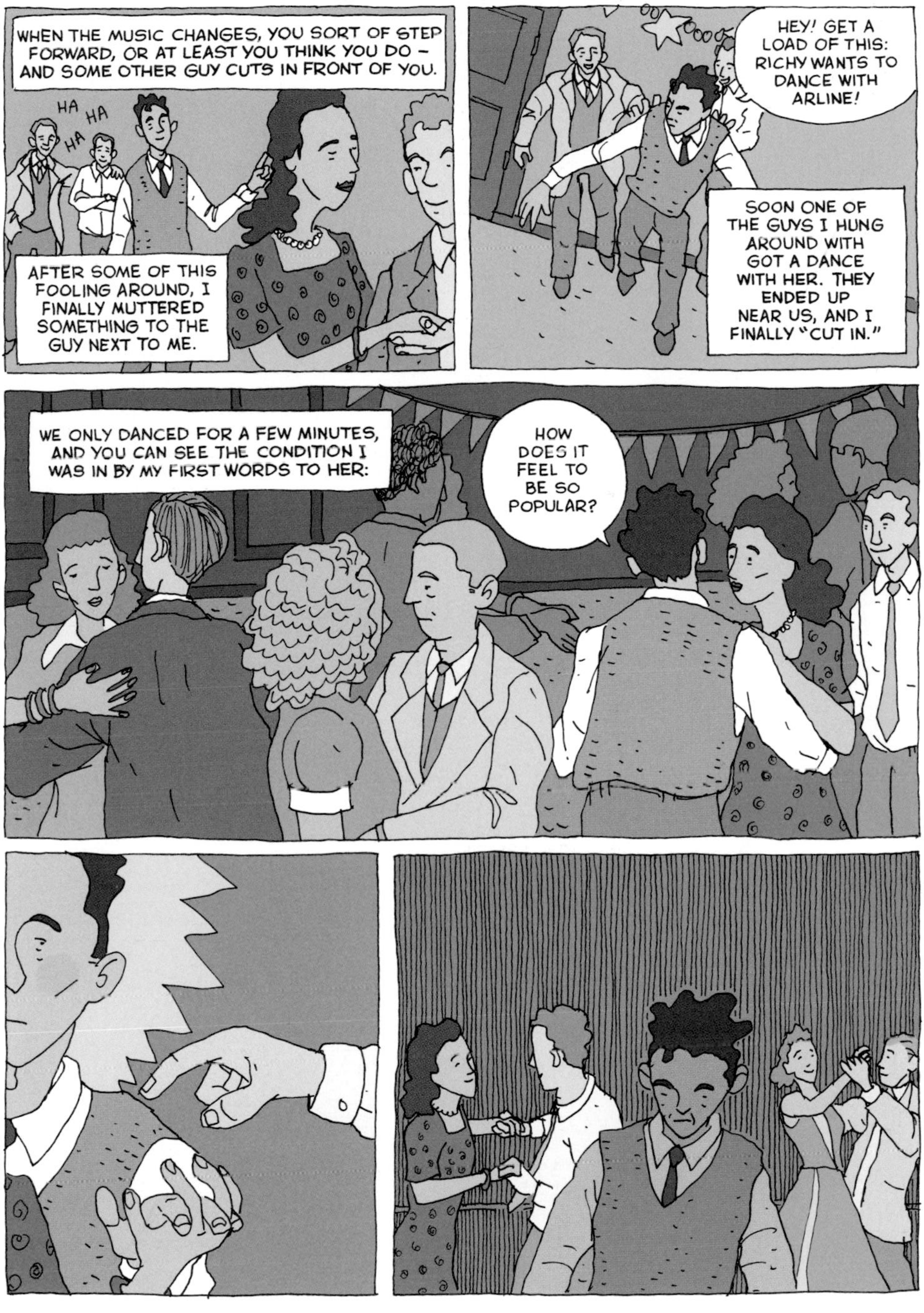
WHEN THE MUSIC CHANGES, YOU SORT OF STEP FORWARD, OR AT LEAST YOU THINK YOU DO – AND SOME OTHER GUY CUTS IN FRONT OF YOU.
HA HA HA HA
AFTER SOME OF THIS FOOLING AROUND, I FINALLY MUTTERED SOMETHING TO THE GUY NEXT TO ME.
HEY! GET A LOAD OF THIS: RICHY WANTS TO DANCE WITH ARLINE!
SOON ONE OF THE GUYS I HUNG AROUND WITH GOT A DANCE WITH HER. THEY ENDED UP NEAR US, AND I FINALLY "CUT IN."
WE ONLY DANCED FOR A FEW MINUTES, AND YOU CAN SEE THE CONDITION I WAS IN BY MY FIRST WORDS TO HER:
HOW DOES IT FEEL TO BE SO POPULAR?

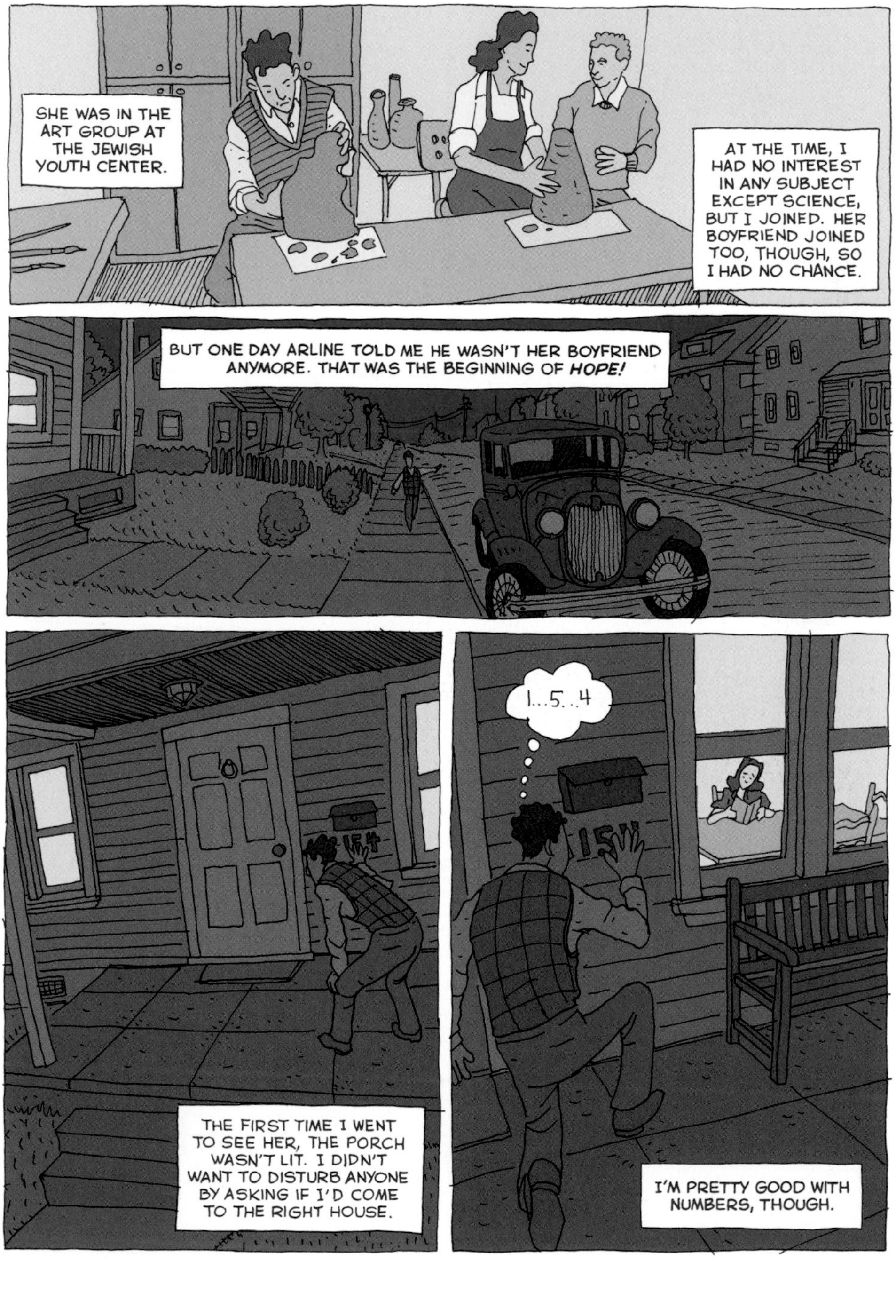
SHE WAS IN THE ART GROUP AT THE JEWISH YOUTH CENTER.
AT THE TIME, I HAD NO INTEREST IN ANY SUBJECT EXCEPT SCIENCE, BUT I JOINED. HER BOYFRIEND JOINED TOO, THOUGH, SO I HAD NO CHANCE.
BUT ONE DAY ARLINE TOLD ME HE WASN'T HER BOYFRIEND ANYMORE. THAT WAS THE BEGINNING OF ***HOPE!***
THE FIRST TIME I WENT TO SEE HER, THE PORCH WASN'T LIT. I DIDN'T WANT TO DISTURB ANYONE BY ASKING IF I'D COME TO THE RIGHT HOUSE.
1...5...4
I'M PRETTY GOOD WITH NUMBERS, THOUGH.

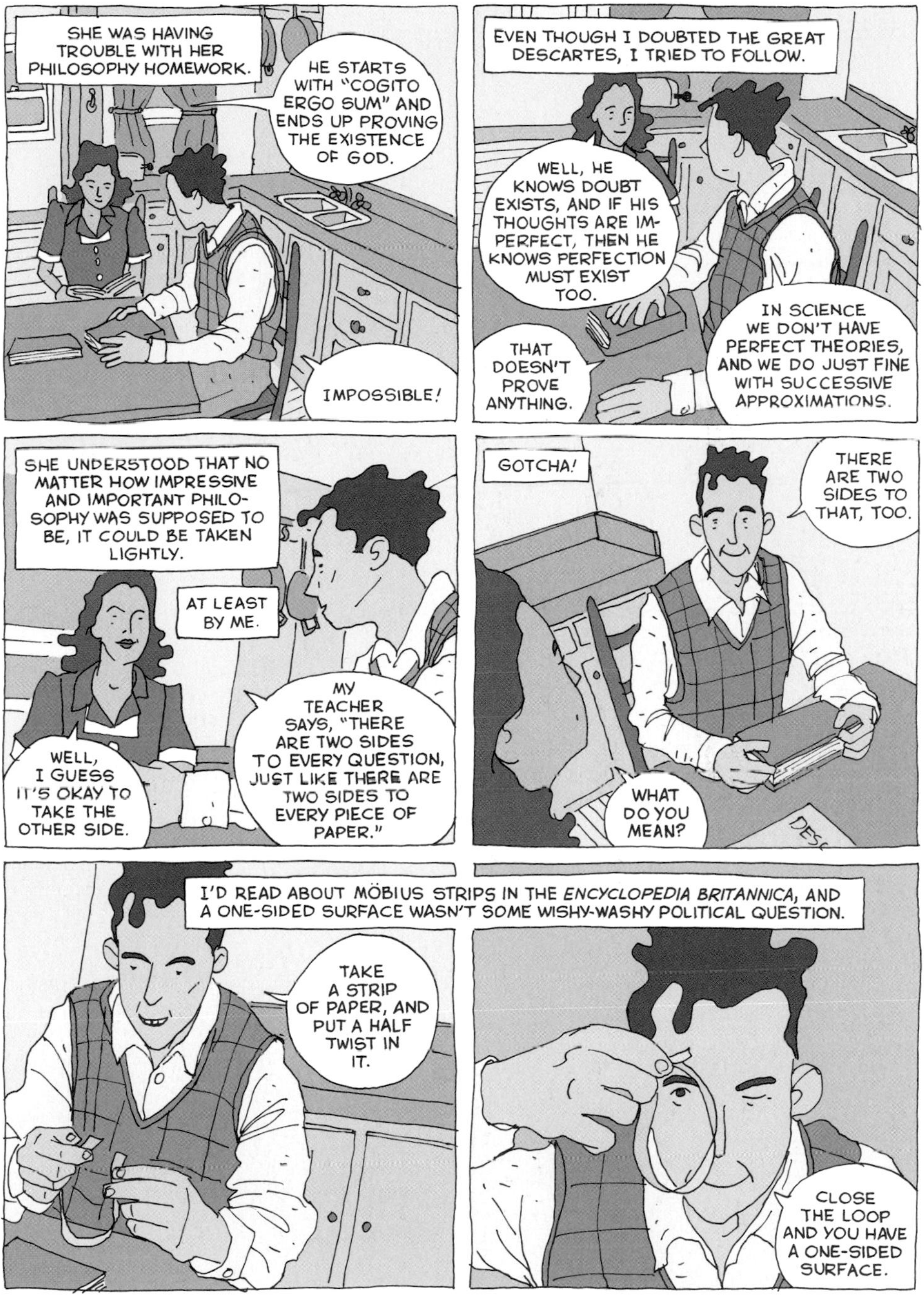
SHE WAS HAVING TROUBLE WITH HER PHILOSOPHY HOMEWORK.
HE STARTS WITH "COGITO ERGO SUM" AND ENDS UP PROVING THE EXISTENCE OF GOD.
IMPOSSIBLE!
EVEN THOUGH I DOUBTED THE GREAT DESCARTES, I TRIED TO FOLLOW.
WELL, HE KNOWS DOUBT EXISTS, AND IF HIS THOUGHTS ARE IMPERFECT, THEN HE KNOWS PERFECTION MUST EXIST TOO.
THAT DOESN'T PROVE ANYTHING.
IN SCIENCE WE DON'T HAVE PERFECT THEORIES, AND WE DO JUST FINE WITH SUCCESSIVE APPROXIMATIONS.
SHE UNDERSTOOD THAT NO MATTER HOW IMPRESSIVE AND IMPORTANT PHILOSOPHY WAS SUPPOSED TO BE, IT COULD BE TAKEN LIGHTLY.
AT LEAST BY ME.
MY TEACHER SAYS, "THERE ARE TWO SIDES TO EVERY QUESTION, JUST LIKE THERE ARE TWO SIDES TO EVERY PIECE OF PAPER."
WELL, I GUESS IT'S OKAY TO TAKE THE OTHER SIDE.
GOTCHA!
THERE ARE TWO SIDES TO THAT, TOO.
WHAT DO YOU MEAN?
I'D READ ABOUT MÖBIUS STRIPS IN THE *ENCYCLOPEDIA BRITANNICA*, AND A ONE-SIDED SURFACE WASN'T SOME WISHY-WASHY POLITICAL QUESTION.
TAKE A STRIP OF PAPER, AND PUT A HALF TWIST IN IT.
CLOSE THE LOOP AND YOU HAVE A ONE-SIDED SURFACE.

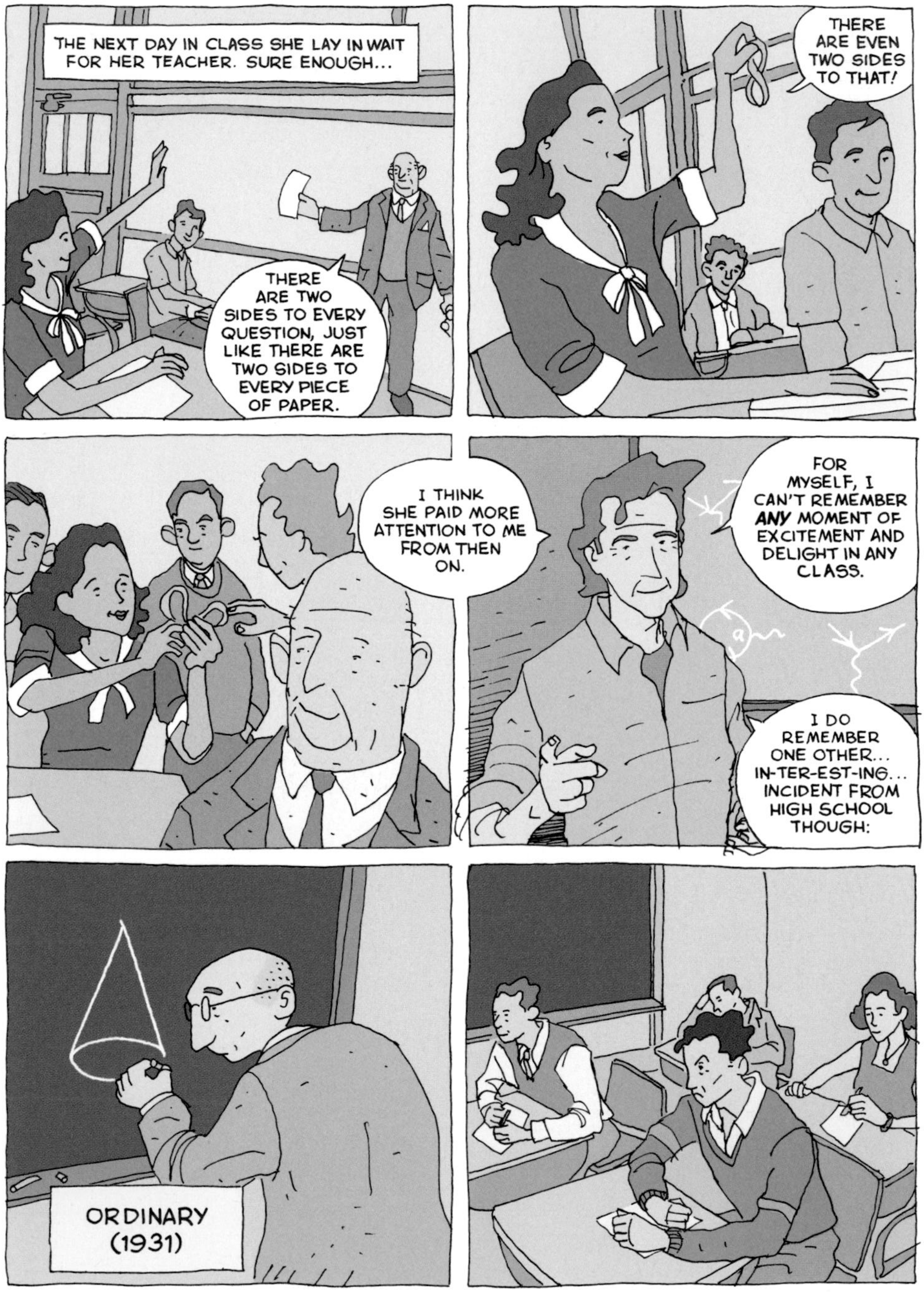
THE NEXT DAY IN CLASS SHE LAY IN WAIT FOR HER TEACHER. SURE ENOUGH...
THERE ARE TWO SIDES TO EVERY QUESTION, JUST LIKE THERE ARE TWO SIDES TO EVERY PIECE OF PAPER.
THERE ARE EVEN TWO SIDES TO THAT!
I THINK SHE PAID MORE ATTENTION TO ME FROM THEN ON.
FOR MYSELF, I CAN'T REMEMBER **ANY** MOMENT OF EXCITEMENT AND DELIGHT IN ANY CLASS.
I DO REMEMBER ONE OTHER... IN-TER-EST-ING... INCIDENT FROM HIGH SCHOOL THOUGH:
ORDINARY (1931)

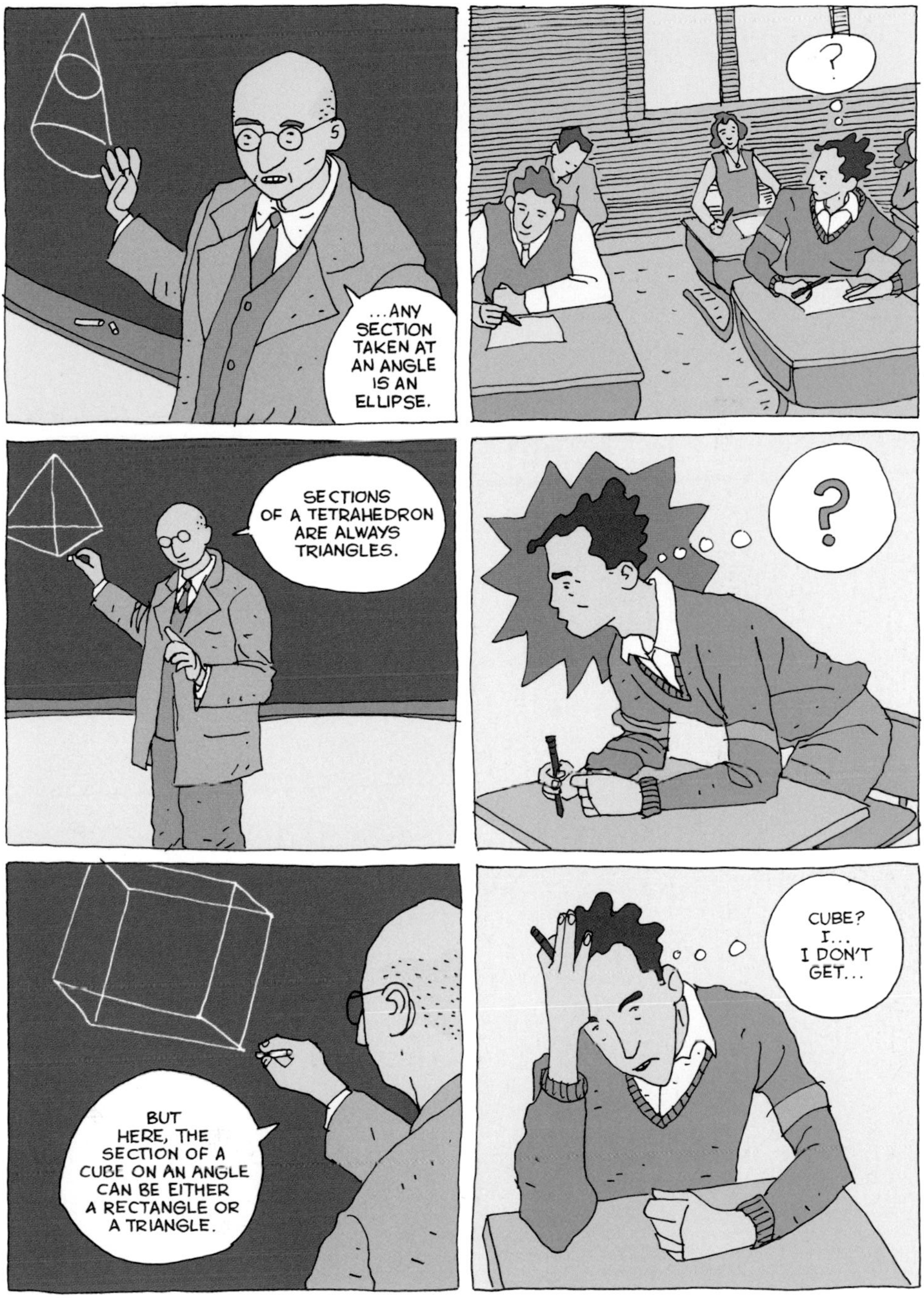
...ANY SECTION TAKEN AT AN ANGLE IS AN ELLIPSE.
?
SECTIONS OF A TETRAHEDRON ARE ALWAYS TRIANGLES.
?
BUT HERE, THE SECTION OF A CUBE ON AN ANGLE CAN BE EITHER A RECTANGLE OR A TRIANGLE.
CUBE? I... I DON'T GET...

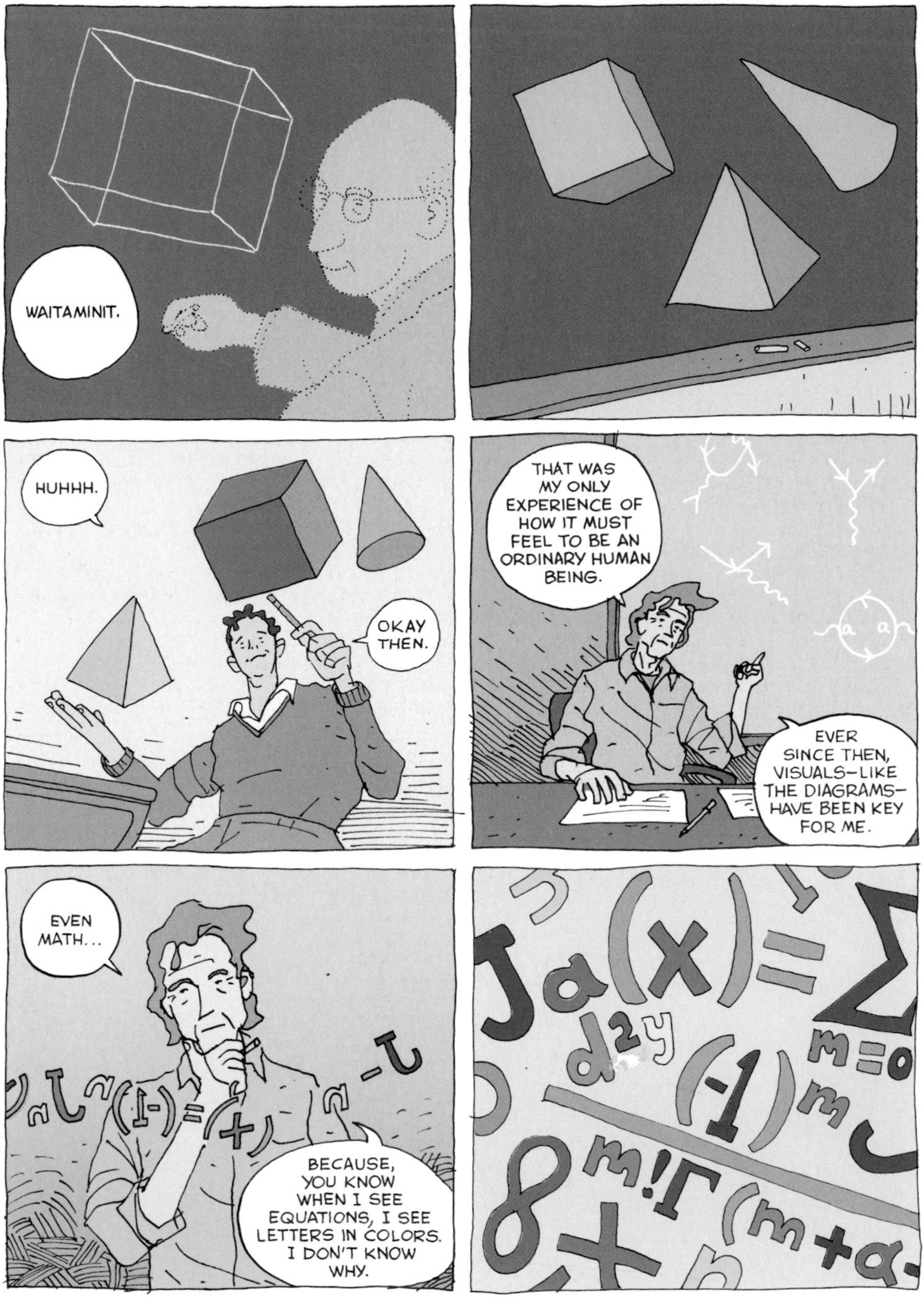
WAITAMINIT.
HUHHH.
OKAY THEN.
THAT WAS MY ONLY EXPERIENCE OF HOW IT MUST FEEL TO BE AN ORDINARY HUMAN BEING.
EVER SINCE THEN, VISUALS—LIKE THE DIAGRAMS—HAVE BEEN KEY FOR ME.
EVEN MATH...
BECAUSE, YOU KNOW WHEN I SEE EQUATIONS, I SEE LETTERS IN COLORS. I DON'T KNOW WHY.

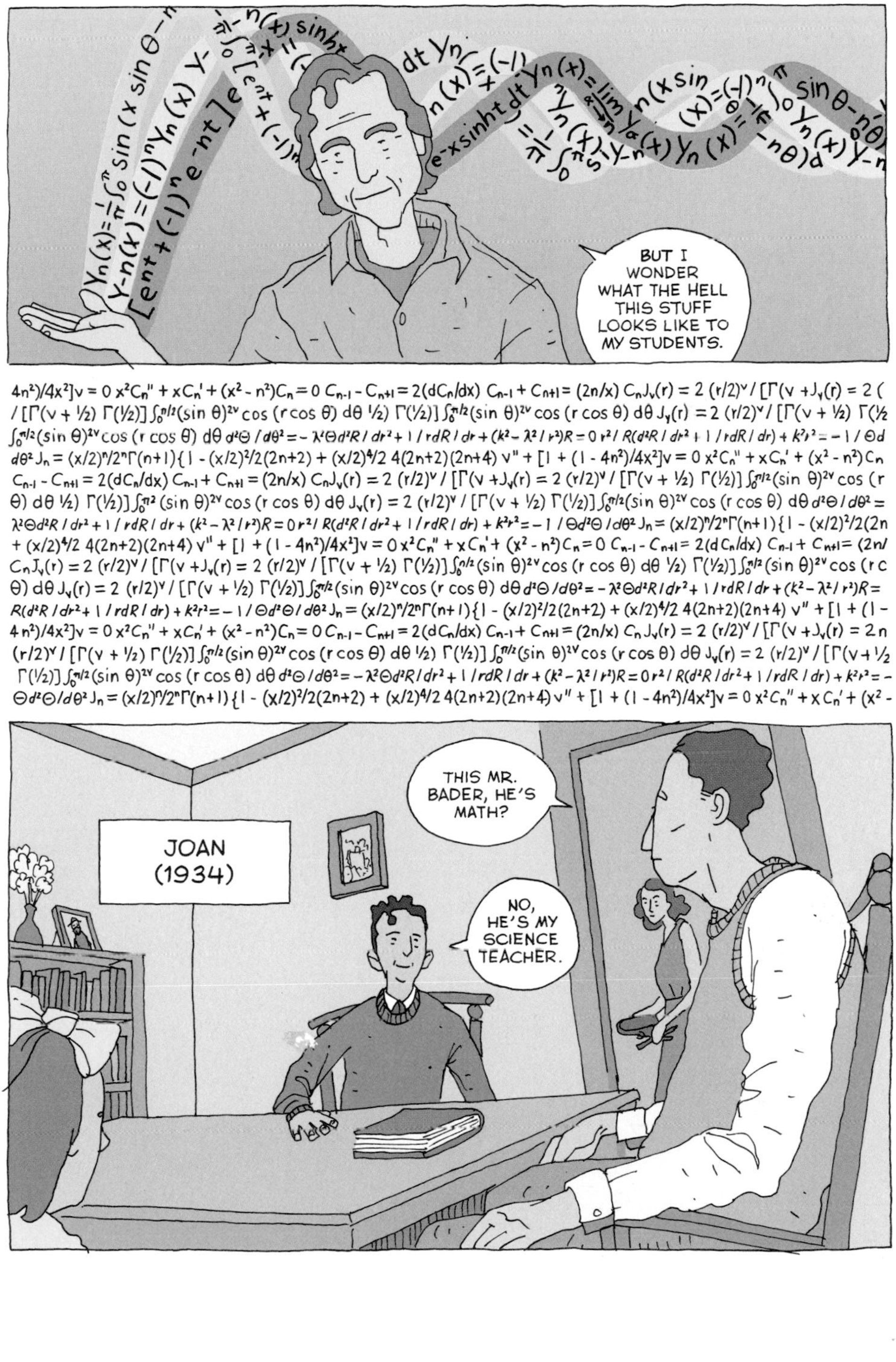
BUT I WONDER WHAT THE HELL THIS STUFF LOOKS LIKE TO MY STUDENTS.
4n^2)/4x^2]v = 0 x^2Cn'' + xCn' + (x^2 - n^2)Cn = 0 Cn-1 - Cn+1 = 2(dCn/dx) Cn-1 + Cn+1 = (2n/x) CnJv(r) = 2 (r/2)^v / [Γ(v + Jv(r) = 2 (
/ [Γ(v + ½) Γ(½)] ∫0^π/2(sin θ)^2v cos (r cos θ) dθ ½) Γ(½)] ∫0^π/2(sin θ)^2v cos (r cos θ) dθ Jv(r) = 2 (r/2)^v / [Γ(v + ½) Γ(½
∫0^π/2(sin θ)^2v cos (r cos θ) dθ d²Θ / dθ² = - λ²Θd²R / dr² + 1 / rdR / dr + (k² - λ² / r²)R = 0 r² / R(d²R / dr² + 1 / rdR / dr) + k²r² = - 1 / Θd
dθ² Jn = (x/2)^n/2^nΓ(n+1){1 - (x/2)²/2(2n+2) + (x/2)^4/2 4(2n+2)(2n+4) v'' + [1 + (1 - 4n²)/4x²]v = 0 x²Cn'' + xCn' + (x² - n²)Cn
Cn-1 - Cn+1 = 2(dCn/dx) Cn-1 + Cn+1 = (2n/x) CnJv(r) = 2 (r/2)^v / [Γ(v + Jv(r) = 2 (r/2)^v / [Γ(v + ½) Γ(½)] ∫0^π/2(sin θ)^2v cos (r
θ) dθ ½) Γ(½)] ∫0^π/2 (sin θ)^2v cos (r cos θ) dθ Jv(r) = 2 (r/2)^v / [Γ(v + ½) Γ(½)] ∫0^π/2(sin θ)^2v cos (r cos θ) dθ d²Θ / dθ² =
λ²Θd²R / dr² + 1 / rdR / dr + (k² - λ² / r²)R = 0 r² / R(d²R / dr² + 1 / rdR / dr) + k²r² = - 1 / Θd²Θ / dθ² Jn = (x/2)^n/2^nΓ(n+1){1 - (x/2)²/2(2n
+ (x/2)^4/2 4(2n+2)(2n+4) v'' + [1 + (1 - 4n²)/4x²]v = 0 x²Cn'' + xCn' + (x² - n²)Cn = 0 Cn-1 - Cn+1 = 2(dCn/dx) Cn-1 + Cn+1 = (2n/
CnJv(r) = 2 (r/2)^v / [Γ(v + Jv(r) = 2 (r/2)^v / [Γ(v + ½) Γ(½)] ∫0^π/2(sin θ)^2v cos (r cos θ) dθ ½) Γ(½)] ∫0^π/2(sin θ)^2v cos (r c
θ) dθ Jv(r) = 2 (r/2)^v / [Γ(v + ½) Γ(½)] ∫0^π/2(sin θ)^2v cos (r cos θ) dθ d²Θ / dθ² = - λ²Θd²R / dr² + 1 / rdR / dr + (k² - λ² / r²)R =
R(d²R / dr² + 1 / rdR / dr) + k²r² = - 1 / Θd²Θ / dθ² Jn = (x/2)^n/2^nΓ(n+1){1 - (x/2)²/2(2n+2) + (x/2)^4/2 4(2n+2)(2n+4) v'' + [1 + (1 -
4n²)/4x²]v = 0 x²Cn'' + xCn' + (x² - n²)Cn = 0 Cn-1 - Cn+1 = 2(dCn/dx) Cn-1 + Cn+1 = (2n/x) CnJv(r) = 2 (r/2)^v / [Γ(v + Jv(r) = 2n
(r/2)^v / [Γ(v + ½) Γ(½)] ∫0^π/2(sin θ)^2v cos (r cos θ) dθ ½) Γ(½)] ∫0^π/2(sin θ)^2v cos (r cos θ) dθ Jv(r) = 2 (r/2)^v / [Γ(v + ½
Γ(½)] ∫0^π/2(sin θ)^2v cos (r cos θ) dθ d²Θ / dθ² = - λ²Θd²R / dr² + 1 / rdR / dr + (k² - λ² / r²)R = 0 r² / R(d²R / dr² + 1 / rdR / dr) + k²r² = -
Θd²Θ / dθ² Jn = (x/2)^n/2^nΓ(n+1){1 - (x/2)²/2(2n+2) + (x/2)^4/2 4(2n+2)(2n+4) v'' + [1 + (1 - 4n²)/4x²]v = 0 x²Cn'' + xCn' + (x² -
JOAN (1934)
THIS MR. BADER, HE'S MATH?
NO, HE'S MY SCIENCE TEACHER.

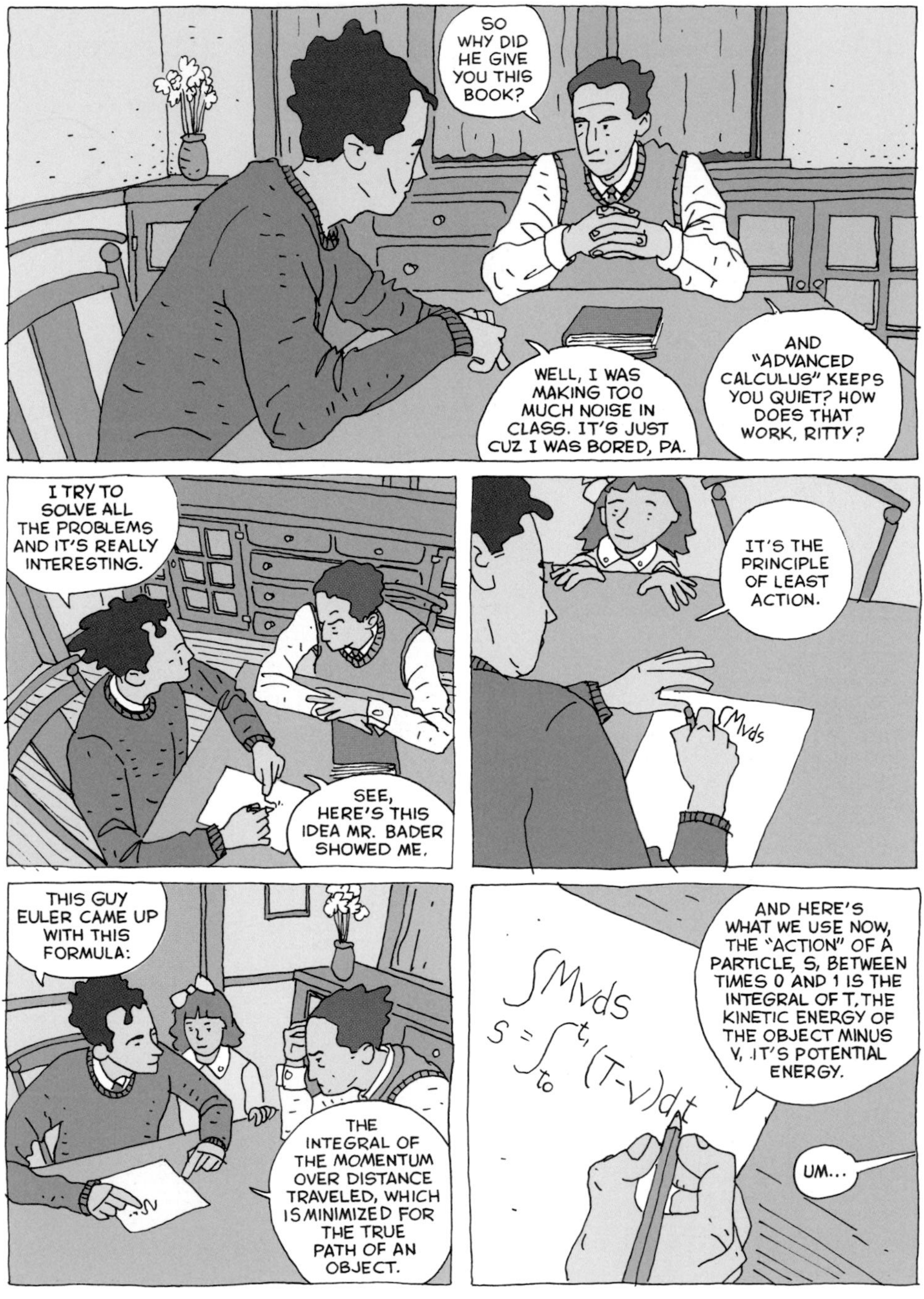
SO WHY DID HE GIVE YOU THIS BOOK?
WELL, I WAS MAKING TOO MUCH NOISE IN CLASS. IT'S JUST CUZ I WAS BORED, PA.
AND "ADVANCED CALCULUS" KEEPS YOU QUIET? HOW DOES THAT WORK, RITTY?
I TRY TO SOLVE ALL THE PROBLEMS AND IT'S REALLY INTERESTING.
SEE, HERE'S THIS IDEA MR. BADER SHOWED ME.
IT'S THE PRINCIPLE OF LEAST ACTION.
∫Mvds
THIS GUY EULER CAME UP WITH THIS FORMULA:
THE INTEGRAL OF THE MOMENTUM OVER DISTANCE TRAVELED, WHICH IS MINIMIZED FOR THE TRUE PATH OF AN OBJECT.
∫Mvds
S = ∫_to^t, (T-v)dt
AND HERE'S WHAT WE USE NOW, THE "ACTION" OF A PARTICLE, S, BETWEEN TIMES 0 AND 1 IS THE INTEGRAL OF T, THE KINETIC ENERGY OF THE OBJECT MINUS V, IT'S POTENTIAL ENERGY.
UM...

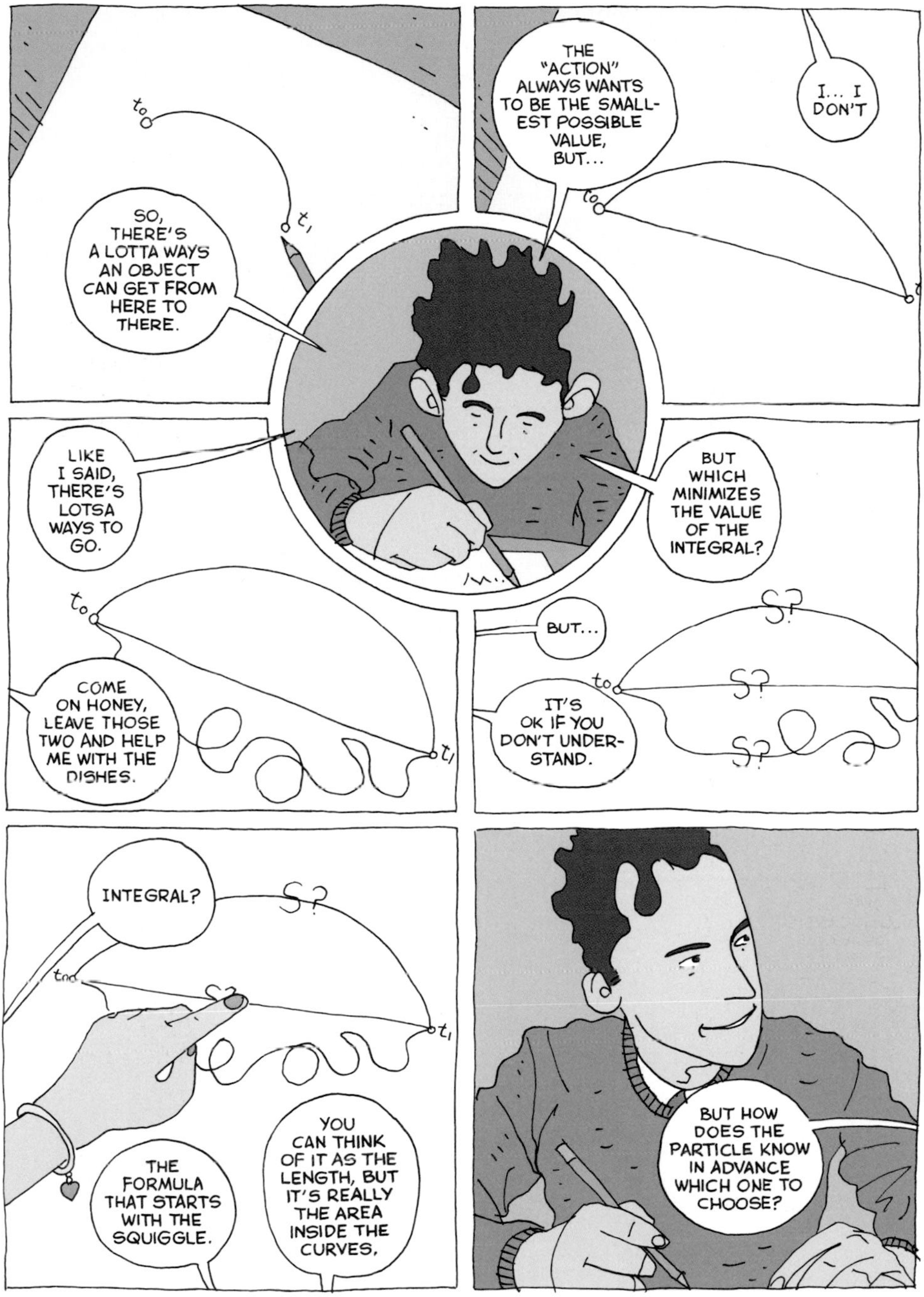

t_0
t_1
SO, THERE'S A LOTTA WAYS AN OBJECT CAN GET FROM HERE TO THERE.
THE "ACTION" ALWAYS WANTS TO BE THE SMALL-EST POSSIBLE VALUE, BUT...
I... I DON'T
LIKE I SAID, THERE'S LOTSA WAYS TO GO.
BUT WHICH MINIMIZES THE VALUE OF THE INTEGRAL?
COME ON HONEY, LEAVE THOSE TWO AND HELP ME WITH THE DISHES.
BUT...
IT'S OK IF YOU DON'T UNDER-STAND.
INTEGRAL?
THE FORMULA THAT STARTS WITH THE SQUIGGLE.
YOU CAN THINK OF IT AS THE LENGTH, BUT IT'S REALLY THE AREA INSIDE THE CURVES.
BUT HOW DOES THE PARTICLE KNOW IN ADVANCE WHICH ONE TO CHOOSE?

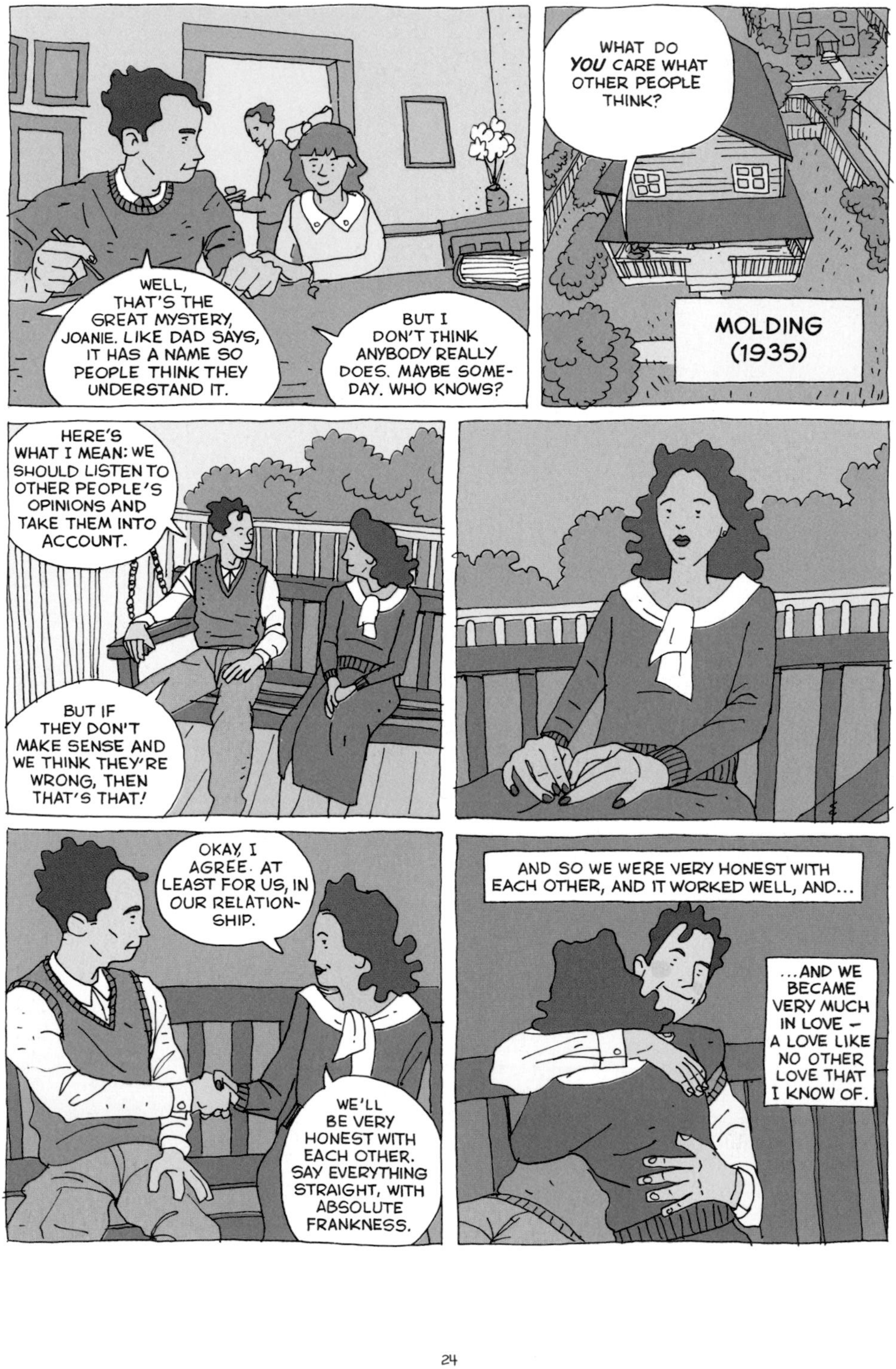
WELL, THAT'S THE GREAT MYSTERY, JOANIE. LIKE DAD SAYS, IT HAS A NAME SO PEOPLE THINK THEY UNDERSTAND IT.
BUT I DON'T THINK ANYBODY REALLY DOES. MAYBE SOME-DAY. WHO KNOWS?
MOLDING (1935)
WHAT DO *YOU* CARE WHAT OTHER PEOPLE THINK?
HERE'S WHAT I MEAN: WE SHOULD LISTEN TO OTHER PEOPLE'S OPINIONS AND TAKE THEM INTO ACCOUNT.
BUT IF THEY DON'T MAKE SENSE AND WE THINK THEY'RE WRONG, THEN THAT'S THAT!
OKAY, I AGREE. AT LEAST FOR US, IN OUR RELATION-SHIP.
WE'LL BE VERY HONEST WITH EACH OTHER. SAY EVERYTHING STRAIGHT, WITH ABSOLUTE FRANKNESS.
AND SO WE WERE VERY HONEST WITH EACH OTHER, AND IT WORKED WELL, AND...
...AND WE BECAME VERY MUCH IN LOVE – A LOVE LIKE NO OTHER LOVE THAT I KNOW OF.

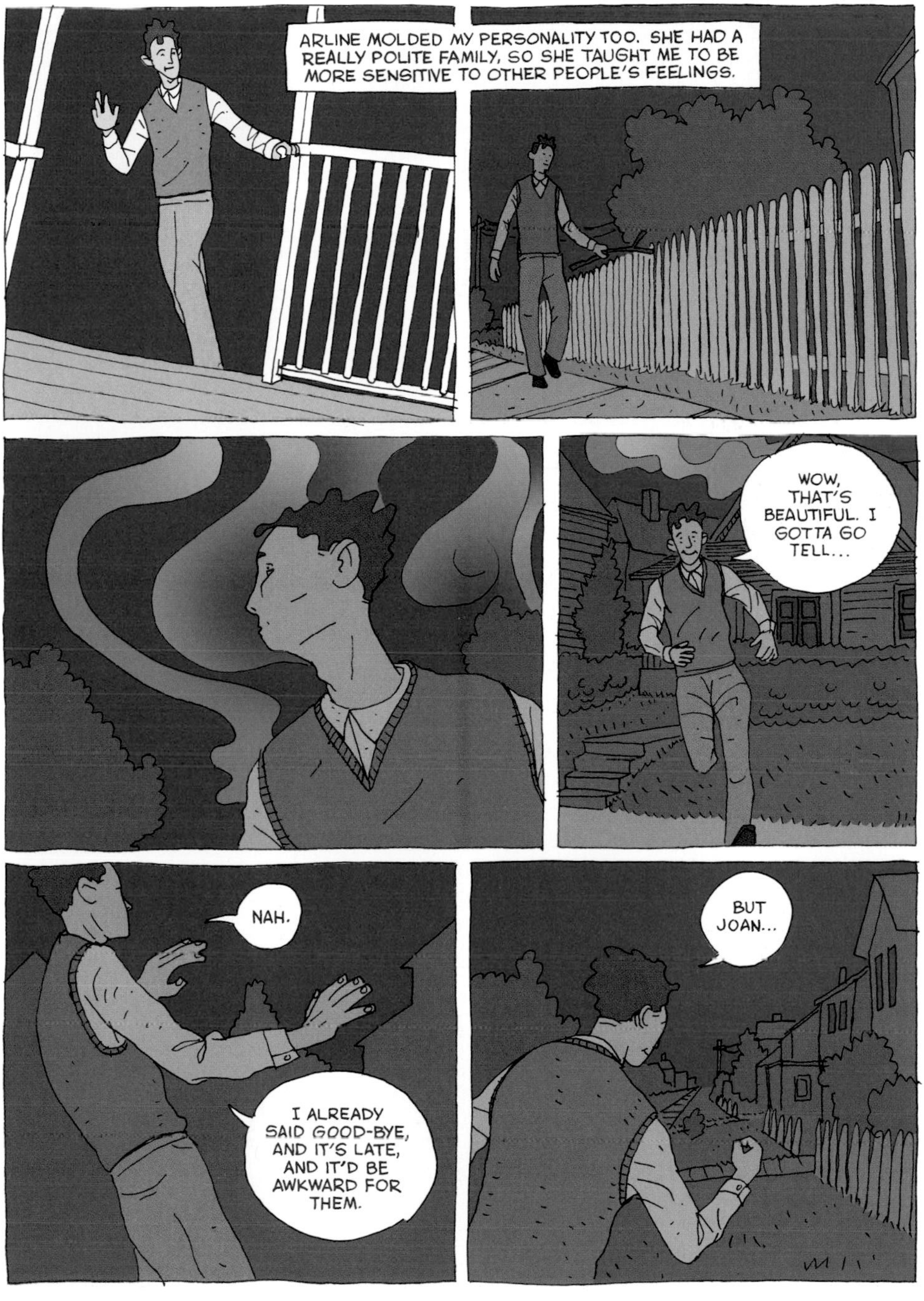
ARLINE MOLDED MY PERSONALITY TOO. SHE HAD A REALLY POLITE FAMILY, SO SHE TAUGHT ME TO BE MORE SENSITIVE TO OTHER PEOPLE'S FEELINGS.
WOW, THAT'S BEAUTIFUL. I GOTTA GO TELL...
NAH.
I ALREADY SAID GOOD-BYE, AND IT'S LATE, AND IT'D BE AWKWARD FOR THEM.
BUT JOAN...

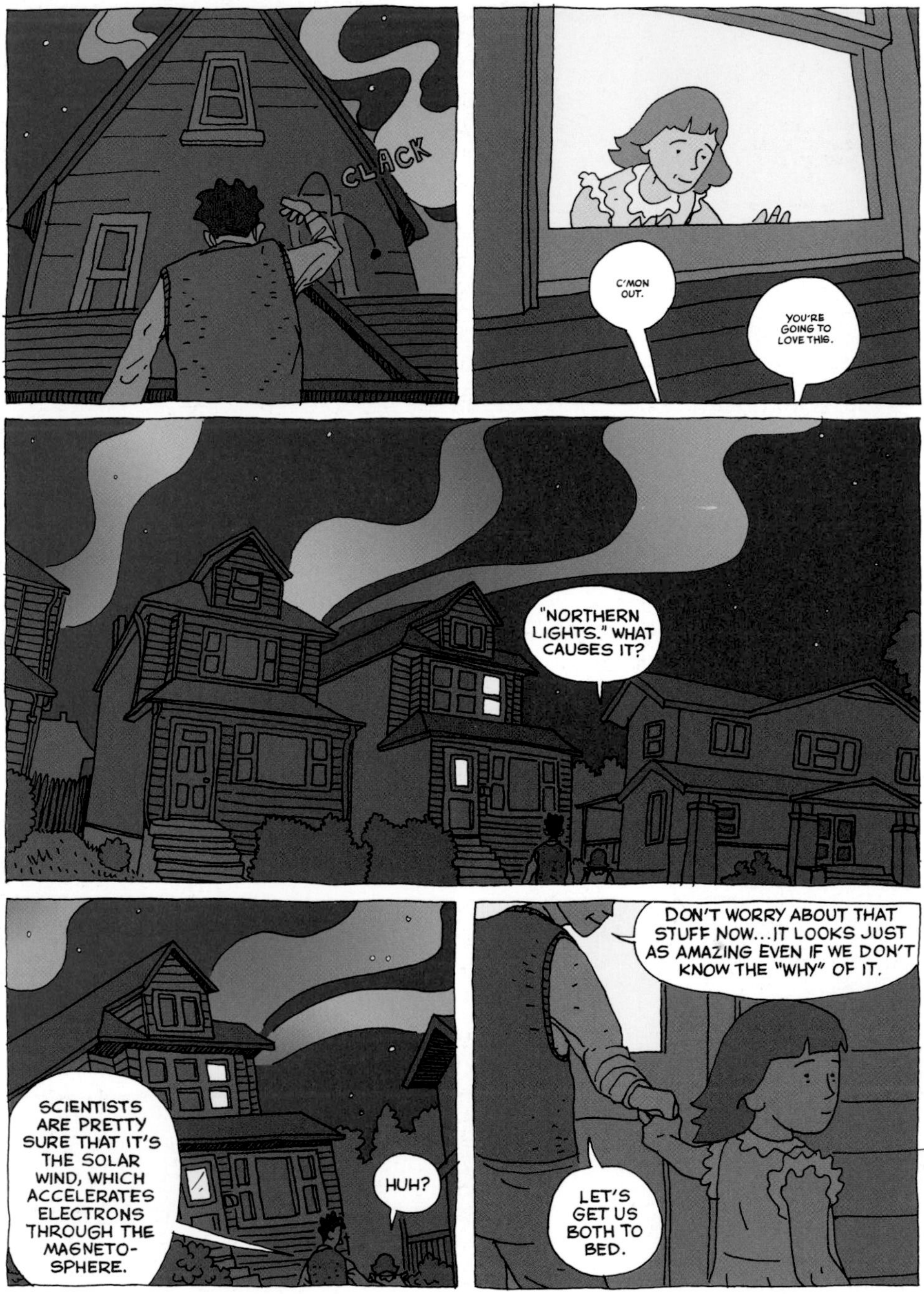
CLACK
C'MON OUT.
YOU'RE GOING TO LOVE THIS.
"NORTHERN LIGHTS." WHAT CAUSES IT?
SCIENTISTS ARE PRETTY SURE THAT IT'S THE SOLAR WIND, WHICH ACCELERATES ELECTRONS THROUGH THE MAGNETO-SPHERE.
HUH?
DON'T WORRY ABOUT THAT STUFF NOW... IT LOOKS JUST AS AMAZING EVEN IF WE DON'T KNOW THE "WHY" OF IT.
LET'S GET US BOTH TO BED.

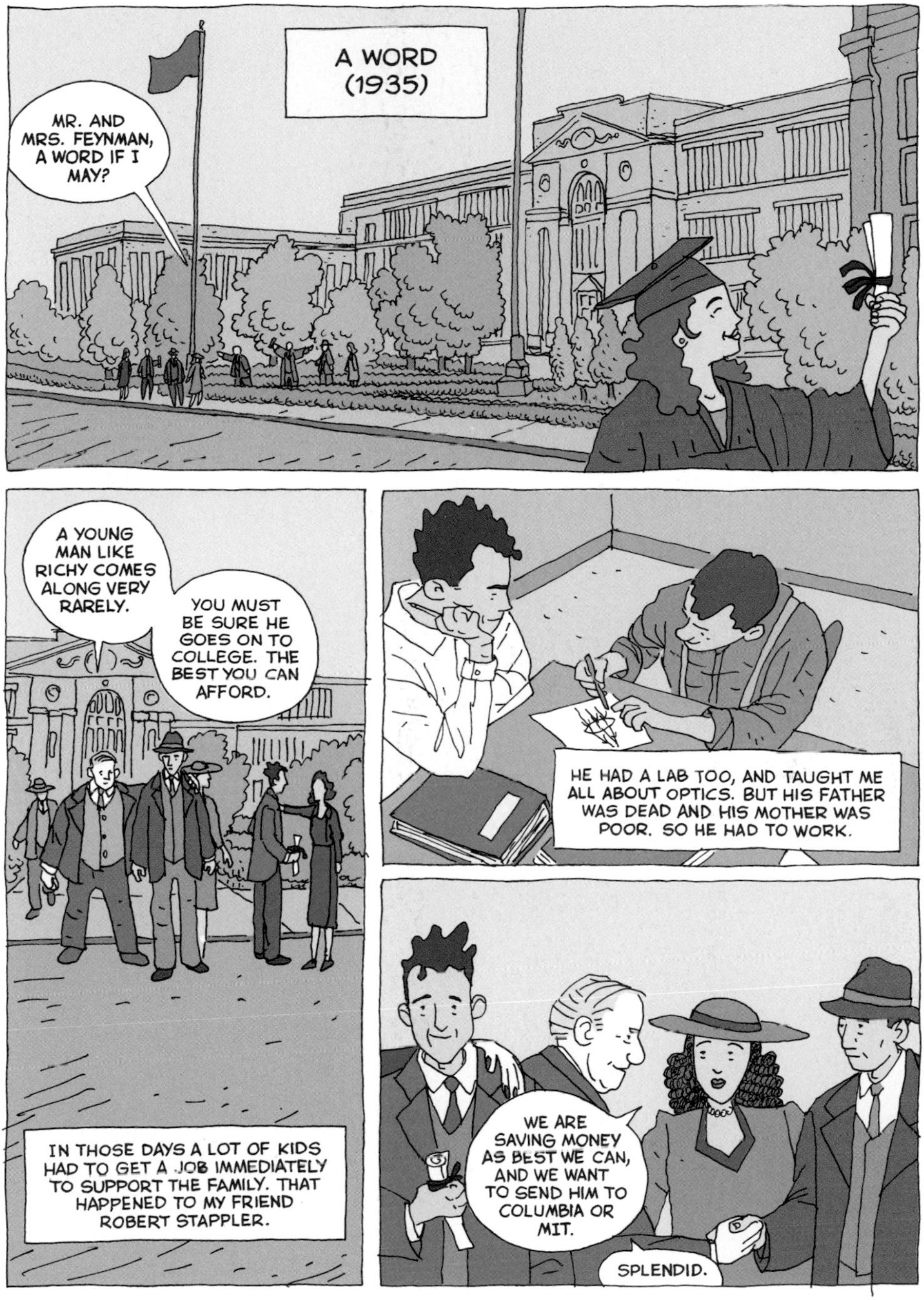
A WORD (1935)
MR. AND MRS. FEYNMAN, A WORD IF I MAY?
A YOUNG MAN LIKE RICHY COMES ALONG VERY RARELY.
YOU MUST BE SURE HE GOES ON TO COLLEGE. THE BEST YOU CAN AFFORD.
IN THOSE DAYS A LOT OF KIDS HAD TO GET A JOB IMMEDIATELY TO SUPPORT THE FAMILY. THAT HAPPENED TO MY FRIEND ROBERT STAPPLER.
HE HAD A LAB TOO, AND TAUGHT ME ALL ABOUT OPTICS. BUT HIS FATHER WAS DEAD AND HIS MOTHER WAS POOR. SO HE HAD TO WORK.
WE ARE SAVING MONEY AS BEST WE CAN, AND WE WANT TO SEND HIM TO COLUMBIA OR MIT.
SPLENDID.

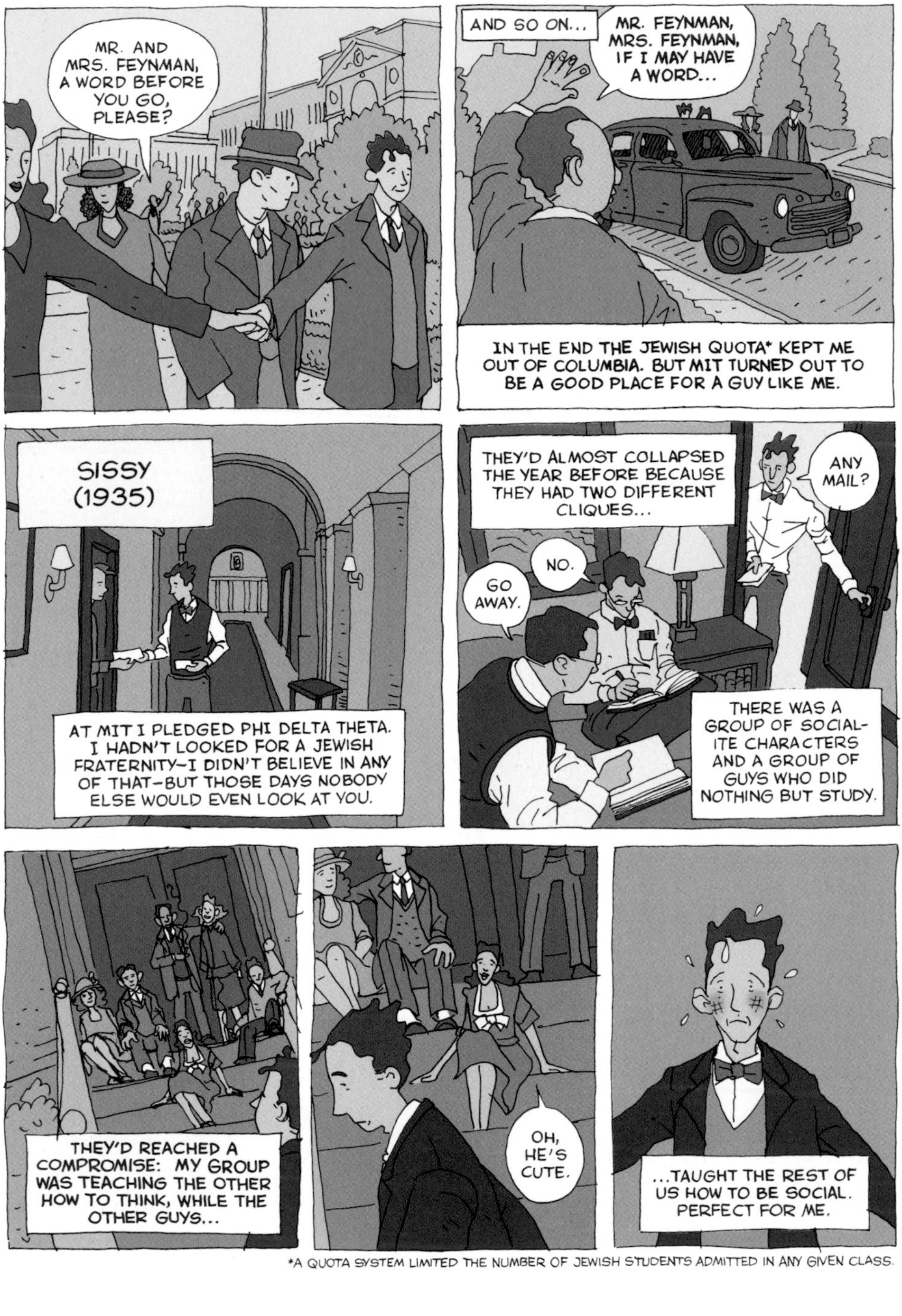
MR. AND MRS. FEYNMAN, A WORD BEFORE YOU GO, PLEASE?
AND SO ON...
MR. FEYNMAN, MRS. FEYNMAN, IF I MAY HAVE A WORD...
IN THE END THE JEWISH QUOTA* KEPT ME OUT OF COLUMBIA. BUT MIT TURNED OUT TO BE A GOOD PLACE FOR A GUY LIKE ME.
SISSY (1935)
AT MIT I PLEDGED PHI DELTA THETA. I HADN'T LOOKED FOR A JEWISH FRATERNITY—I DIDN'T BELIEVE IN ANY OF THAT—BUT THOSE DAYS NOBODY ELSE WOULD EVEN LOOK AT YOU.
THEY'D ALMOST COLLAPSED THE YEAR BEFORE BECAUSE THEY HAD TWO DIFFERENT CLIQUES...
ANY MAIL?
NO.
GO AWAY.
THERE WAS A GROUP OF SOCIAL-ITE CHARACTERS AND A GROUP OF GUYS WHO DID NOTHING BUT STUDY.
THEY'D REACHED A COMPROMISE: MY GROUP WAS TEACHING THE OTHER HOW TO THINK, WHILE THE OTHER GUYS...
OH, HE'S CUTE.
...TAUGHT THE REST OF US HOW TO BE SOCIAL. PERFECT FOR ME.

*A QUOTA SYSTEM LIMITED THE NUMBER OF JEWISH STUDENTS ADMITTED IN ANY GIVEN CLASS.

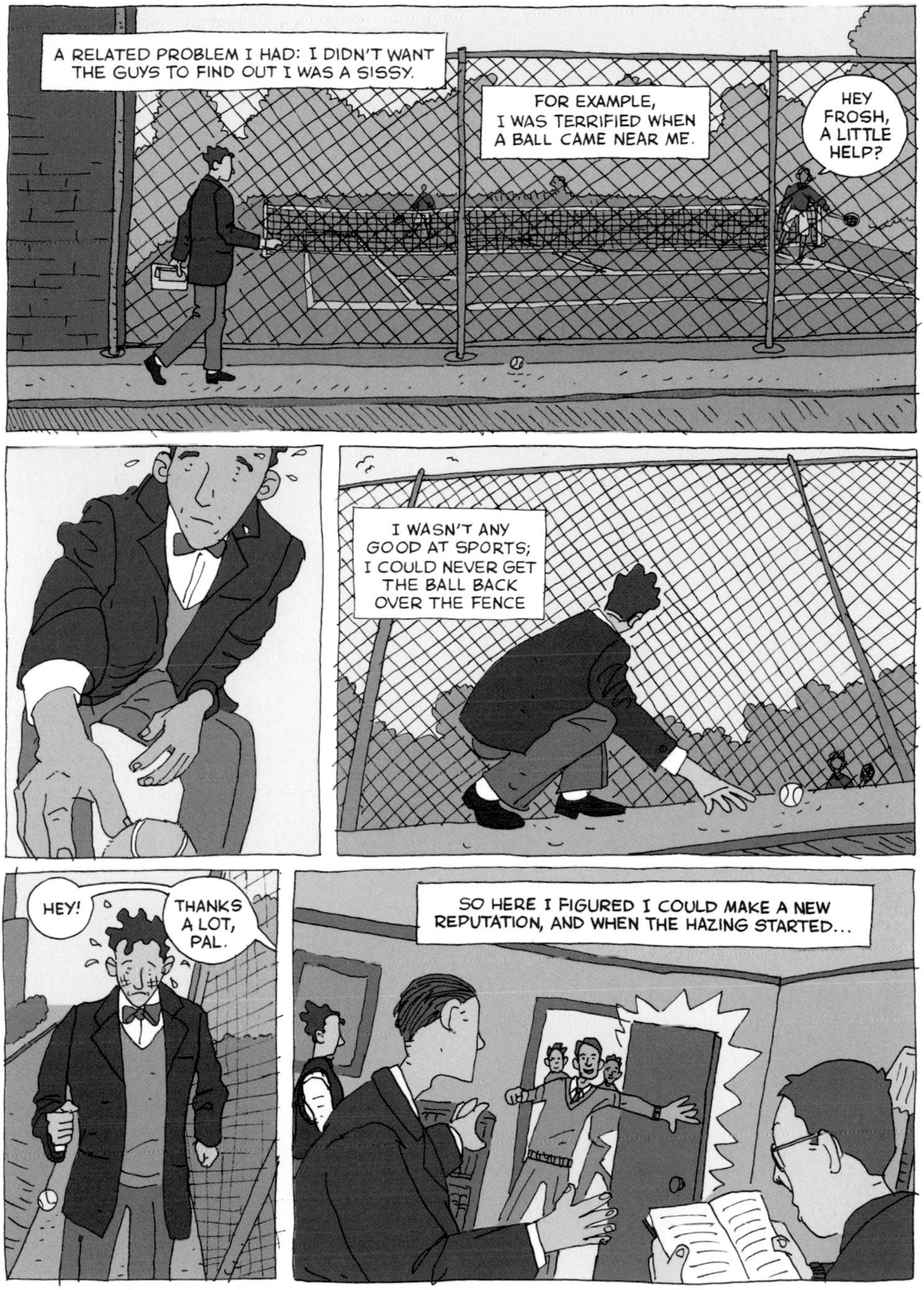
A RELATED PROBLEM I HAD: I DIDN'T WANT THE GUYS TO FIND OUT I WAS A SISSY.
FOR EXAMPLE, I WAS TERRIFIED WHEN A BALL CAME NEAR ME.
HEY FROSH, A LITTLE HELP?
I WASN'T ANY GOOD AT SPORTS; I COULD NEVER GET THE BALL BACK OVER THE FENCE
HEY!
THANKS A LOT, PAL.
SO HERE I FIGURED I COULD MAKE A NEW REPUTATION, AND WHEN THE HAZING STARTED...

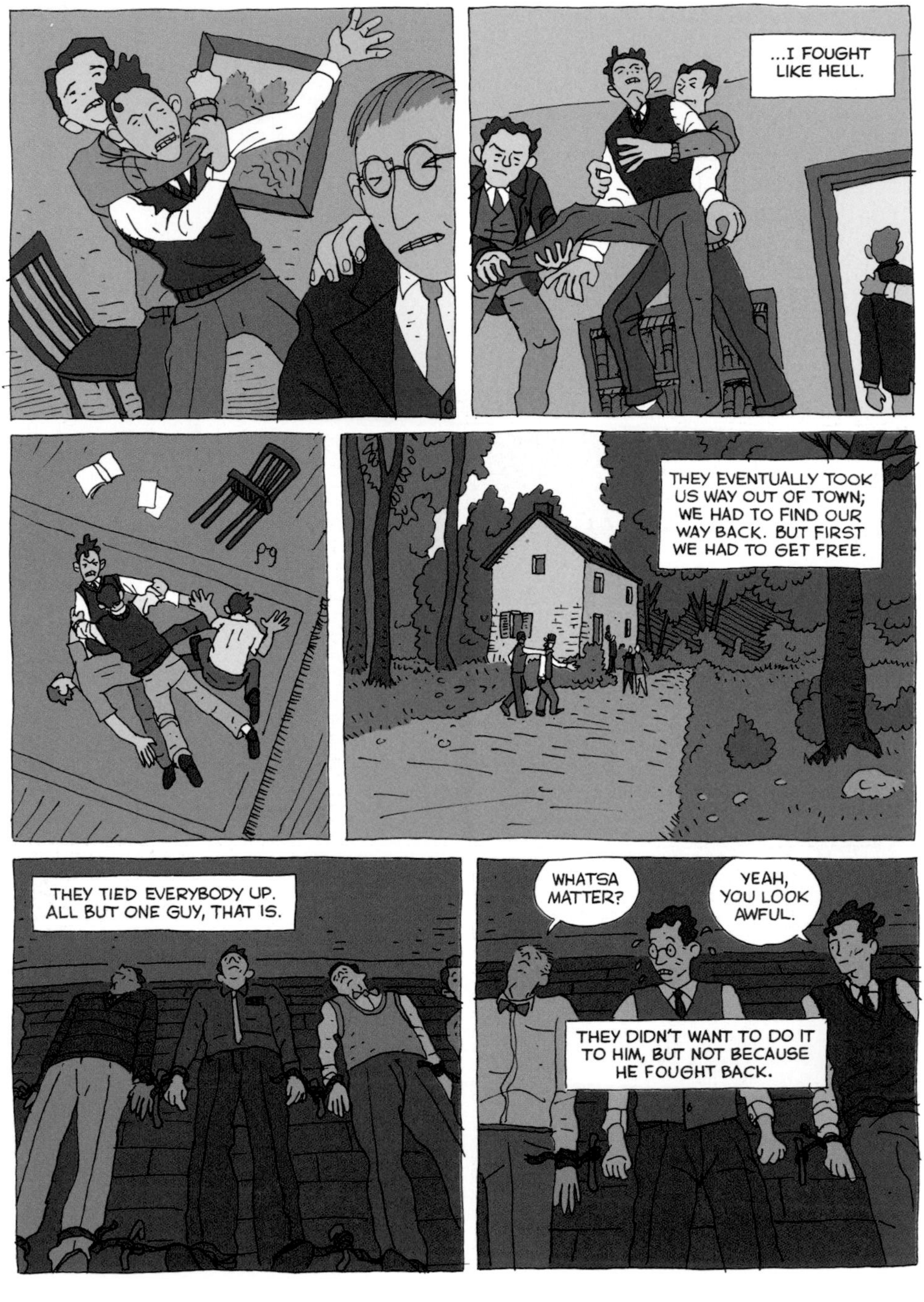
...I FOUGHT LIKE HELL.
THEY EVENTUALLY TOOK US WAY OUT OF TOWN; WE HAD TO FIND OUR WAY BACK. BUT FIRST WE HAD TO GET FREE.
THEY TIED EVERYBODY UP. ALL BUT ONE GUY, THAT IS.
WHATSA MATTER?
YEAH, YOU LOOK AWFUL.
THEY DIDN'T WANT TO DO IT TO HIM, BUT NOT BECAUSE HE FOUGHT BACK.

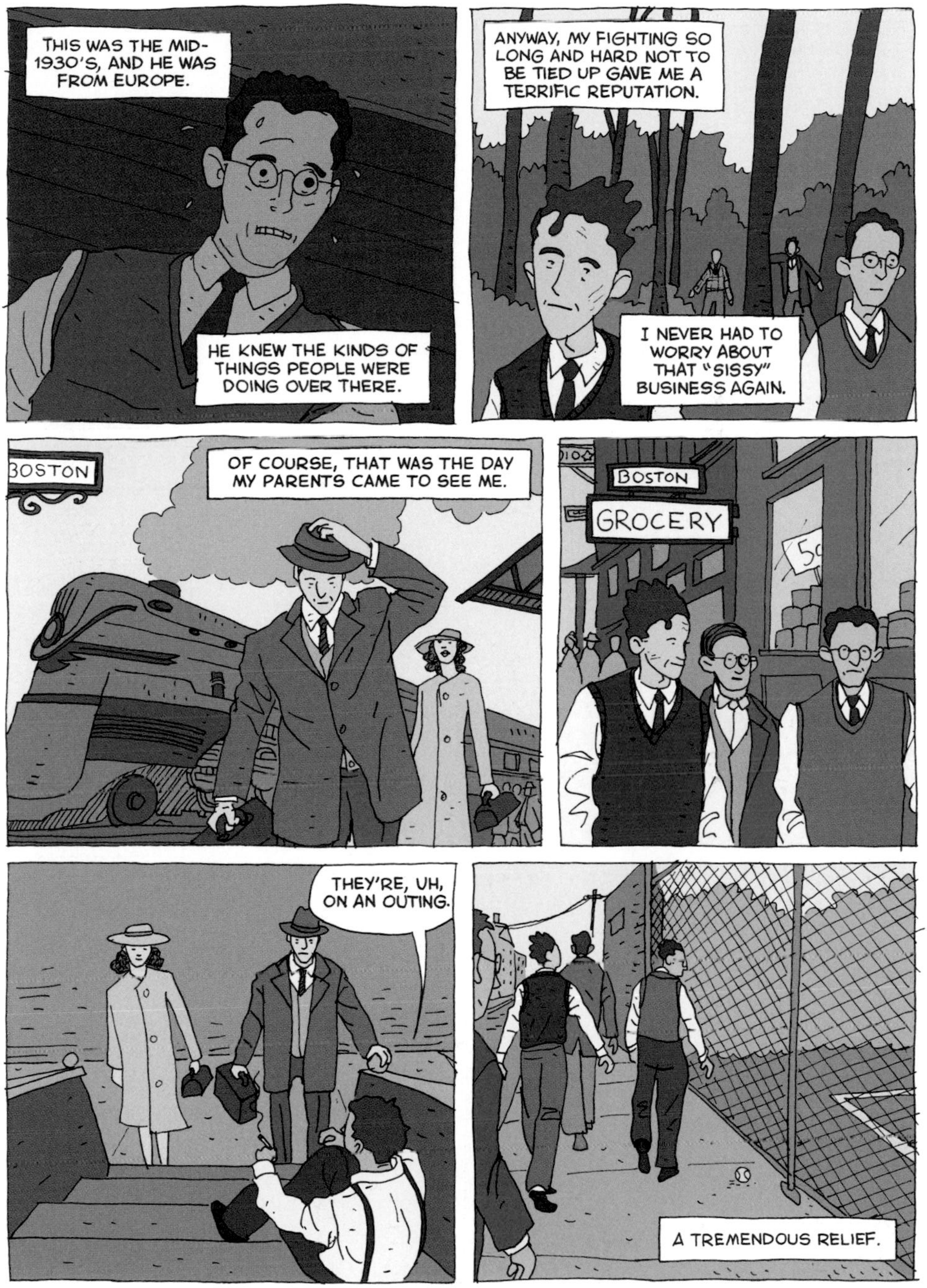
THIS WAS THE MID-1930'S, AND HE WAS FROM EUROPE.
HE KNEW THE KINDS OF THINGS PEOPLE WERE DOING OVER THERE.
ANYWAY, MY FIGHTING SO LONG AND HARD NOT TO BE TIED UP GAVE ME A TERRIFIC REPUTATION.
I NEVER HAD TO WORRY ABOUT THAT "SISSY" BUSINESS AGAIN.
BOSTON
OF COURSE, THAT WAS THE DAY MY PARENTS CAME TO SEE ME.
BOSTON
GROCERY
THEY'RE, UH, ON AN OUTING.
A TREMENDOUS RELIEF.

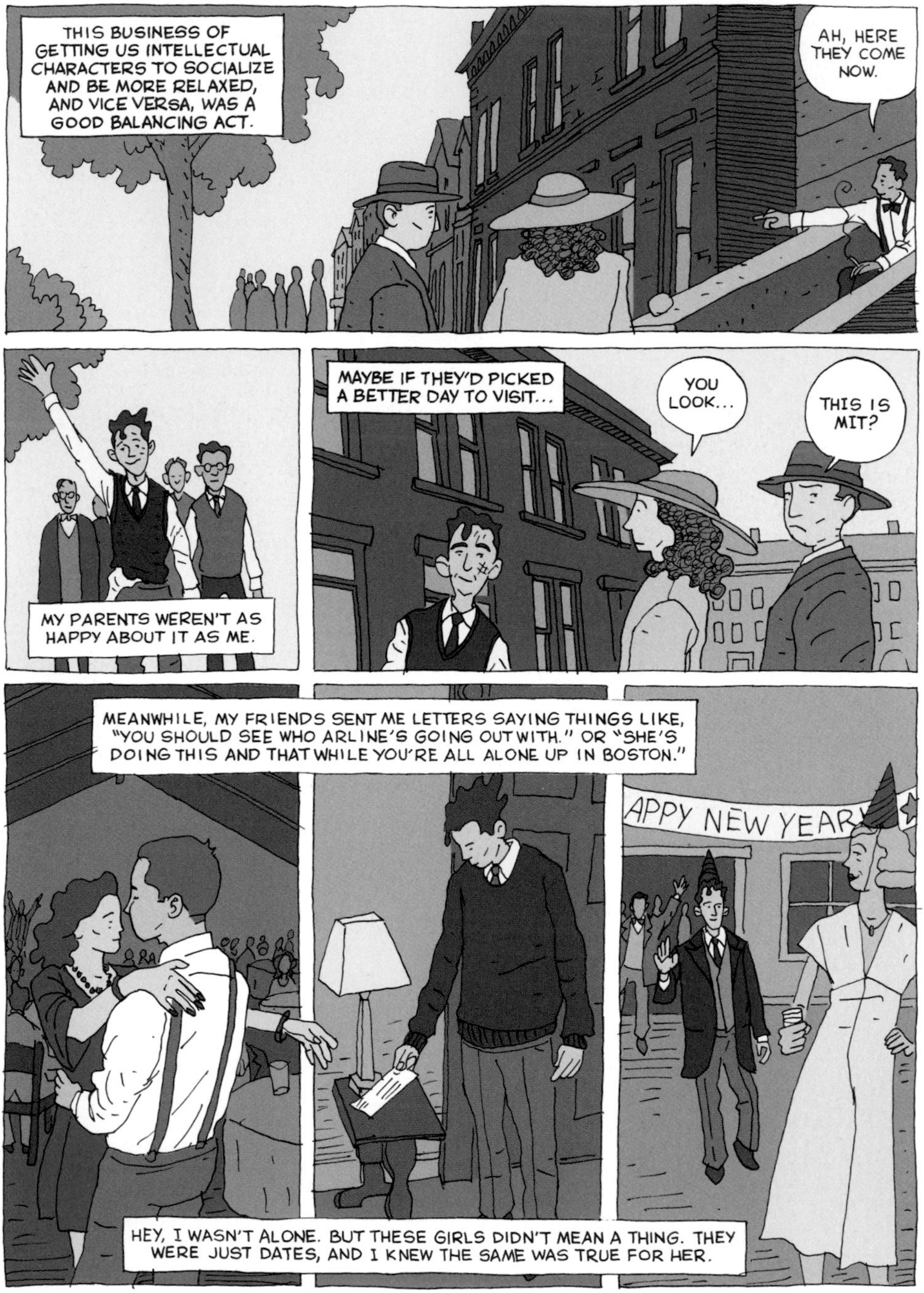

THIS BUSINESS OF GETTING US INTELLECTUAL CHARACTERS TO SOCIALIZE AND BE MORE RELAXED, AND VICE VERSA, WAS A GOOD BALANCING ACT.
AH, HERE THEY COME NOW.
MY PARENTS WEREN'T AS HAPPY ABOUT IT AS ME.
MAYBE IF THEY'D PICKED A BETTER DAY TO VISIT...
YOU LOOK...
THIS IS MIT?
MEANWHILE, MY FRIENDS SENT ME LETTERS SAYING THINGS LIKE, "YOU SHOULD SEE WHO ARLINE'S GOING OUT WITH." OR "SHE'S DOING THIS AND THAT WHILE YOU'RE ALL ALONE UP IN BOSTON."
APPY NEW YEAR
HEY, I WASN'T ALONE. BUT THESE GIRLS DIDN'T MEAN A THING. THEY WERE JUST DATES, AND I KNEW THE SAME WAS TRUE FOR HER.

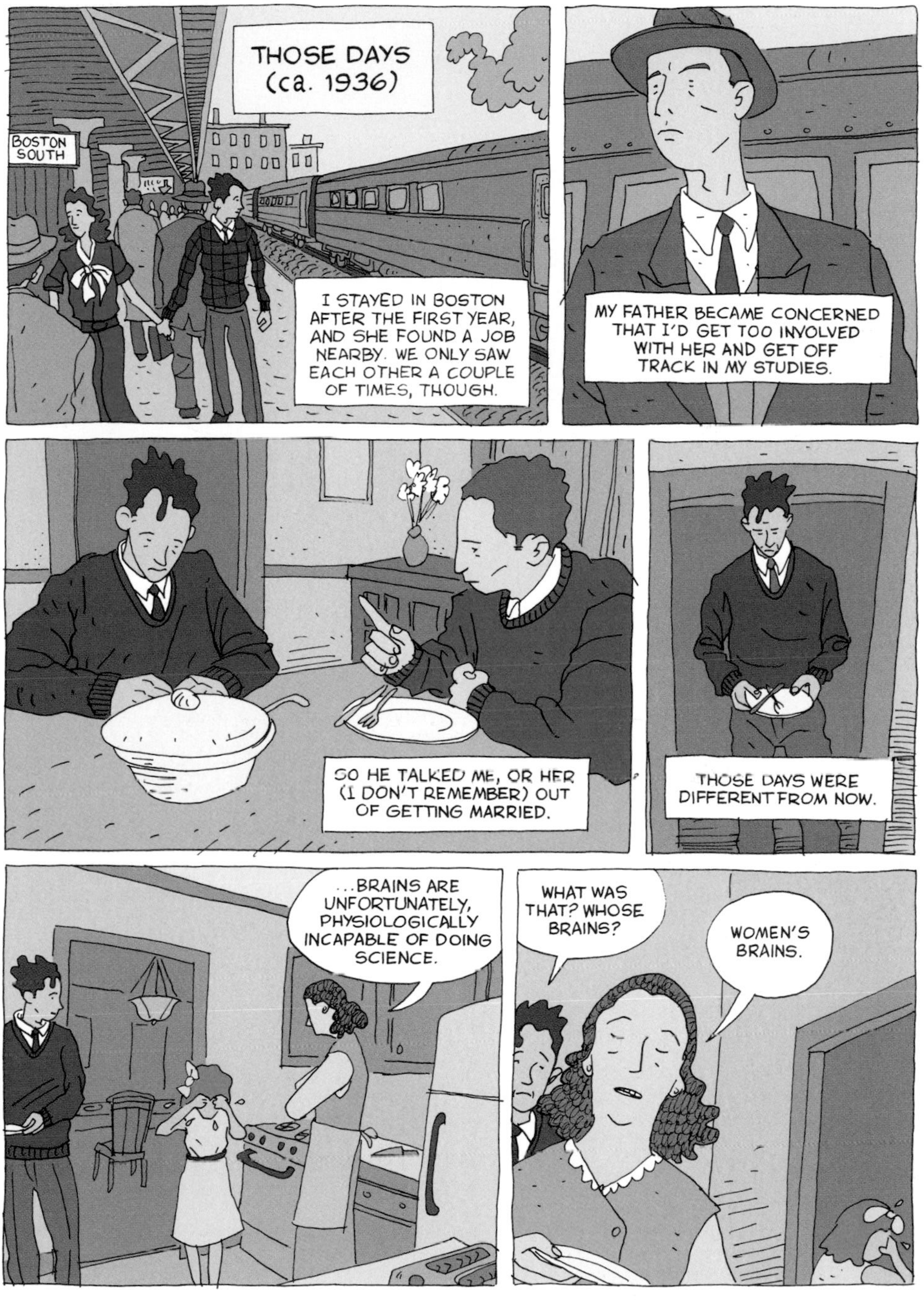
THOSE DAYS (ca. 1936)
BOSTON SOUTH
I STAYED IN BOSTON AFTER THE FIRST YEAR, AND SHE FOUND A JOB NEARBY. WE ONLY SAW EACH OTHER A COUPLE OF TIMES, THOUGH.
MY FATHER BECAME CONCERNED THAT I'D GET TOO INVOLVED WITH HER AND GET OFF TRACK IN MY STUDIES.
SO HE TALKED ME, OR HER (I DON'T REMEMBER) OUT OF GETTING MARRIED.
THOSE DAYS WERE DIFFERENT FROM NOW.
...BRAINS ARE UNFORTUNATELY, PHYSIOLOGICALLY INCAPABLE OF DOING SCIENCE.
WHAT WAS THAT? WHOSE BRAINS?
WOMEN'S BRAINS.

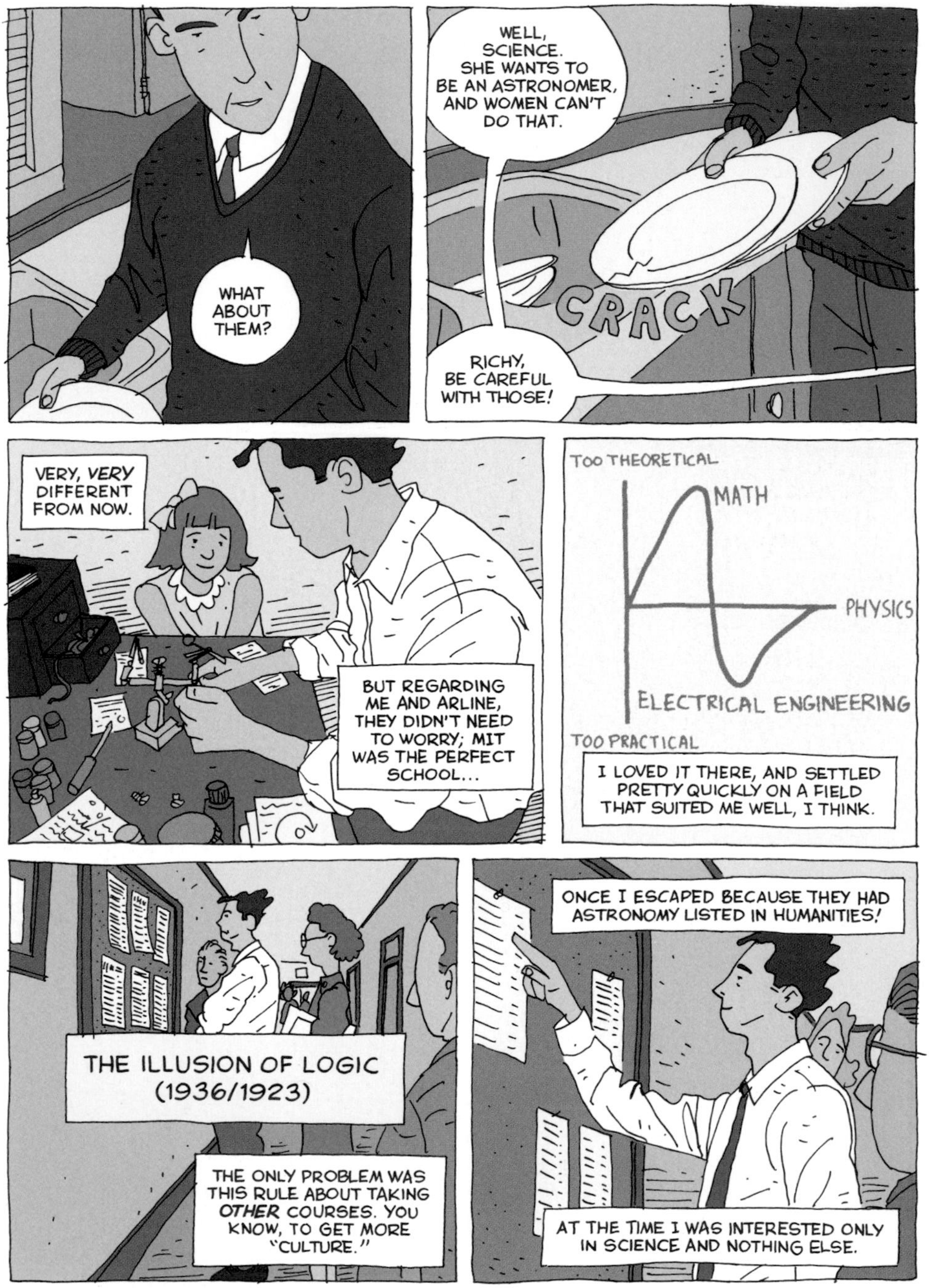
WHAT ABOUT THEM?
WELL, SCIENCE. SHE WANTS TO BE AN ASTRONOMER, AND WOMEN CAN'T DO THAT.
CRACK
RICHY, BE CAREFUL WITH THOSE!
VERY, *VERY* DIFFERENT FROM NOW.
BUT REGARDING ME AND ARLINE, THEY DIDN'T NEED TO WORRY; MIT WAS THE PERFECT SCHOOL...
TOO THEORETICAL
MATH
PHYSICS
ELECTRICAL ENGINEERING
TOO PRACTICAL
I LOVED IT THERE, AND SETTLED PRETTY QUICKLY ON A FIELD THAT SUITED ME WELL, I THINK.
THE ILLUSION OF LOGIC (1936/1923)
THE ONLY PROBLEM WAS THIS RULE ABOUT TAKING *OTHER* COURSES. YOU KNOW, TO GET MORE "CULTURE."
ONCE I ESCAPED BECAUSE THEY HAD ASTRONOMY LISTED IN HUMANITIES!
AT THE TIME I WAS INTERESTED ONLY IN SCIENCE AND NOTHING ELSE.

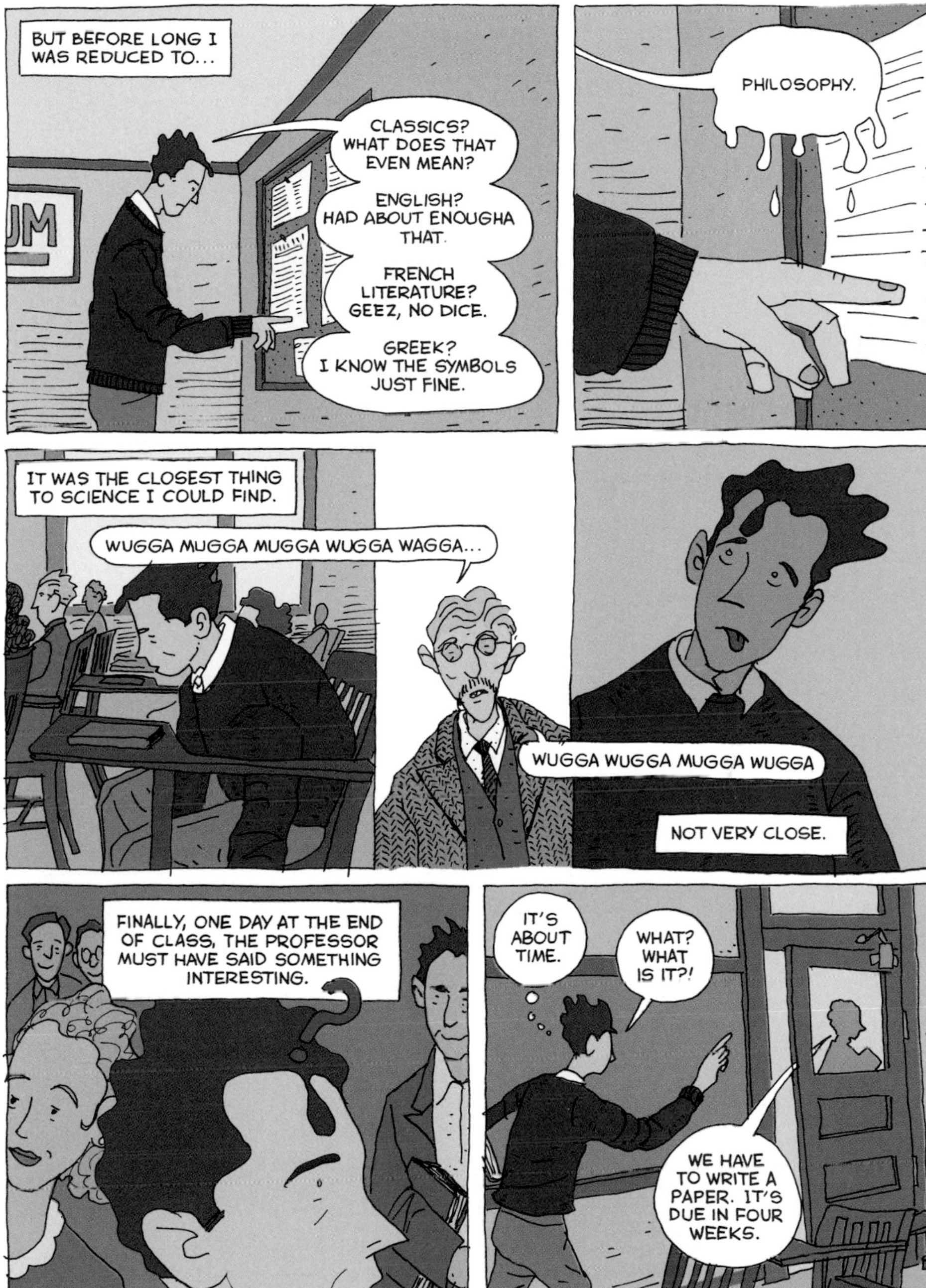
BUT BEFORE LONG I WAS REDUCED TO...
CLASSICS? WHAT DOES THAT EVEN MEAN?
ENGLISH? HAD ABOUT ENOUGHA THAT.
FRENCH LITERATURE? GEEZ, NO DICE.
GREEK? I KNOW THE SYMBOLS JUST FINE.
PHILOSOPHY.
IT WAS THE CLOSEST THING TO SCIENCE I COULD FIND.
WUGGA MUGGA MUGGA WUGGA WAGGA...
WUGGA WUGGA MUGGA WUGGA
NOT VERY CLOSE.
FINALLY, ONE DAY AT THE END OF CLASS, THE PROFESSOR MUST HAVE SAID SOMETHING INTERESTING.
IT'S ABOUT TIME.
WHAT? WHAT IS IT?!
WE HAVE TO WRITE A PAPER. IT'S DUE IN FOUR WEEKS.

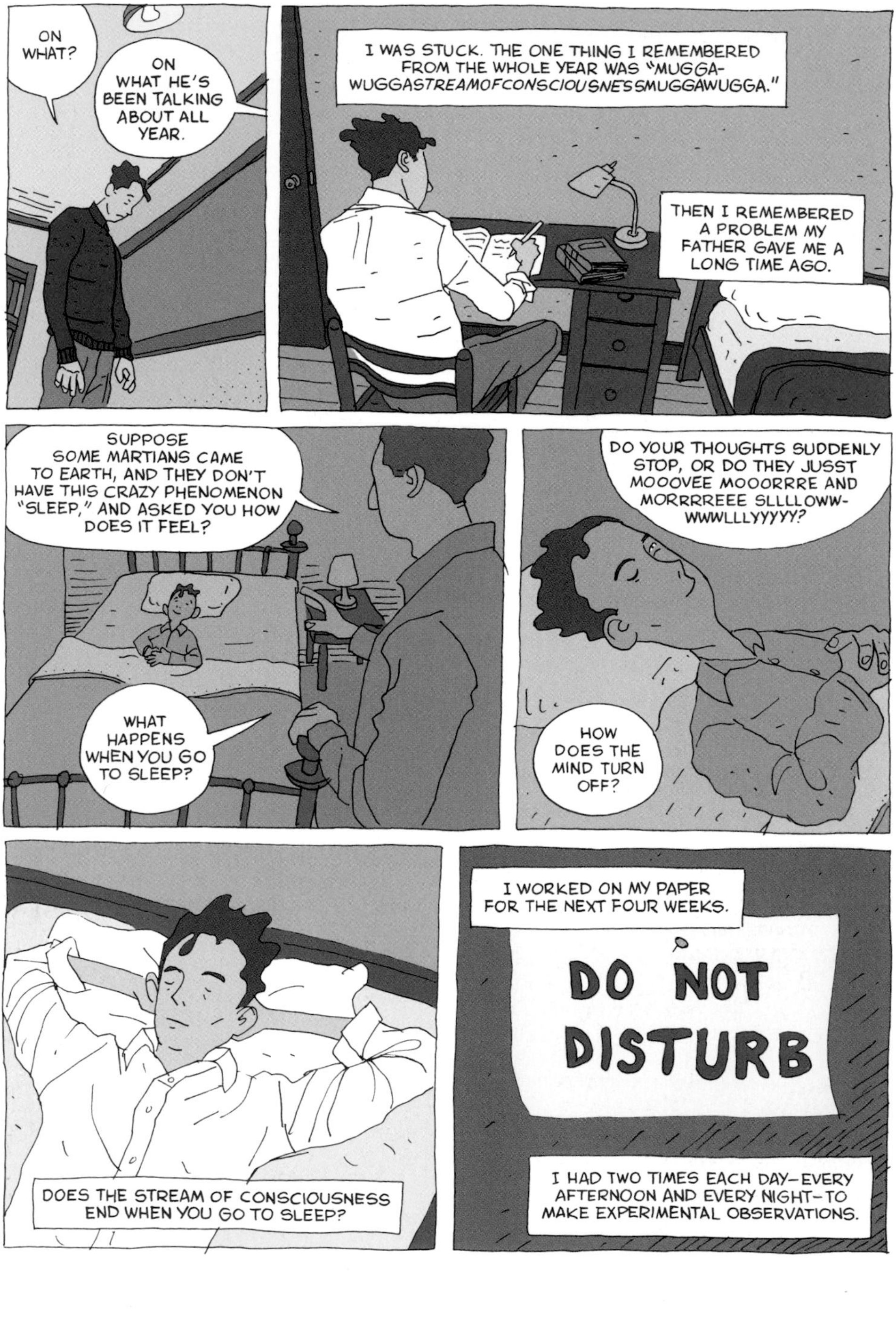

ON WHAT?
ON WHAT HE'S BEEN TALKING ABOUT ALL YEAR.
I WAS STUCK. THE ONE THING I REMEMBERED FROM THE WHOLE YEAR WAS "MUGGA-WUGGASTREAMOFCONSCIOUSNESSMUGGAWUGGA."
THEN I REMEMBERED A PROBLEM MY FATHER GAVE ME A LONG TIME AGO.
SUPPOSE SOME MARTIANS CAME TO EARTH, AND THEY DON'T HAVE THIS CRAZY PHENOMENON "SLEEP," AND ASKED YOU HOW DOES IT FEEL?
WHAT HAPPENS WHEN YOU GO TO SLEEP?
DO YOUR THOUGHTS SUDDENLY STOP, OR DO THEY JUSST MOOOVEE MOOORRRE AND MORRRREEE SLLLLOWW-WWWLLLYYYYY?
HOW DOES THE MIND TURN OFF?
DOES THE STREAM OF CONSCIOUSNESS END WHEN YOU GO TO SLEEP?
I WORKED ON MY PAPER FOR THE NEXT FOUR WEEKS.
DO NOT DISTURB
I HAD TWO TIMES EACH DAY—EVERY AFTERNOON AND EVERY NIGHT—TO MAKE EXPERIMENTAL OBSERVATIONS.

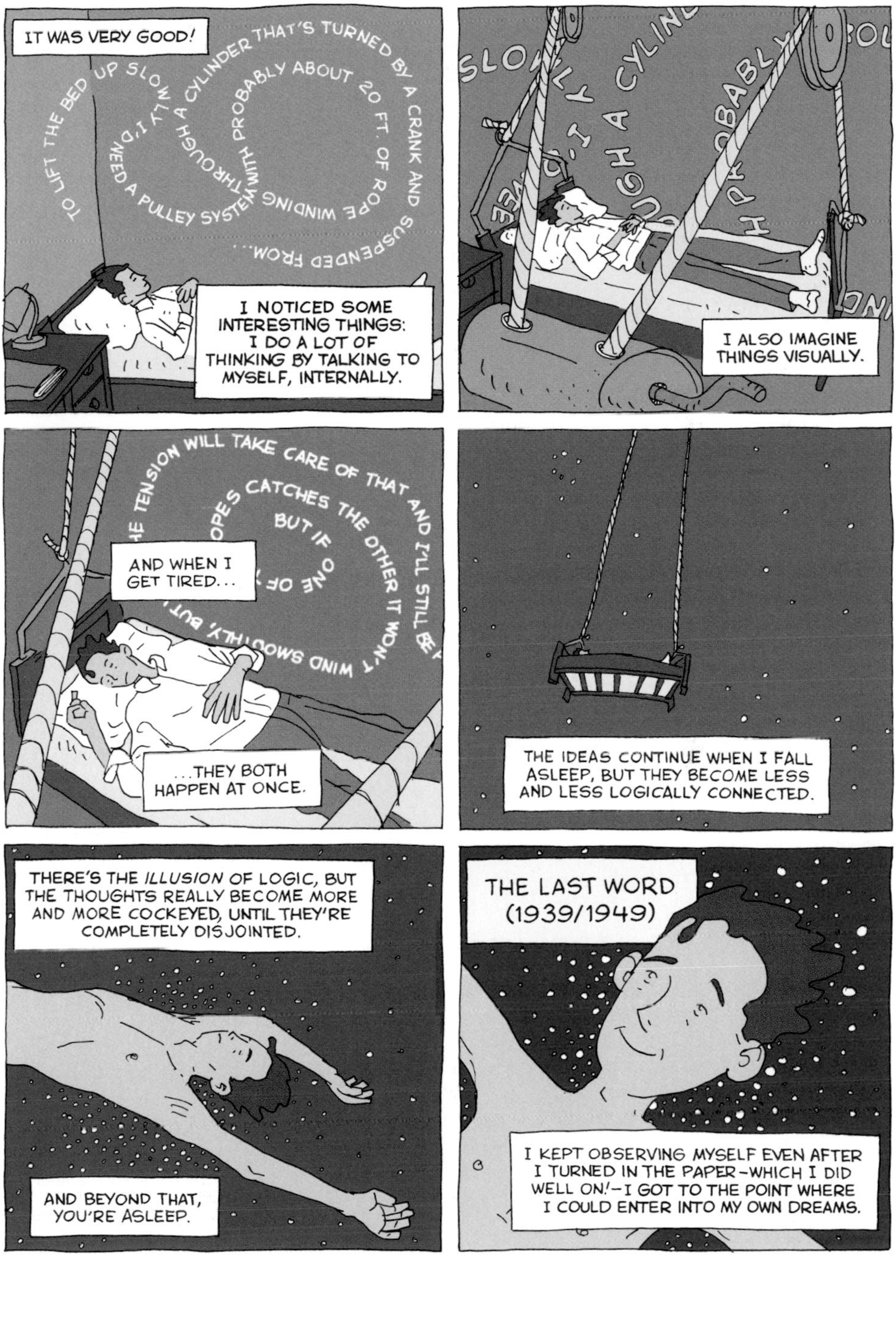

IT WAS VERY GOOD!
TO LIFT THE BED UP SLOWLY, I NEED A PULLEY SYSTEM WITH PROBABLY ABOUT 20 FT. OF ROPE WINDING THROUGH A CYLINDER THAT'S TURNED BY A CRANK AND SUSPENDED FROM...
I NOTICED SOME INTERESTING THINGS: I DO A LOT OF THINKING BY TALKING TO MYSELF, INTERNALLY.
I ALSO IMAGINE THINGS VISUALLY.
BUT IF ONE OF THE ROPES CATCHES THE OTHER IT WON'T WIND SMOOTHLY, BUT THE TENSION WILL TAKE CARE OF THAT AND I'LL STILL BE
AND WHEN I GET TIRED...
...THEY BOTH HAPPEN AT ONCE.
THE IDEAS CONTINUE WHEN I FALL ASLEEP, BUT THEY BECOME LESS AND LESS LOGICALLY CONNECTED.
THERE'S THE *ILLUSION* OF LOGIC, BUT THE THOUGHTS REALLY BECOME MORE AND MORE COCKEYED, UNTIL THEY'RE COMPLETELY DISJOINTED.
AND BEYOND THAT, YOU'RE ASLEEP.
THE LAST WORD (1939/1949)
I KEPT OBSERVING MYSELF EVEN AFTER I TURNED IN THE PAPER—WHICH I DID WELL ON!—I GOT TO THE POINT WHERE I COULD ENTER INTO MY OWN DREAMS.

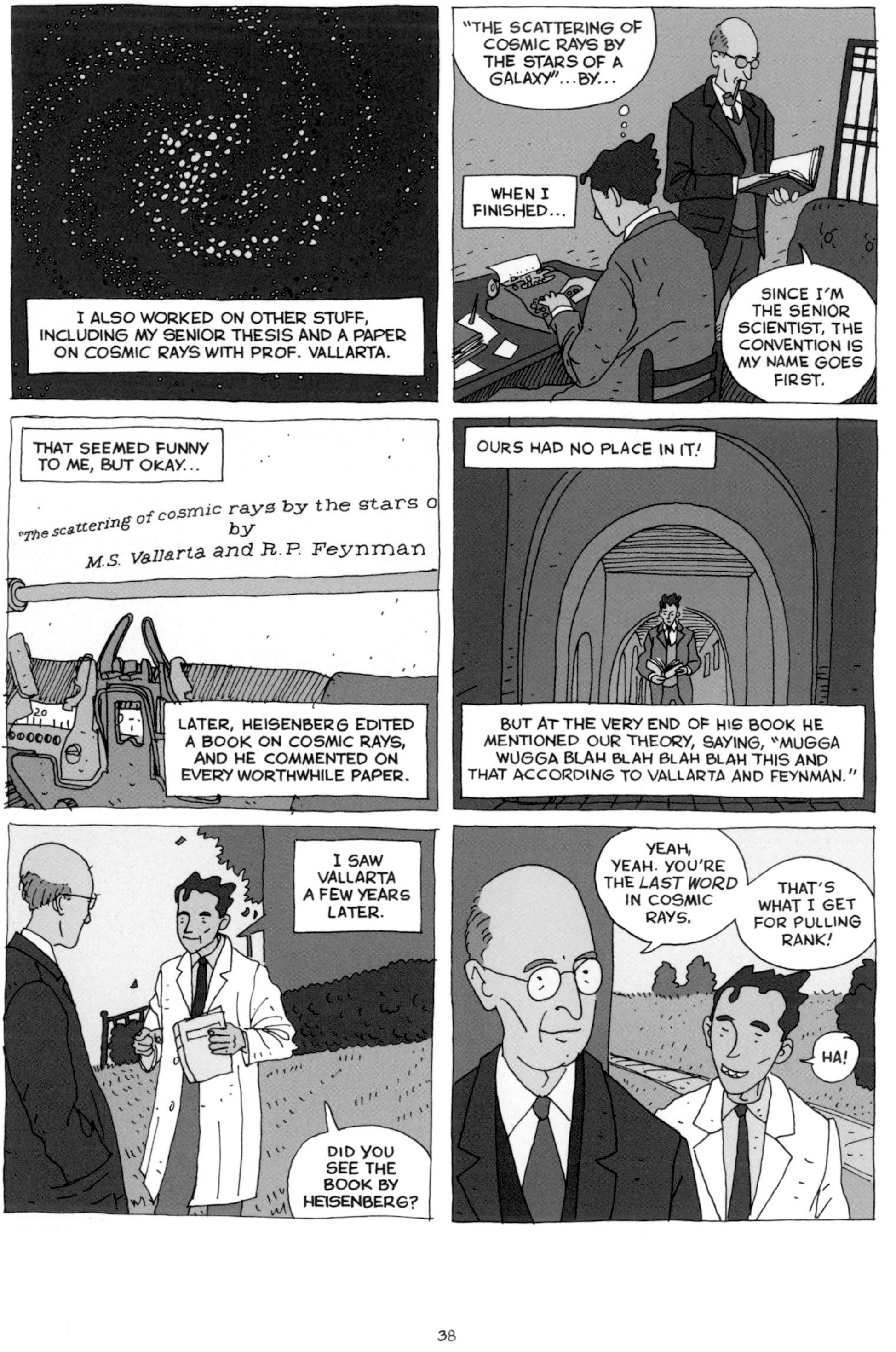
I ALSO WORKED ON OTHER STUFF, INCLUDING MY SENIOR THESIS AND A PAPER ON COSMIC RAYS WITH PROF. VALLARTA.
"THE SCATTERING OF COSMIC RAYS BY THE STARS OF A GALAXY"...BY...
WHEN I FINISHED...
SINCE I'M THE SENIOR SCIENTIST, THE CONVENTION IS MY NAME GOES FIRST.
THAT SEEMED FUNNY TO ME, BUT OKAY...
"The scattering of cosmic rays by the stars o
by
M.S. Vallarta and R.P. Feynman
LATER, HEISENBERG EDITED A BOOK ON COSMIC RAYS, AND HE COMMENTED ON EVERY WORTHWHILE PAPER.
OURS HAD NO PLACE IN IT!
BUT AT THE VERY END OF HIS BOOK HE MENTIONED OUR THEORY, SAYING, "MUGGA WUGGA BLAH BLAH BLAH BLAH THIS AND THAT ACCORDING TO VALLARTA AND FEYNMAN."
I SAW VALLARTA A FEW YEARS LATER.
DID YOU SEE THE BOOK BY HEISENBERG?
YEAH, YEAH. YOU'RE THE *LAST WORD* IN COSMIC RAYS.
THAT'S WHAT I GET FOR PULLING RANK!
HA!

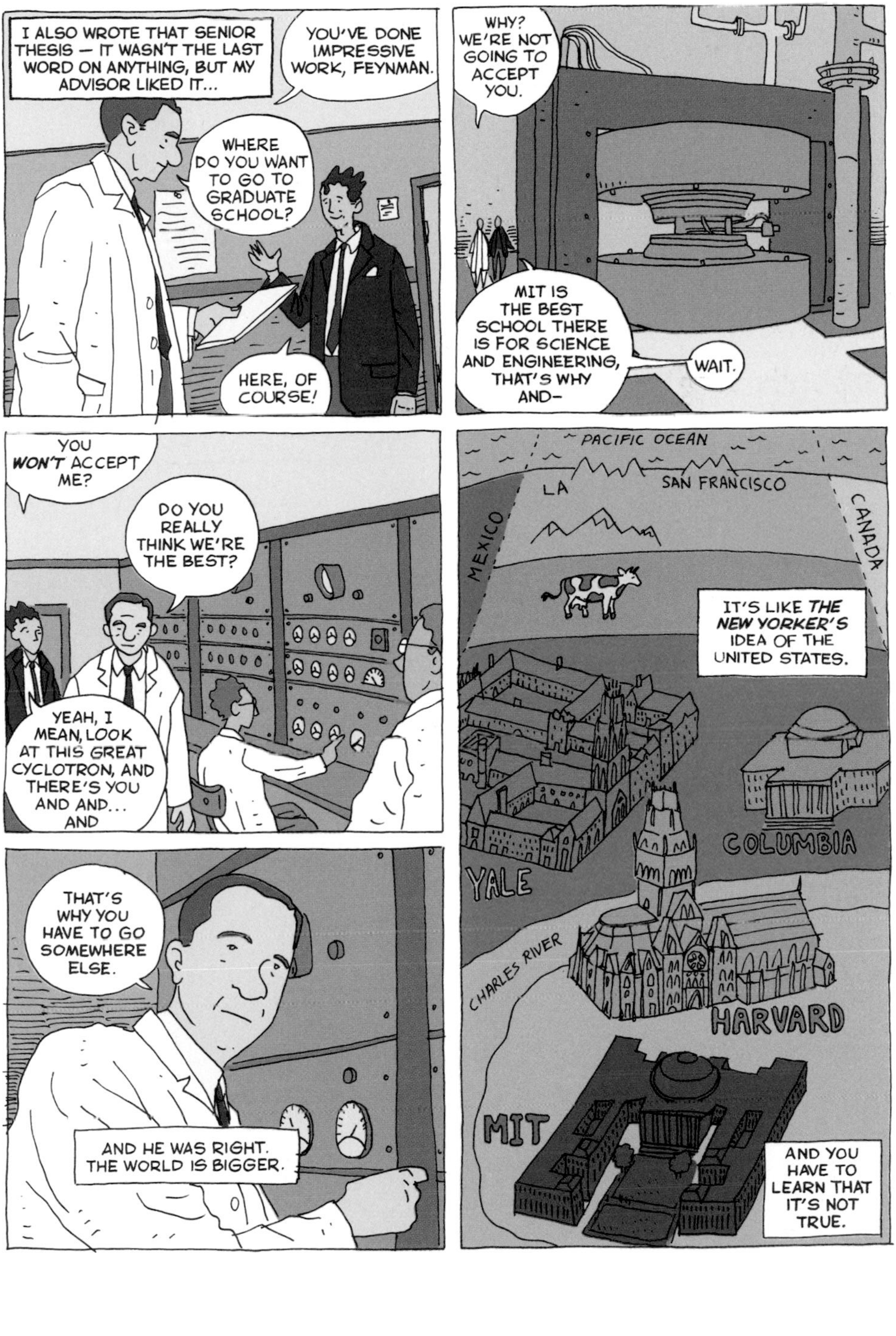
I ALSO WROTE THAT SENIOR THESIS — IT WASN'T THE LAST WORD ON ANYTHING, BUT MY ADVISOR LIKED IT...
YOU'VE DONE IMPRESSIVE WORK, FEYNMAN.
WHERE DO YOU WANT TO GO TO GRADUATE SCHOOL?
HERE, OF COURSE!
WHY? WE'RE NOT GOING TO ACCEPT YOU.
MIT IS THE BEST SCHOOL THERE IS FOR SCIENCE AND ENGINEERING, THAT'S WHY AND–
WAIT.
YOU WON'T ACCEPT ME?
DO YOU REALLY THINK WE'RE THE BEST?
YEAH, I MEAN, LOOK AT THIS GREAT CYCLOTRON, AND THERE'S YOU AND AND... AND
THAT'S WHY YOU HAVE TO GO SOMEWHERE ELSE.
AND HE WAS RIGHT. THE WORLD IS BIGGER.
PACIFIC OCEAN
LA
SAN FRANCISCO
MEXICO
CANADA
IT'S LIKE THE NEW YORKER'S IDEA OF THE UNITED STATES.
COLUMBIA
YALE
CHARLES RIVER
HARVARD
MIT
AND YOU HAVE TO LEARN THAT IT'S NOT TRUE.

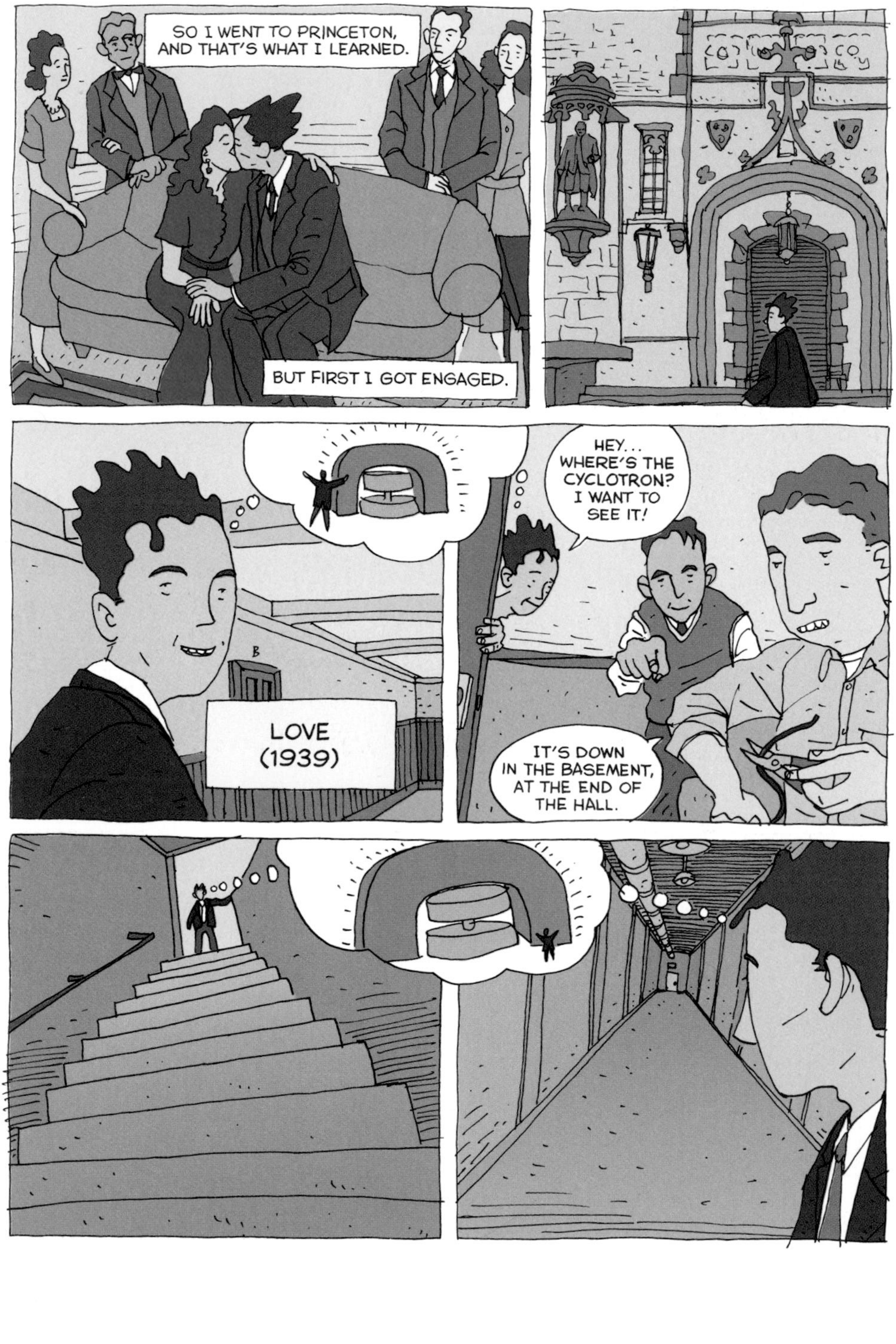
SO I WENT TO PRINCETON, AND THAT'S WHAT I LEARNED.
BUT FIRST I GOT ENGAGED.
LOVE (1939)
B
HEY... WHERE'S THE CYCLOTRON? I WANT TO SEE IT!
IT'S DOWN IN THE BASEMENT, AT THE END OF THE HALL.

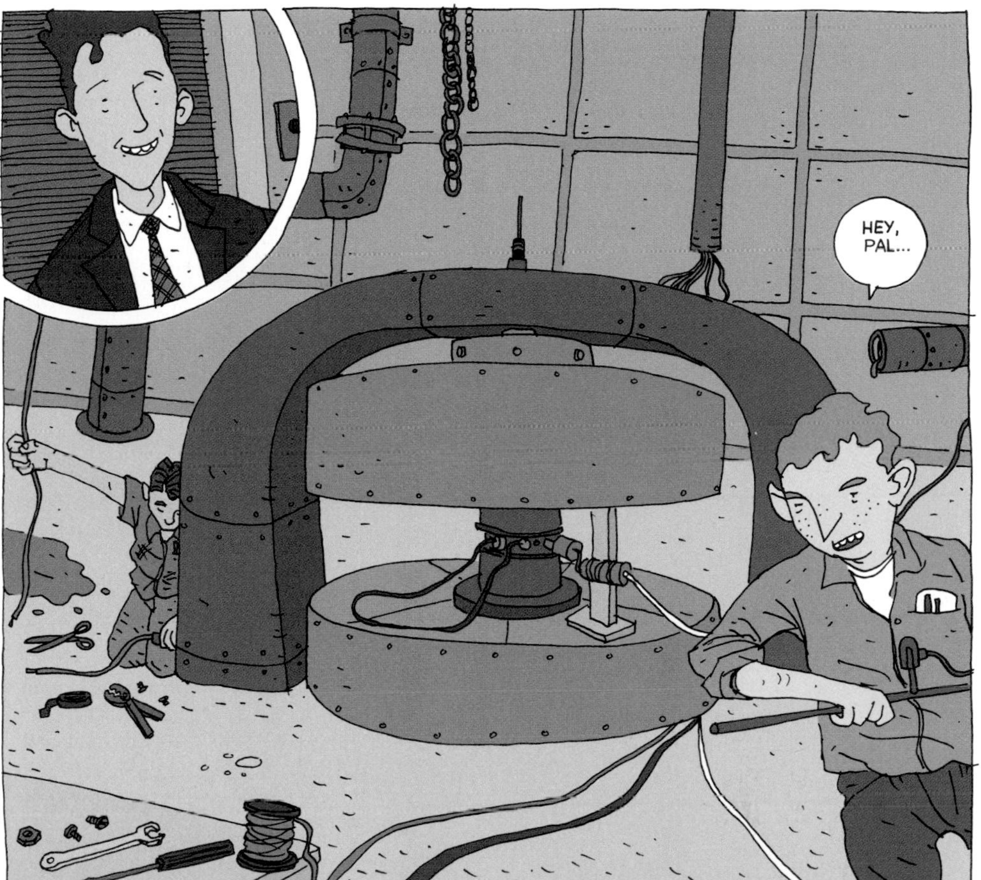
HEY, PAL...

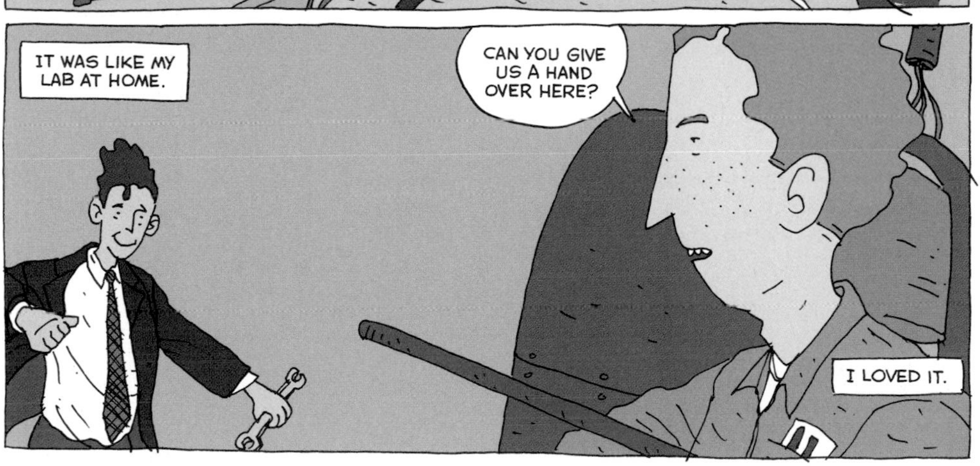
IT WAS LIKE MY LAB AT HOME.
CAN YOU GIVE US A HAND OVER HERE?
I LOVED IT.

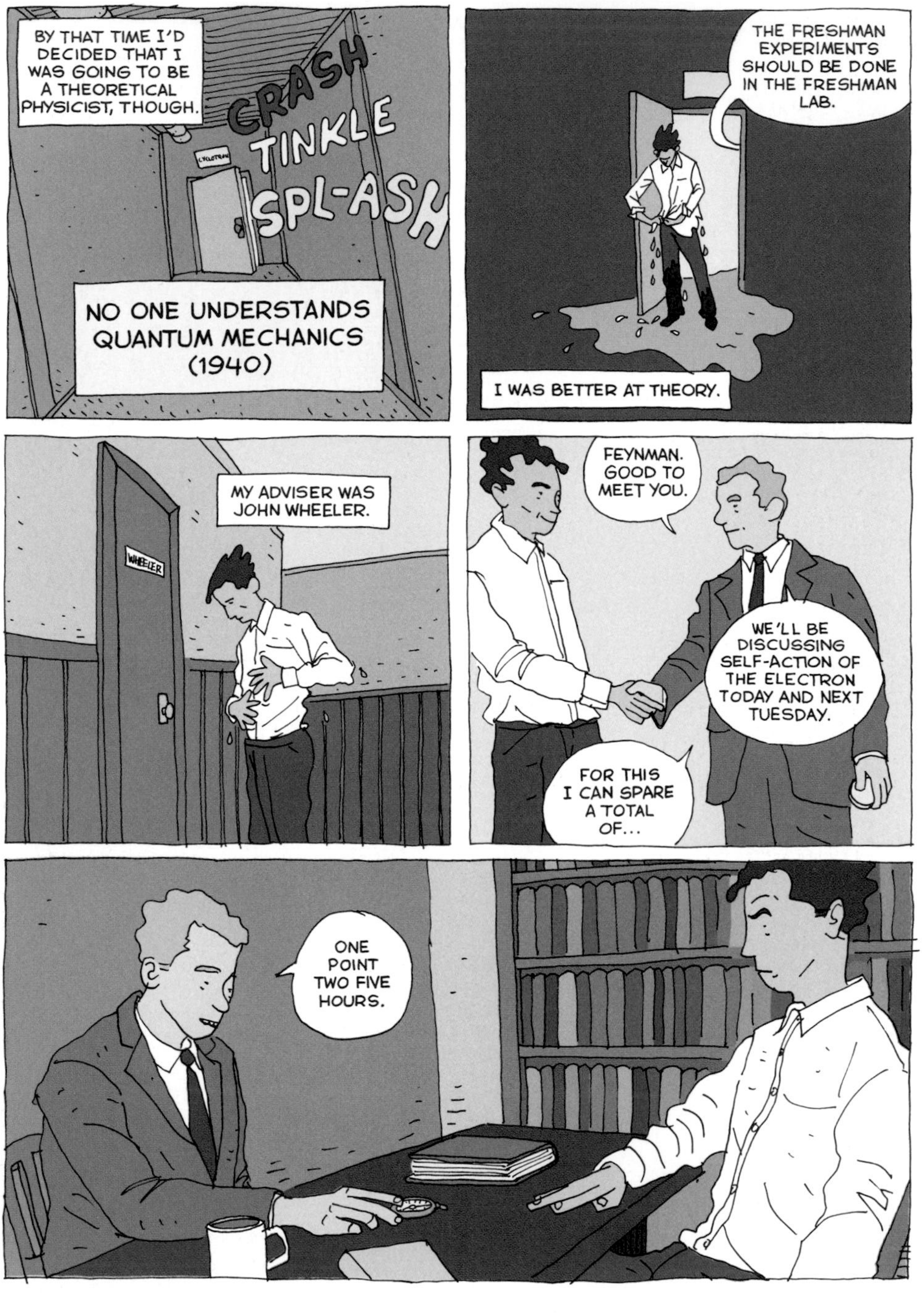
BY THAT TIME I'D DECIDED THAT I WAS GOING TO BE A THEORETICAL PHYSICIST, THOUGH.
CRASH
TINKLE
SPL-ASH
CYCLOTRON
NO ONE UNDERSTANDS QUANTUM MECHANICS (1940)
THE FRESHMAN EXPERIMENTS SHOULD BE DONE IN THE FRESHMAN LAB.
I WAS BETTER AT THEORY.
MY ADVISER WAS JOHN WHEELER.
WHEELER
FEYNMAN. GOOD TO MEET YOU.
WE'LL BE DISCUSSING SELF-ACTION OF THE ELECTRON TODAY AND NEXT TUESDAY.
FOR THIS I CAN SPARE A TOTAL OF...
ONE POINT TWO FIVE HOURS.

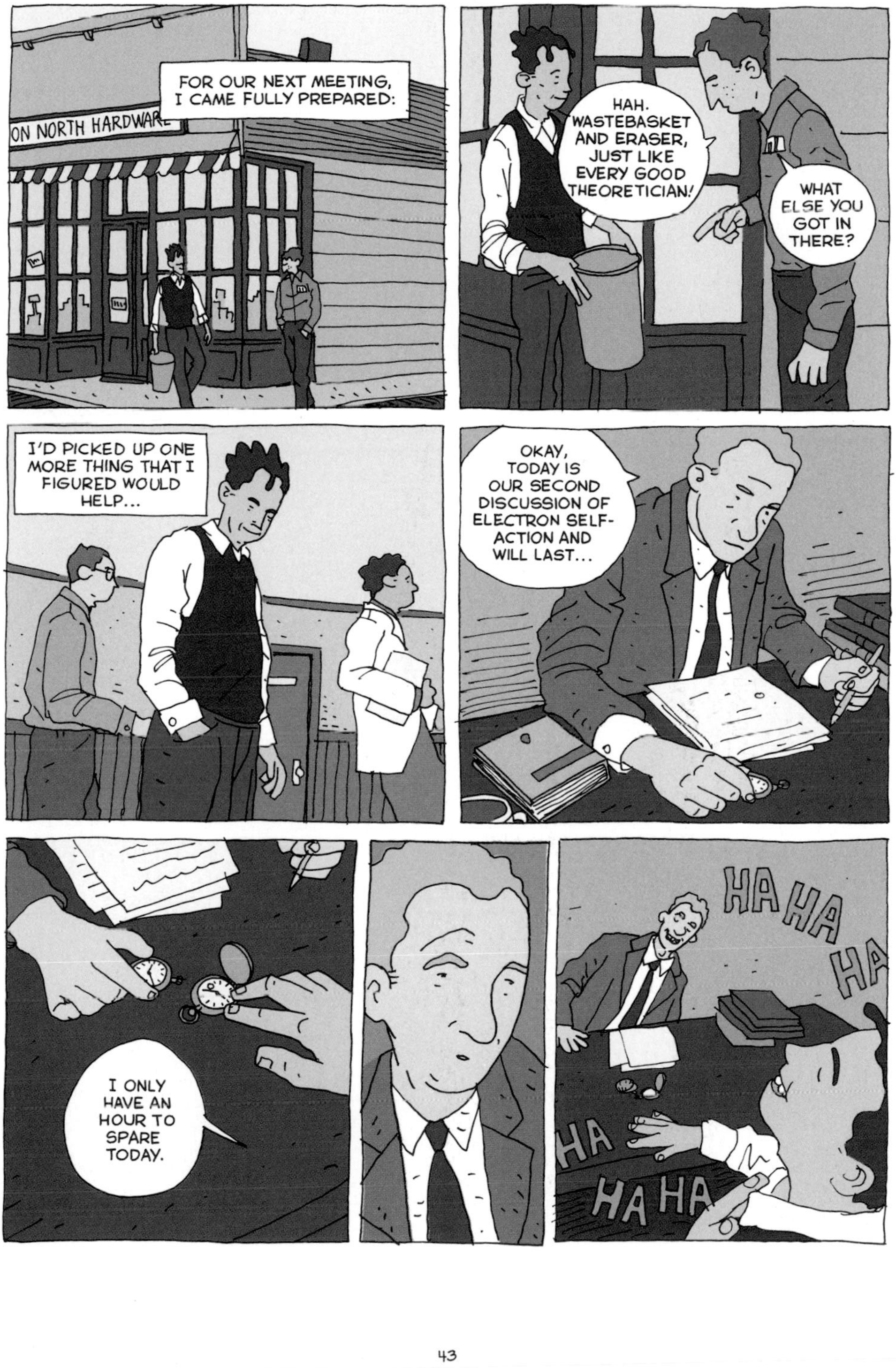
FOR OUR NEXT MEETING, I CAME FULLY PREPARED:
ON NORTH HARDWARE
HAH. WASTEBASKET AND ERASER, JUST LIKE EVERY GOOD THEORETICIAN!
WHAT ELSE YOU GOT IN THERE?
I'D PICKED UP ONE MORE THING THAT I FIGURED WOULD HELP...
OKAY, TODAY IS OUR SECOND DISCUSSION OF ELECTRON SELF-ACTION AND WILL LAST...
I ONLY HAVE AN HOUR TO SPARE TODAY.
HA HA HA HA
HA
HA HA HA

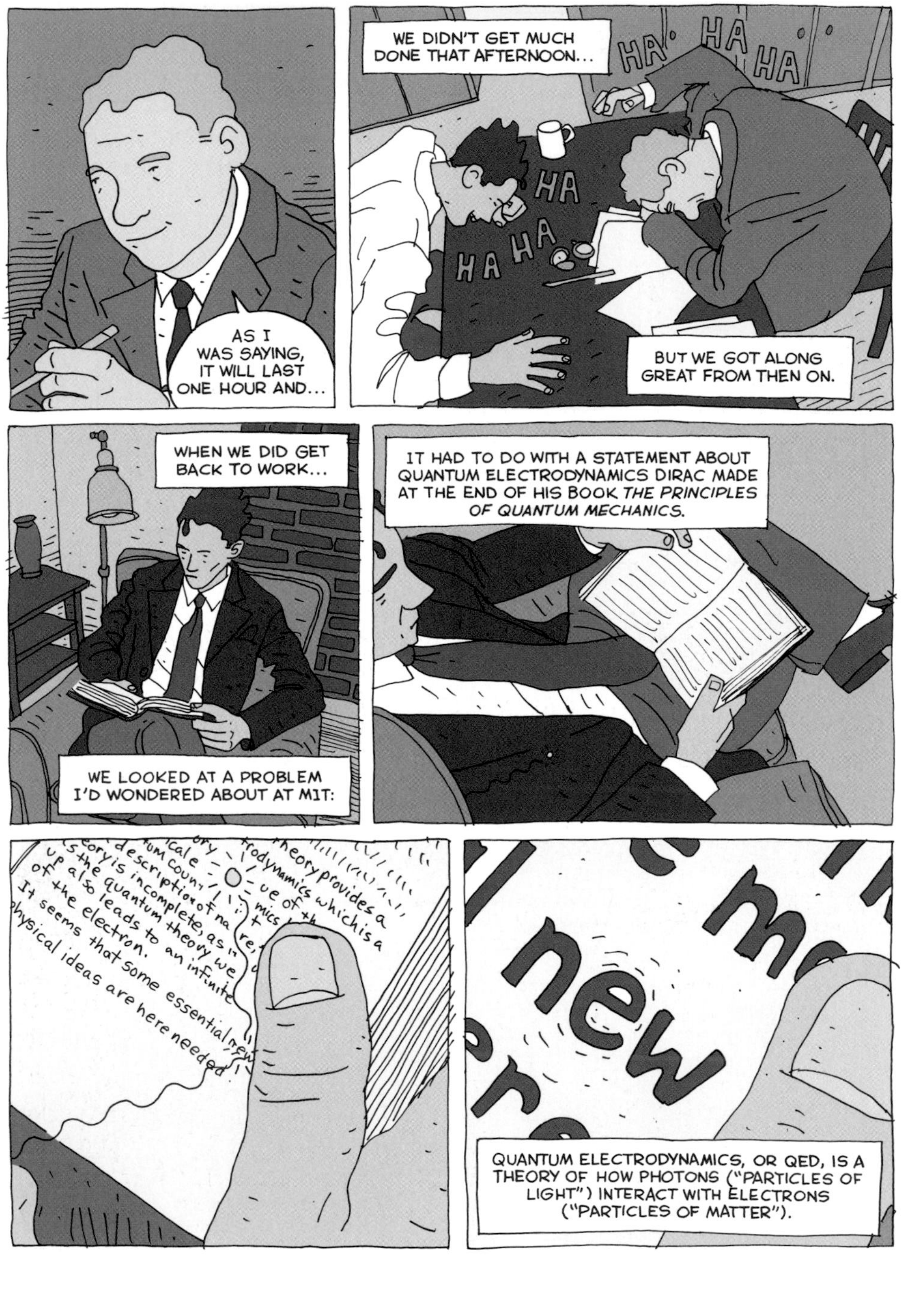
AS I WAS SAYING, IT WILL LAST ONE HOUR AND...
WE DIDN'T GET MUCH DONE THAT AFTERNOON...
HA HA HA
HA HA HA HA
BUT WE GOT ALONG GREAT FROM THEN ON.
WHEN WE DID GET BACK TO WORK...
WE LOOKED AT A PROBLEM I'D WONDERED ABOUT AT MIT:
IT HAD TO DO WITH A STATEMENT ABOUT QUANTUM ELECTRODYNAMICS DIRAC MADE AT THE END OF HIS BOOK *THE PRINCIPLES OF QUANTUM MECHANICS*.
the electron.
It seems that some essential
physical ideas are here needed
new
QUANTUM ELECTRODYNAMICS, OR QED, IS A THEORY OF HOW PHOTONS ("PARTICLES OF LIGHT") INTERACT WITH ELECTRONS ("PARTICLES OF MATTER").

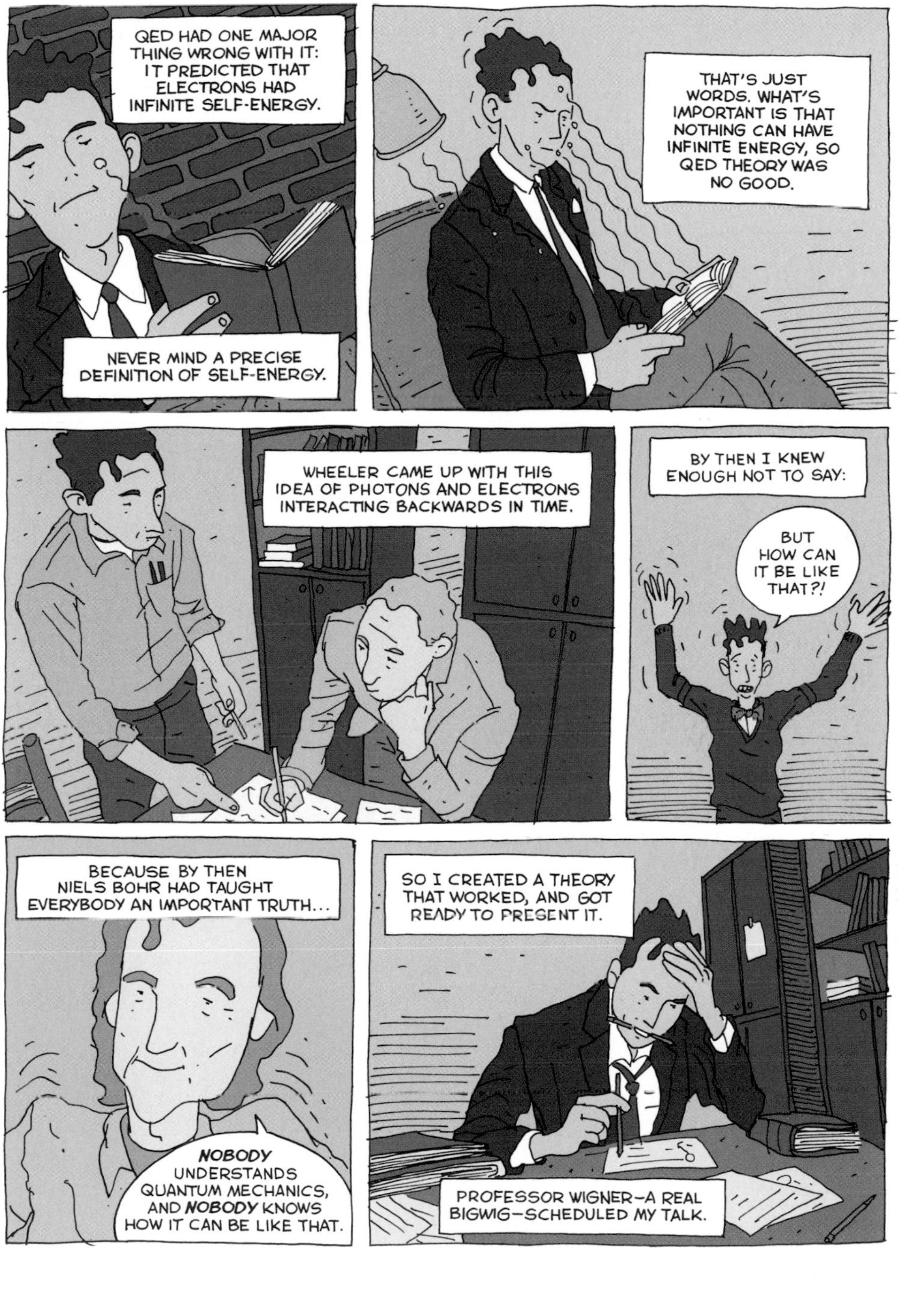
QED HAD ONE MAJOR THING WRONG WITH IT: IT PREDICTED THAT ELECTRONS HAD INFINITE SELF-ENERGY.
NEVER MIND A PRECISE DEFINITION OF SELF-ENERGY.
THAT'S JUST WORDS. WHAT'S IMPORTANT IS THAT NOTHING CAN HAVE INFINITE ENERGY, SO QED THEORY WAS NO GOOD.
WHEELER CAME UP WITH THIS IDEA OF PHOTONS AND ELECTRONS INTERACTING BACKWARDS IN TIME.
BY THEN I KNEW ENOUGH NOT TO SAY:
BUT HOW CAN IT BE LIKE THAT?!
BECAUSE BY THEN NIELS BOHR HAD TAUGHT EVERYBODY AN IMPORTANT TRUTH...
NOBODY UNDERSTANDS QUANTUM MECHANICS, AND NOBODY KNOWS HOW IT CAN BE LIKE THAT.
SO I CREATED A THEORY THAT WORKED, AND GOT READY TO PRESENT IT.
PROFESSOR WIGNER—A REAL BIGWIG—SCHEDULED MY TALK.

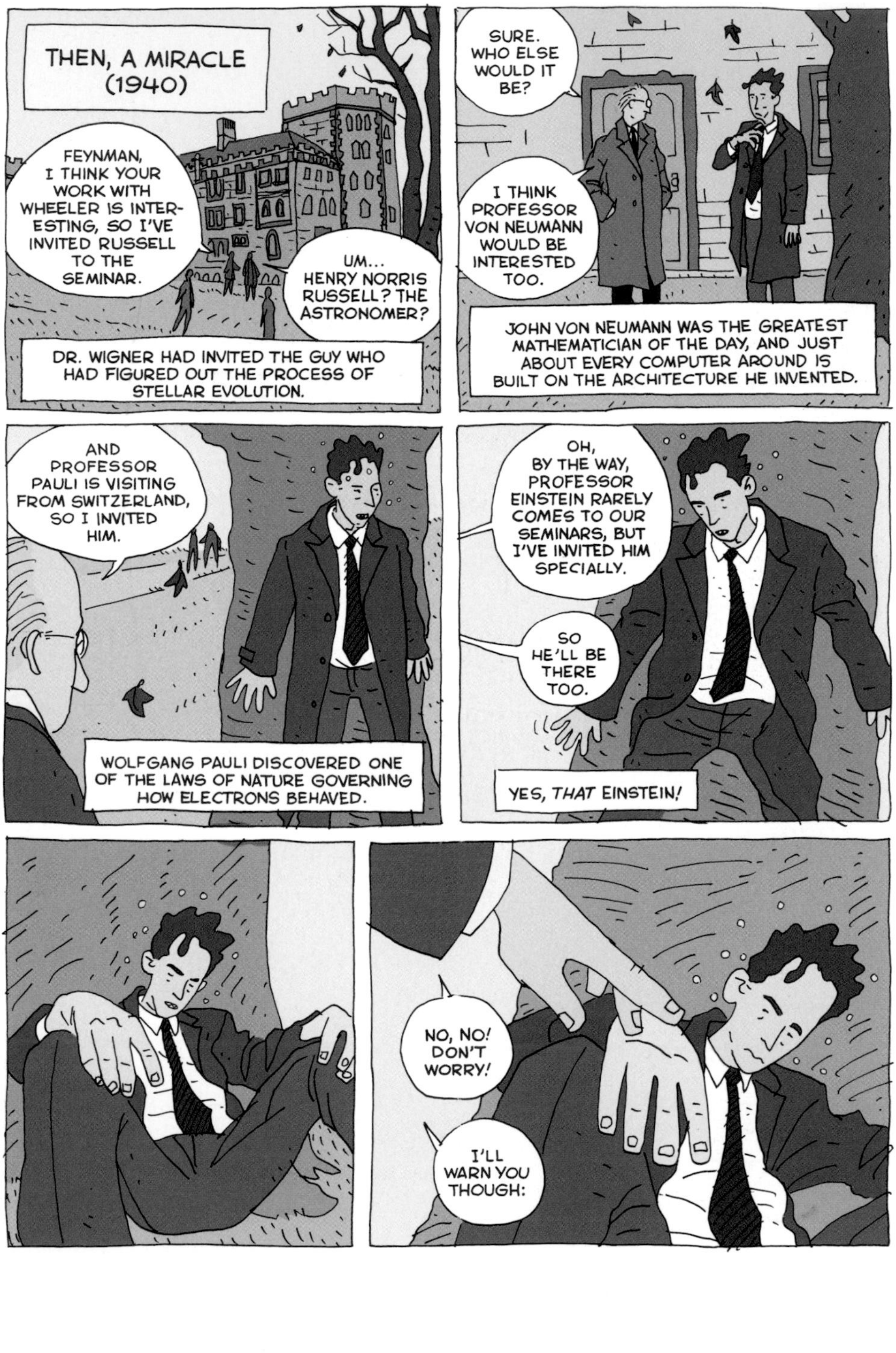
THEN, A MIRACLE (1940)
FEYNMAN, I THINK YOUR WORK WITH WHEELER IS INTERESTING, SO I'VE INVITED RUSSELL TO THE SEMINAR.
UM... HENRY NORRIS RUSSELL? THE ASTRONOMER?
DR. WIGNER HAD INVITED THE GUY WHO HAD FIGURED OUT THE PROCESS OF STELLAR EVOLUTION.
SURE. WHO ELSE WOULD IT BE?
I THINK PROFESSOR VON NEUMANN WOULD BE INTERESTED TOO.
JOHN VON NEUMANN WAS THE GREATEST MATHEMATICIAN OF THE DAY, AND JUST ABOUT EVERY COMPUTER AROUND IS BUILT ON THE ARCHITECTURE HE INVENTED.
AND PROFESSOR PAULI IS VISITING FROM SWITZERLAND, SO I INVITED HIM.
WOLFGANG PAULI DISCOVERED ONE OF THE LAWS OF NATURE GOVERNING HOW ELECTRONS BEHAVED.
OH, BY THE WAY, PROFESSOR EINSTEIN RARELY COMES TO OUR SEMINARS, BUT I'VE INVITED HIM SPECIALLY.
SO HE'LL BE THERE TOO.
YES, *THAT* EINSTEIN!
NO, NO! DON'T WORRY!
I'LL WARN YOU THOUGH:

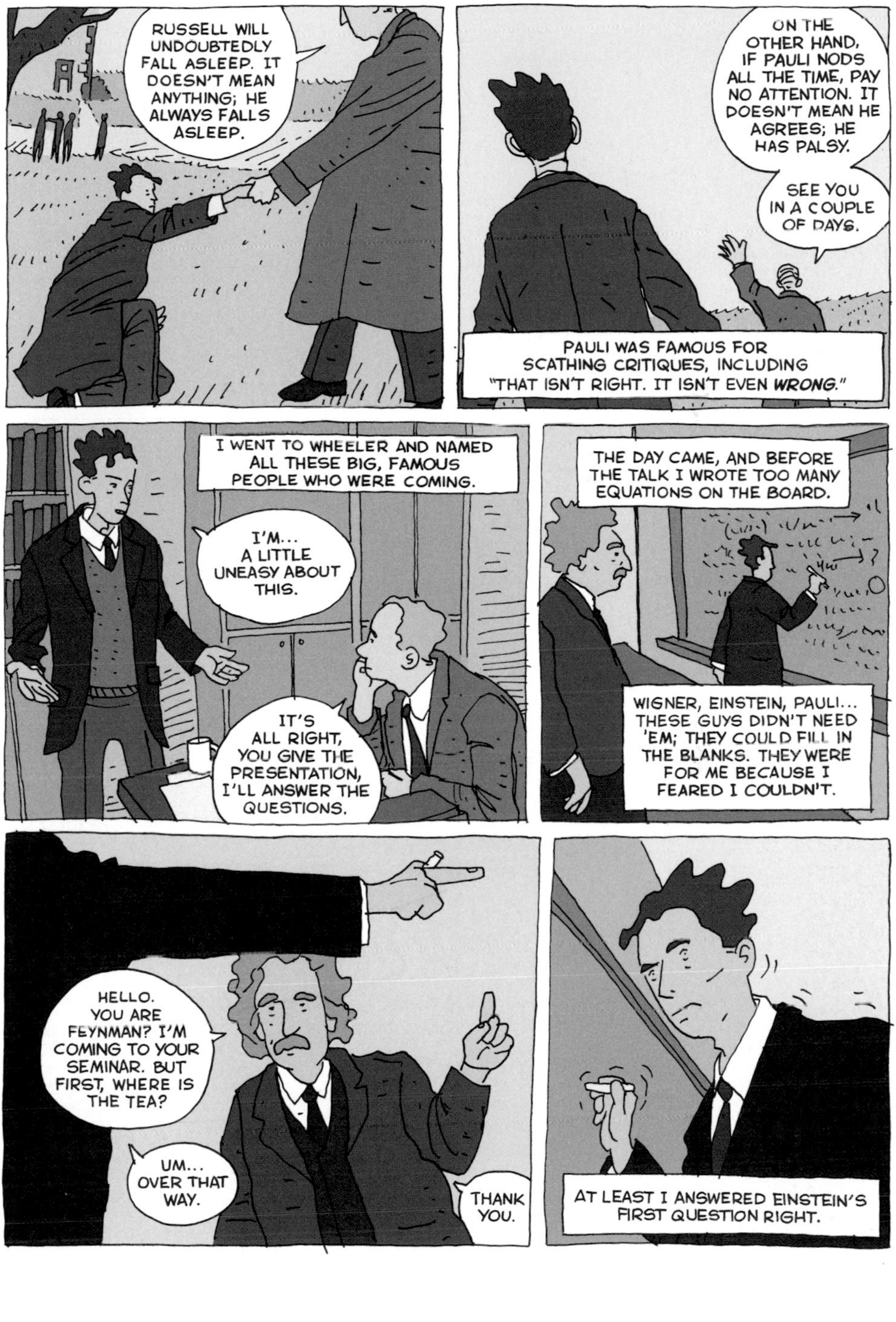
RUSSELL WILL UNDOUBTEDLY FALL ASLEEP. IT DOESN'T MEAN ANYTHING; HE ALWAYS FALLS ASLEEP.
ON THE OTHER HAND, IF PAULI NODS ALL THE TIME, PAY NO ATTENTION. IT DOESN'T MEAN HE AGREES; HE HAS PALSY.
SEE YOU IN A COUPLE OF DAYS.
PAULI WAS FAMOUS FOR SCATHING CRITIQUES, INCLUDING "THAT ISN'T RIGHT. IT ISN'T EVEN WRONG."
I WENT TO WHEELER AND NAMED ALL THESE BIG, FAMOUS PEOPLE WHO WERE COMING.
I'M... A LITTLE UNEASY ABOUT THIS.
IT'S ALL RIGHT, YOU GIVE THE PRESENTATION, I'LL ANSWER THE QUESTIONS.
THE DAY CAME, AND BEFORE THE TALK I WROTE TOO MANY EQUATIONS ON THE BOARD.
WIGNER, EINSTEIN, PAULI... THESE GUYS DIDN'T NEED 'EM; THEY COULD FILL IN THE BLANKS. THEY WERE FOR ME BECAUSE I FEARED I COULDN'T.
HELLO. YOU ARE FEYNMAN? I'M COMING TO YOUR SEMINAR. BUT FIRST, WHERE IS THE TEA?
UM... OVER THAT WAY.
THANK YOU.
AT LEAST I ANSWERED EINSTEIN'S FIRST QUESTION RIGHT.

MY FIRST TALK, AND HERE ARE THESE MONSTER MINDS IN FRONT OF ME.

BUT THEN A MIRACLE OCCURRED.

AND IT'S OCCURRED AGAIN AND AGAIN IN MY LIFE, AND IT'S VERY LUCKY FOR ME.

TODAY I'LL PRESENT A CLASSICAL THEORY OF ACTION-AT-A-DISTANCE IN ELECTRO-DYNAMICS...

THE MOMENT I START TO THINK ABOUT PHYSICS AND CONCENTRATE ON WHAT I'M EXPLAINING, I'M COMPLETELY IMMUNE TO BEING NERVOUS.

NO WORRIES ABOUT THE AUDIENCE AND THE PERSONALITIES. I WAS CALM, EVERYTHING WAS GOOD.

QUESTIONS, THEN?

MY TALK WASN'T GOOD BECAUSE I WASN'T USED TO GIVING LECTURES, BUT THERE WAS NO MORE NERVOUSNESS UNTIL I SAT DOWN.

I DO NOT THINK THIS THEORY CAN BE RIGHT BECAUSE OF THIS, THAT, AND THE OTHER THING.

DON'T YOU AGREE, PROFESSOR EINSTEIN?

NO. I FIND ONLY THAT IT WOULD BE DIFFICULT TO MAKE A CORRESPONDING THEORY FOR GRAVITY.

BUT SINCE WE DO NOT HAVE A GREAT DEAL OF EXPERIMENTAL EVIDENCE, I AM NOT SURE OF THE CORRECT GRAVITATIONAL THEORY.

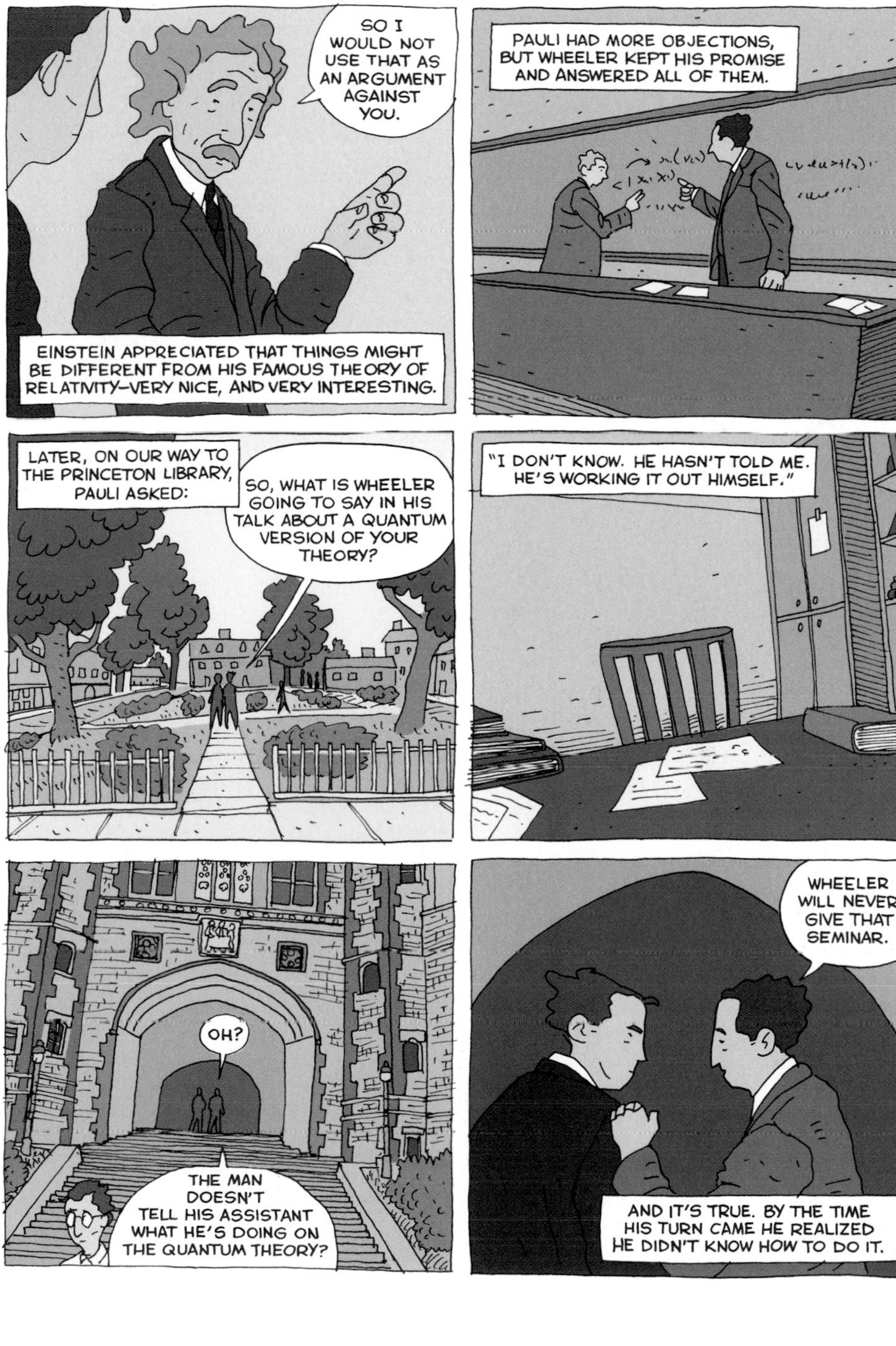
SO I WOULD NOT USE THAT AS AN ARGUMENT AGAINST YOU.
EINSTEIN APPRECIATED THAT THINGS MIGHT BE DIFFERENT FROM HIS FAMOUS THEORY OF RELATIVITY—VERY NICE, AND VERY INTERESTING.
PAULI HAD MORE OBJECTIONS, BUT WHEELER KEPT HIS PROMISE AND ANSWERED ALL OF THEM.
LATER, ON OUR WAY TO THE PRINCETON LIBRARY, PAULI ASKED:
SO, WHAT IS WHEELER GOING TO SAY IN HIS TALK ABOUT A QUANTUM VERSION OF YOUR THEORY?
"I DON'T KNOW. HE HASN'T TOLD ME. HE'S WORKING IT OUT HIMSELF."
OH?
THE MAN DOESN'T TELL HIS ASSISTANT WHAT HE'S DOING ON THE QUANTUM THEORY?
WHEELER WILL NEVER GIVE THAT SEMINAR.
AND IT'S TRUE. BY THE TIME HIS TURN CAME HE REALIZED HE DIDN'T KNOW HOW TO DO IT.

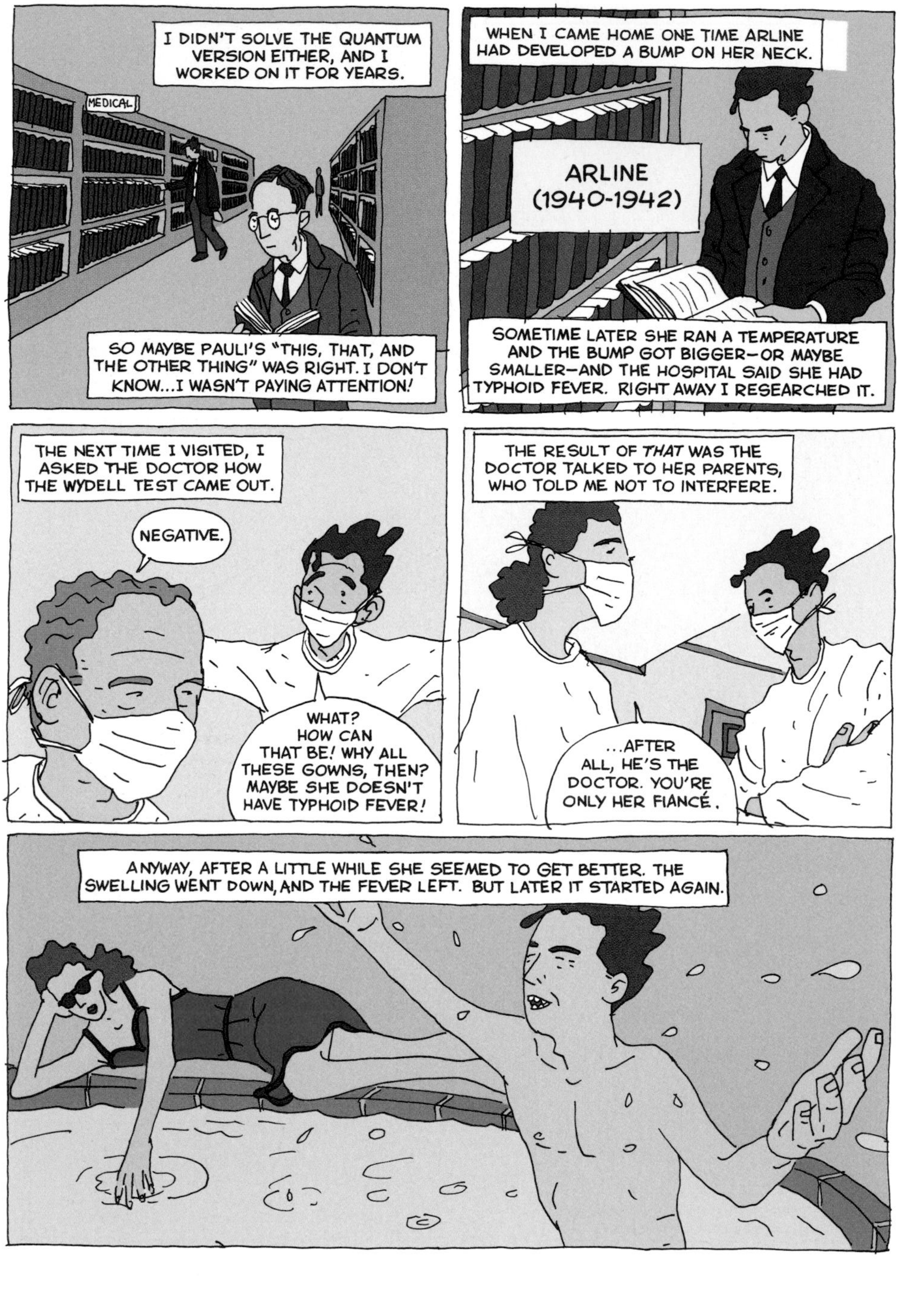
I DIDN'T SOLVE THE QUANTUM VERSION EITHER, AND I WORKED ON IT FOR YEARS.
MEDICAL
SO MAYBE PAULI'S "THIS, THAT, AND THE OTHER THING" WAS RIGHT. I DON'T KNOW...I WASN'T PAYING ATTENTION!
WHEN I CAME HOME ONE TIME ARLINE HAD DEVELOPED A BUMP ON HER NECK.
ARLINE (1940-1942)
SOMETIME LATER SHE RAN A TEMPERATURE AND THE BUMP GOT BIGGER—OR MAYBE SMALLER—AND THE HOSPITAL SAID SHE HAD TYPHOID FEVER. RIGHT AWAY I RESEARCHED IT.
THE NEXT TIME I VISITED, I ASKED THE DOCTOR HOW THE WYDELL TEST CAME OUT.
NEGATIVE.
WHAT? HOW CAN THAT BE! WHY ALL THESE GOWNS, THEN? MAYBE SHE DOESN'T HAVE TYPHOID FEVER!
THE RESULT OF *THAT* WAS THE DOCTOR TALKED TO HER PARENTS, WHO TOLD ME NOT TO INTERFERE.
...AFTER ALL, HE'S THE DOCTOR. YOU'RE ONLY HER FIANCÉ.
ANYWAY, AFTER A LITTLE WHILE SHE SEEMED TO GET BETTER. THE SWELLING WENT DOWN, AND THE FEVER LEFT. BUT LATER IT STARTED AGAIN.

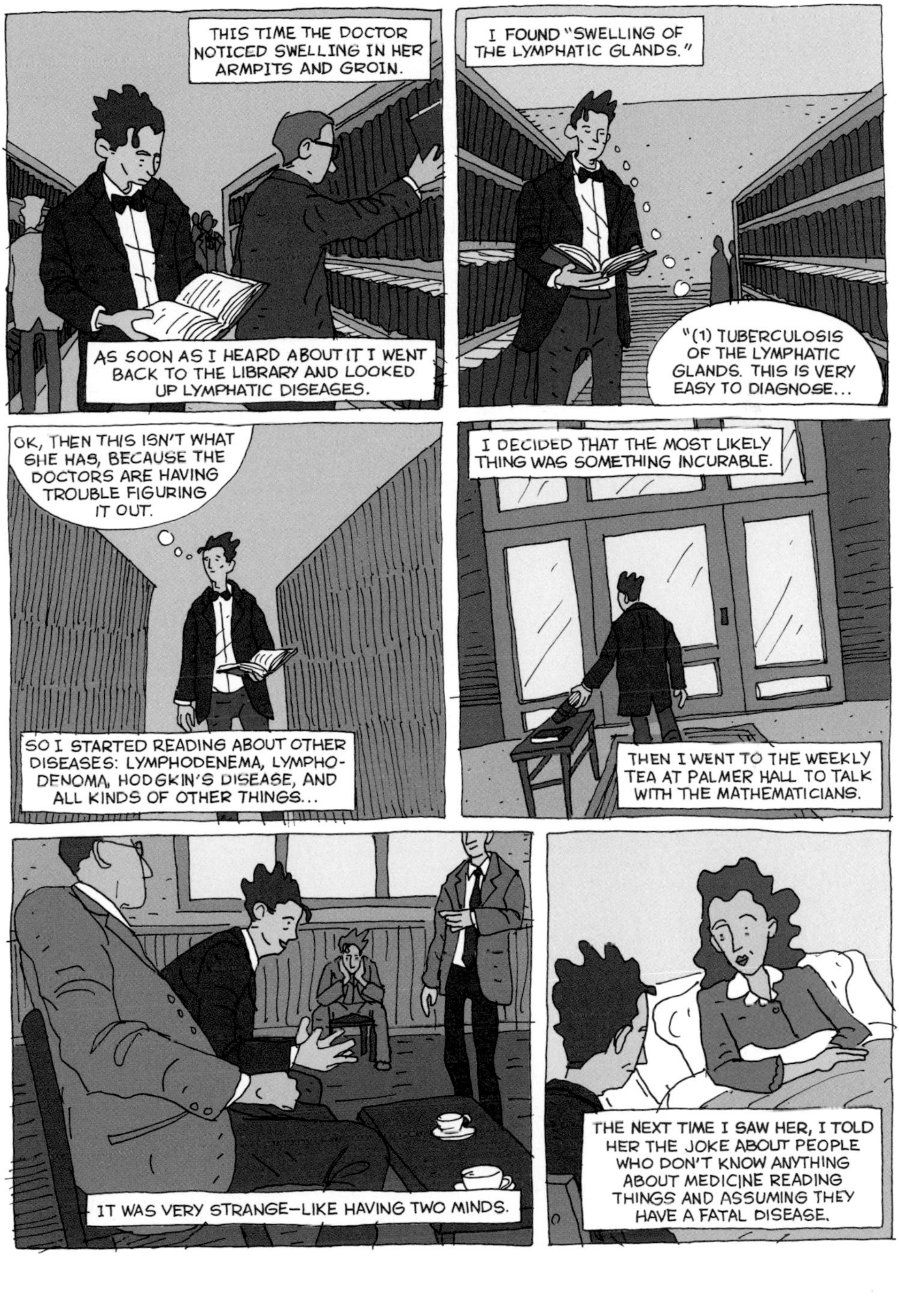
THIS TIME THE DOCTOR NOTICED SWELLING IN HER ARMPITS AND GROIN.
AS SOON AS I HEARD ABOUT IT I WENT BACK TO THE LIBRARY AND LOOKED UP LYMPHATIC DISEASES.
I FOUND "SWELLING OF THE LYMPHATIC GLANDS."
"(1) TUBERCULOSIS OF THE LYMPHATIC GLANDS. THIS IS VERY EASY TO DIAGNOSE...
OK, THEN THIS ISN'T WHAT SHE HAS, BECAUSE THE DOCTORS ARE HAVING TROUBLE FIGURING IT OUT.
SO I STARTED READING ABOUT OTHER DISEASES: LYMPHODENEMA, LYMPHO-DENOMA, HODGKIN'S DISEASE, AND ALL KINDS OF OTHER THINGS...
I DECIDED THAT THE MOST LIKELY THING WAS SOMETHING INCURABLE.
THEN I WENT TO THE WEEKLY TEA AT PALMER HALL TO TALK WITH THE MATHEMATICIANS.
IT WAS VERY STRANGE—LIKE HAVING TWO MINDS.
THE NEXT TIME I SAW HER, I TOLD HER THE JOKE ABOUT PEOPLE WHO DON'T KNOW ANYTHING ABOUT MEDICINE READING THINGS AND ASSUMING THEY HAVE A FATAL DISEASE.

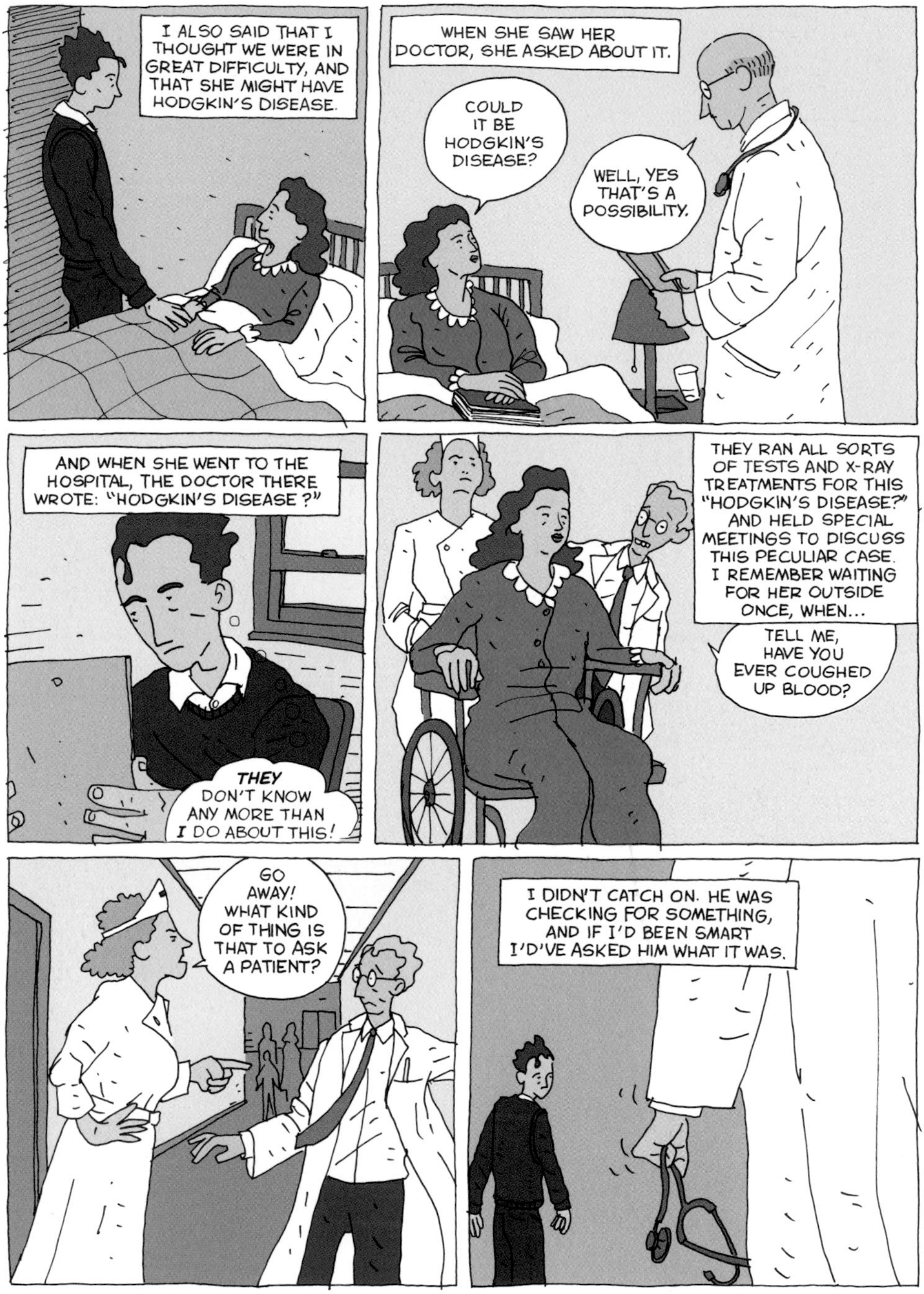
I ALSO SAID THAT I THOUGHT WE WERE IN GREAT DIFFICULTY, AND THAT SHE MIGHT HAVE HODGKIN'S DISEASE.
WHEN SHE SAW HER DOCTOR, SHE ASKED ABOUT IT.
COULD IT BE HODGKIN'S DISEASE?
WELL, YES THAT'S A POSSIBILITY.
AND WHEN SHE WENT TO THE HOSPITAL, THE DOCTOR THERE WROTE: "HODGKIN'S DISEASE?"
THEY DON'T KNOW ANY MORE THAN I DO ABOUT THIS!
THEY RAN ALL SORTS OF TESTS AND X-RAY TREATMENTS FOR THIS "HODGKIN'S DISEASE?" AND HELD SPECIAL MEETINGS TO DISCUSS THIS PECULIAR CASE. I REMEMBER WAITING FOR HER OUTSIDE ONCE, WHEN...
TELL ME, HAVE YOU EVER COUGHED UP BLOOD?
GO AWAY! WHAT KIND OF THING IS THAT TO ASK A PATIENT?
I DIDN'T CATCH ON. HE WAS CHECKING FOR SOMETHING, AND IF I'D BEEN SMART I'D'VE ASKED HIM WHAT IT WAS.

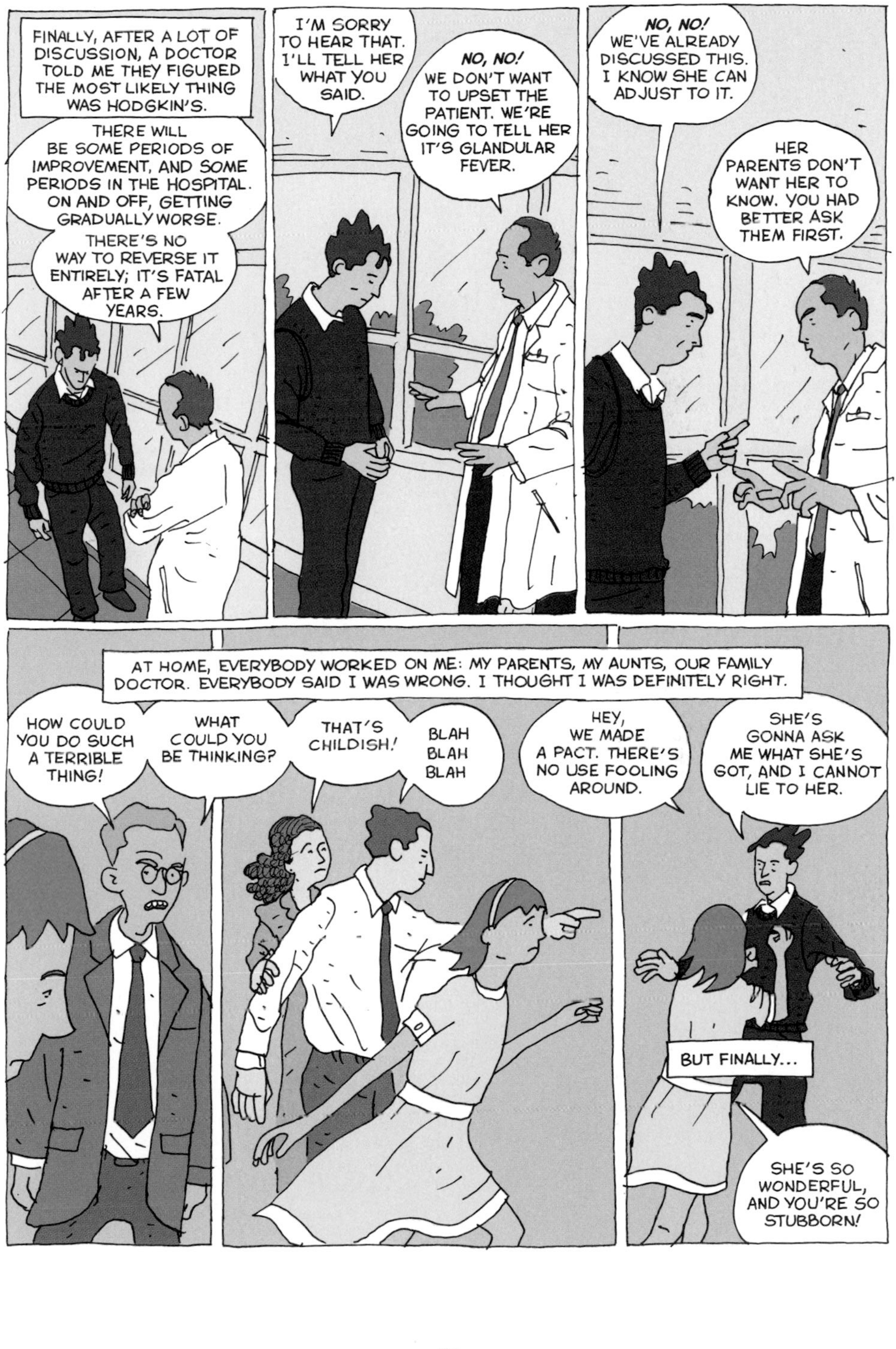
FINALLY, AFTER A LOT OF DISCUSSION, A DOCTOR TOLD ME THEY FIGURED THE MOST LIKELY THING WAS HODGKIN'S.
THERE WILL BE SOME PERIODS OF IMPROVEMENT, AND SOME PERIODS IN THE HOSPITAL. ON AND OFF, GETTING GRADUALLY WORSE.
THERE'S NO WAY TO REVERSE IT ENTIRELY; IT'S FATAL AFTER A FEW YEARS.
I'M SORRY TO HEAR THAT. I'LL TELL HER WHAT YOU SAID.
NO, NO! WE DON'T WANT TO UPSET THE PATIENT. WE'RE GOING TO TELL HER IT'S GLANDULAR FEVER.
NO, NO! WE'VE ALREADY DISCUSSED THIS. I KNOW SHE CAN ADJUST TO IT.
HER PARENTS DON'T WANT HER TO KNOW. YOU HAD BETTER ASK THEM FIRST.
AT HOME, EVERYBODY WORKED ON ME: MY PARENTS, MY AUNTS, OUR FAMILY DOCTOR. EVERYBODY SAID I WAS WRONG. I THOUGHT I WAS DEFINITELY RIGHT.
HOW COULD YOU DO SUCH A TERRIBLE THING!
WHAT COULD YOU BE THINKING?
THAT'S CHILDISH!
BLAH BLAH BLAH
HEY, WE MADE A PACT. THERE'S NO USE FOOLING AROUND.
SHE'S GONNA ASK ME WHAT SHE'S GOT, AND I CANNOT LIE TO HER.
BUT FINALLY...
SHE'S SO WONDERFUL, AND YOU'RE SO STUBBORN!

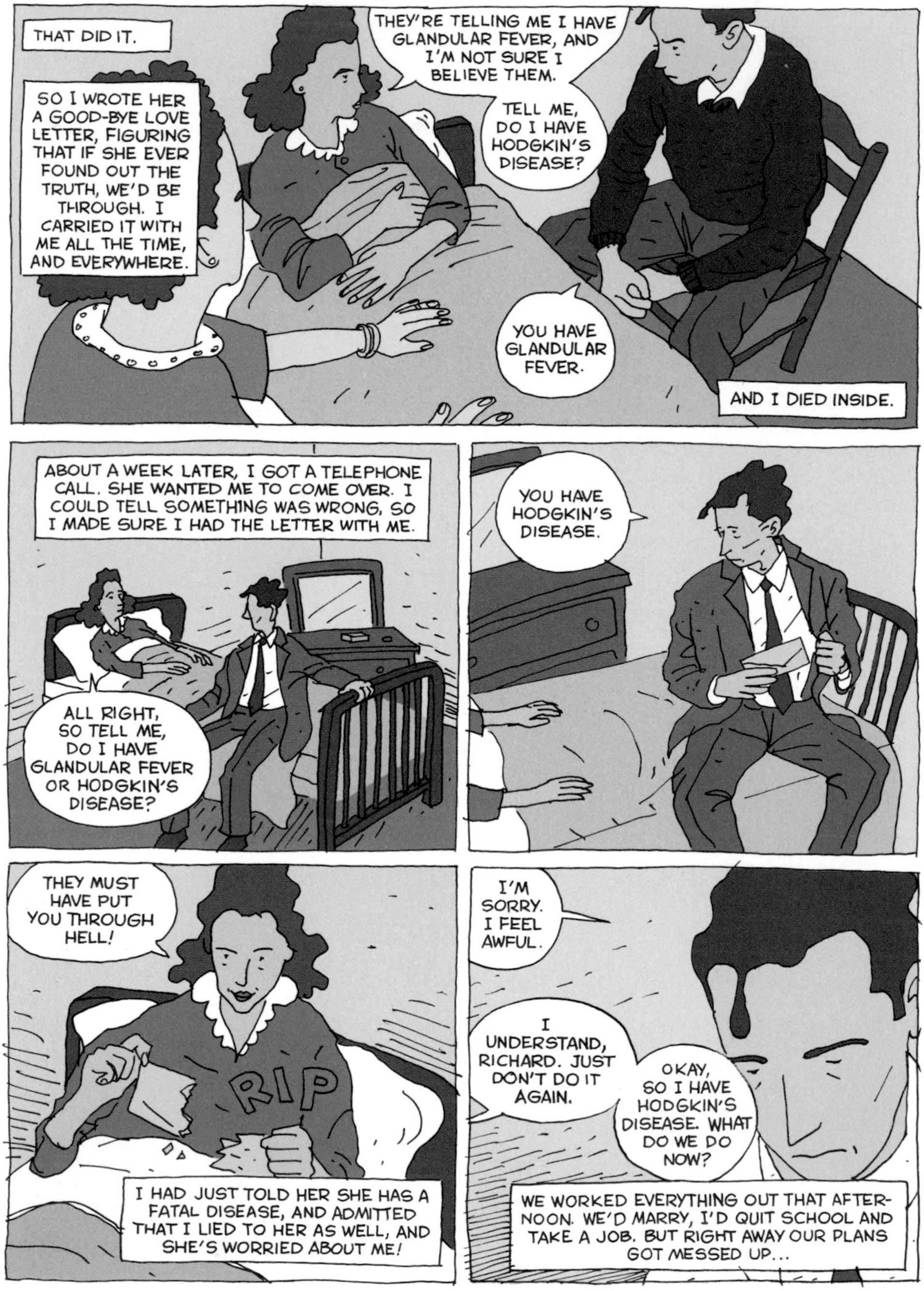
THAT DID IT.
SO I WROTE HER A GOOD-BYE LOVE LETTER, FIGURING THAT IF SHE EVER FOUND OUT THE TRUTH, WE'D BE THROUGH. I CARRIED IT WITH ME ALL THE TIME, AND EVERYWHERE.
THEY'RE TELLING ME I HAVE GLANDULAR FEVER, AND I'M NOT SURE I BELIEVE THEM.
TELL ME, DO I HAVE HODGKIN'S DISEASE?
YOU HAVE GLANDULAR FEVER.
AND I DIED INSIDE.
ABOUT A WEEK LATER, I GOT A TELEPHONE CALL. SHE WANTED ME TO COME OVER. I COULD TELL SOMETHING WAS WRONG, SO I MADE SURE I HAD THE LETTER WITH ME.
ALL RIGHT, SO TELL ME, DO I HAVE GLANDULAR FEVER OR HODGKIN'S DISEASE?
YOU HAVE HODGKIN'S DISEASE.
THEY MUST HAVE PUT YOU THROUGH HELL!
RIP
I HAD JUST TOLD HER SHE HAS A FATAL DISEASE, AND ADMITTED THAT I LIED TO HER AS WELL, AND SHE'S WORRIED ABOUT ME!
I'M SORRY. I FEEL AWFUL.
I UNDERSTAND, RICHARD. JUST DON'T DO IT AGAIN.
OKAY, SO I HAVE HODGKIN'S DISEASE. WHAT DO WE DO NOW?
WE WORKED EVERYTHING OUT THAT AFTERNOON. WE'D MARRY, I'D QUIT SCHOOL AND TAKE A JOB. BUT RIGHT AWAY OUR PLANS GOT MESSED UP...

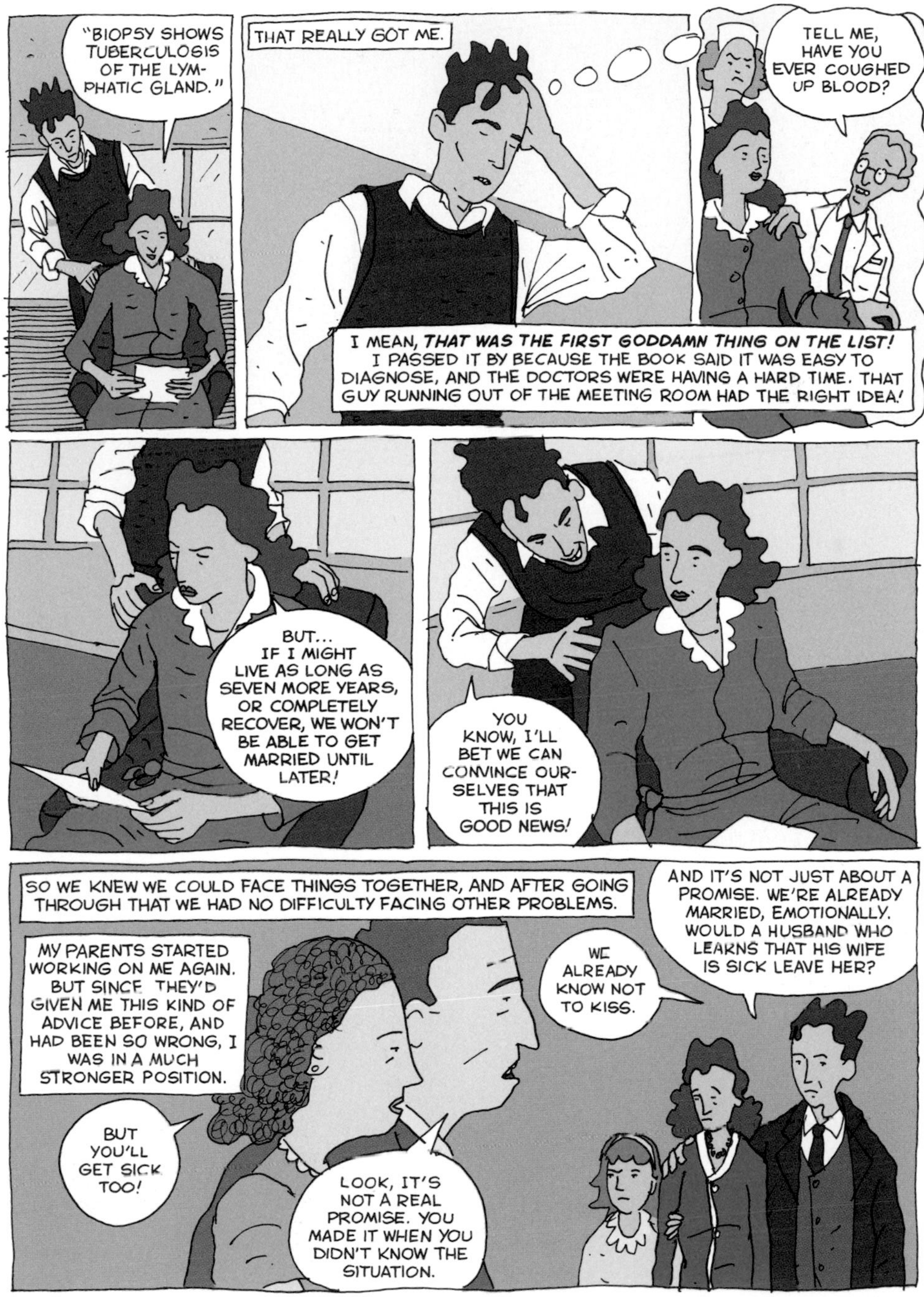
"BIOPSY SHOWS TUBERCULOSIS OF THE LYMPHATIC GLAND."
THAT REALLY GOT ME.
TELL ME, HAVE YOU EVER COUGHED UP BLOOD?
I MEAN, THAT WAS THE FIRST GODDAMN THING ON THE LIST! I PASSED IT BY BECAUSE THE BOOK SAID IT WAS EASY TO DIAGNOSE, AND THE DOCTORS WERE HAVING A HARD TIME. THAT GUY RUNNING OUT OF THE MEETING ROOM HAD THE RIGHT IDEA!
BUT... IF I MIGHT LIVE AS LONG AS SEVEN MORE YEARS, OR COMPLETELY RECOVER, WE WON'T BE ABLE TO GET MARRIED UNTIL LATER!
YOU KNOW, I'LL BET WE CAN CONVINCE OURSELVES THAT THIS IS GOOD NEWS!
SO WE KNEW WE COULD FACE THINGS TOGETHER, AND AFTER GOING THROUGH THAT WE HAD NO DIFFICULTY FACING OTHER PROBLEMS.
MY PARENTS STARTED WORKING ON ME AGAIN. BUT SINCE THEY'D GIVEN ME THIS KIND OF ADVICE BEFORE, AND HAD BEEN SO WRONG, I WAS IN A MUCH STRONGER POSITION.
BUT YOU'LL GET SICK TOO!
LOOK, IT'S NOT A REAL PROMISE. YOU MADE IT WHEN YOU DIDN'T KNOW THE SITUATION.
WE ALREADY KNOW NOT TO KISS.
AND IT'S NOT JUST ABOUT A PROMISE. WE'RE ALREADY MARRIED, EMOTIONALLY. WOULD A HUSBAND WHO LEARNS THAT HIS WIFE IS SICK LEAVE HER?

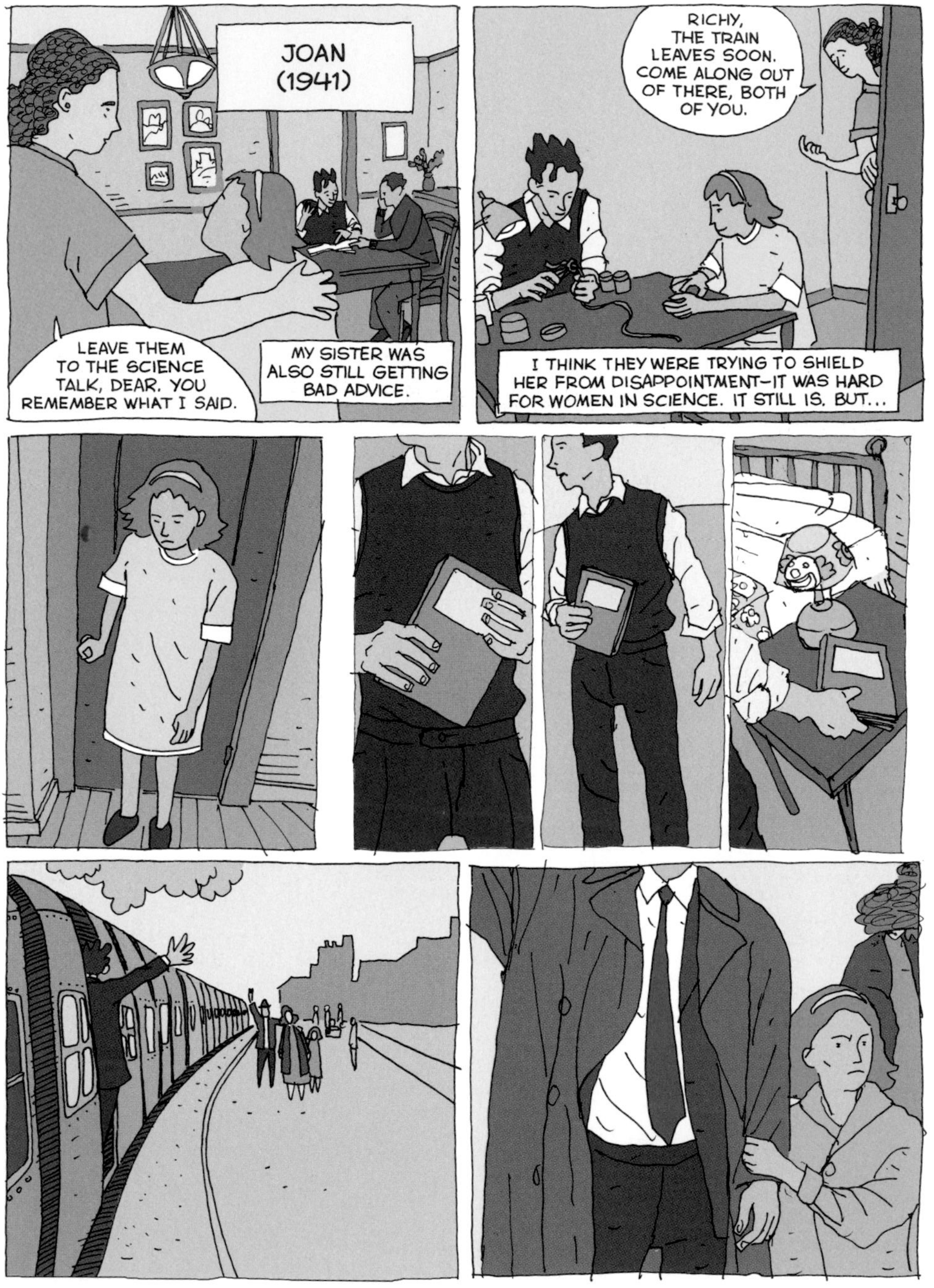
JOAN (1941)
LEAVE THEM TO THE SCIENCE TALK, DEAR. YOU REMEMBER WHAT I SAID.
MY SISTER WAS ALSO STILL GETTING BAD ADVICE.
RICHY, THE TRAIN LEAVES SOON. COME ALONG OUT OF THERE, BOTH OF YOU.
I THINK THEY WERE TRYING TO SHIELD HER FROM DISAPPOINTMENT—IT WAS HARD FOR WOMEN IN SCIENCE. IT STILL IS, BUT...

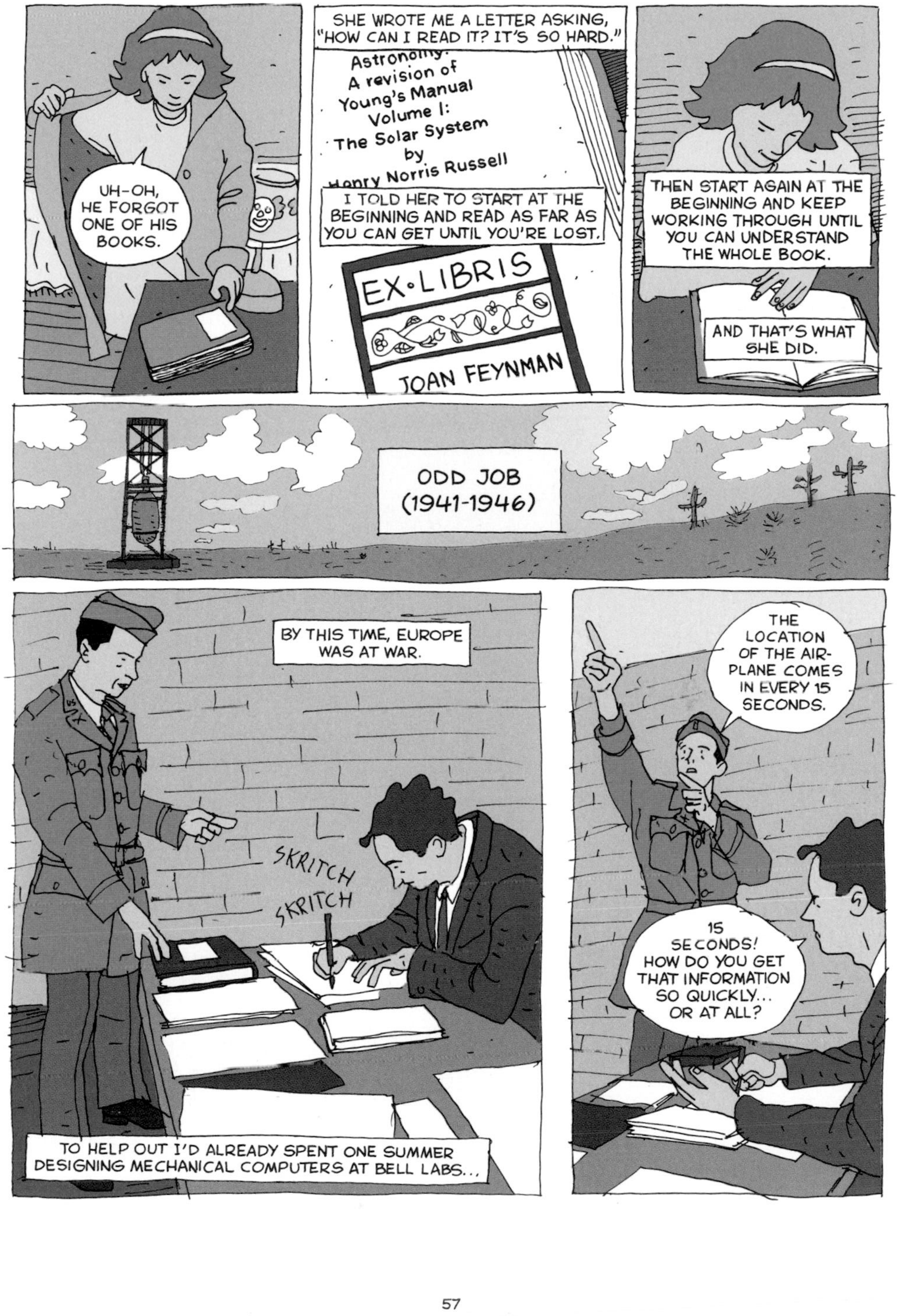

UH-OH, HE FORGOT ONE OF HIS BOOKS.
SHE WROTE ME A LETTER ASKING, "HOW CAN I READ IT? IT'S SO HARD."
Astronomy:
A revision of
Young's Manual
Volume I:
The Solar System
by
Henry Norris Russell
I TOLD HER TO START AT THE BEGINNING AND READ AS FAR AS YOU CAN GET UNTIL YOU'RE LOST.
EX•LIBRIS
JOAN FEYNMAN
THEN START AGAIN AT THE BEGINNING AND KEEP WORKING THROUGH UNTIL YOU CAN UNDERSTAND THE WHOLE BOOK.
AND THAT'S WHAT SHE DID.
ODD JOB
(1941-1946)
BY THIS TIME, EUROPE WAS AT WAR.
SKRITCH
SKRITCH
TO HELP OUT I'D ALREADY SPENT ONE SUMMER DESIGNING MECHANICAL COMPUTERS AT BELL LABS...
THE LOCATION OF THE AIR-PLANE COMES IN EVERY 15 SECONDS.
15 SECONDS! HOW DO YOU GET THAT INFORMATION SO QUICKLY... OR AT ALL?

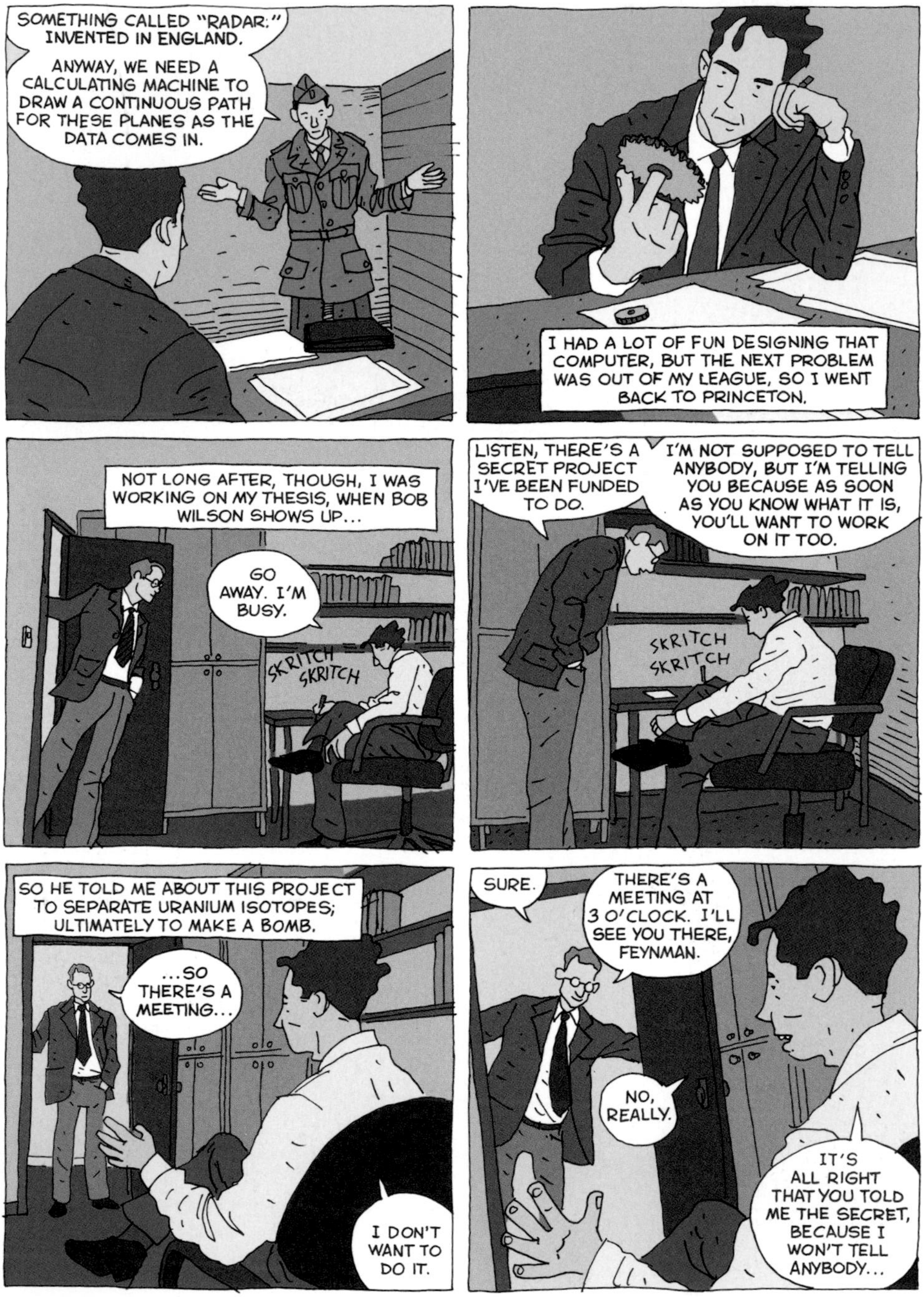
SOMETHING CALLED "RADAR." INVENTED IN ENGLAND.
ANYWAY, WE NEED A CALCULATING MACHINE TO DRAW A CONTINUOUS PATH FOR THESE PLANES AS THE DATA COMES IN.
I HAD A LOT OF FUN DESIGNING THAT COMPUTER, BUT THE NEXT PROBLEM WAS OUT OF MY LEAGUE, SO I WENT BACK TO PRINCETON.
NOT LONG AFTER, THOUGH, I WAS WORKING ON MY THESIS, WHEN BOB WILSON SHOWS UP...
GO AWAY. I'M BUSY.
SKRITCH SKRITCH
LISTEN, THERE'S A SECRET PROJECT I'VE BEEN FUNDED TO DO.
I'M NOT SUPPOSED TO TELL ANYBODY, BUT I'M TELLING YOU BECAUSE AS SOON AS YOU KNOW WHAT IT IS, YOU'LL WANT TO WORK ON IT TOO.
SKRITCH SKRITCH
SO HE TOLD ME ABOUT THIS PROJECT TO SEPARATE URANIUM ISOTOPES; ULTIMATELY TO MAKE A BOMB.
...SO THERE'S A MEETING...
I DON'T WANT TO DO IT.
SURE.
THERE'S A MEETING AT 3 O'CLOCK. I'LL SEE YOU THERE, FEYNMAN.
NO, REALLY.
IT'S ALL RIGHT THAT YOU TOLD ME THE SECRET, BECAUSE I WON'T TELL ANYBODY...

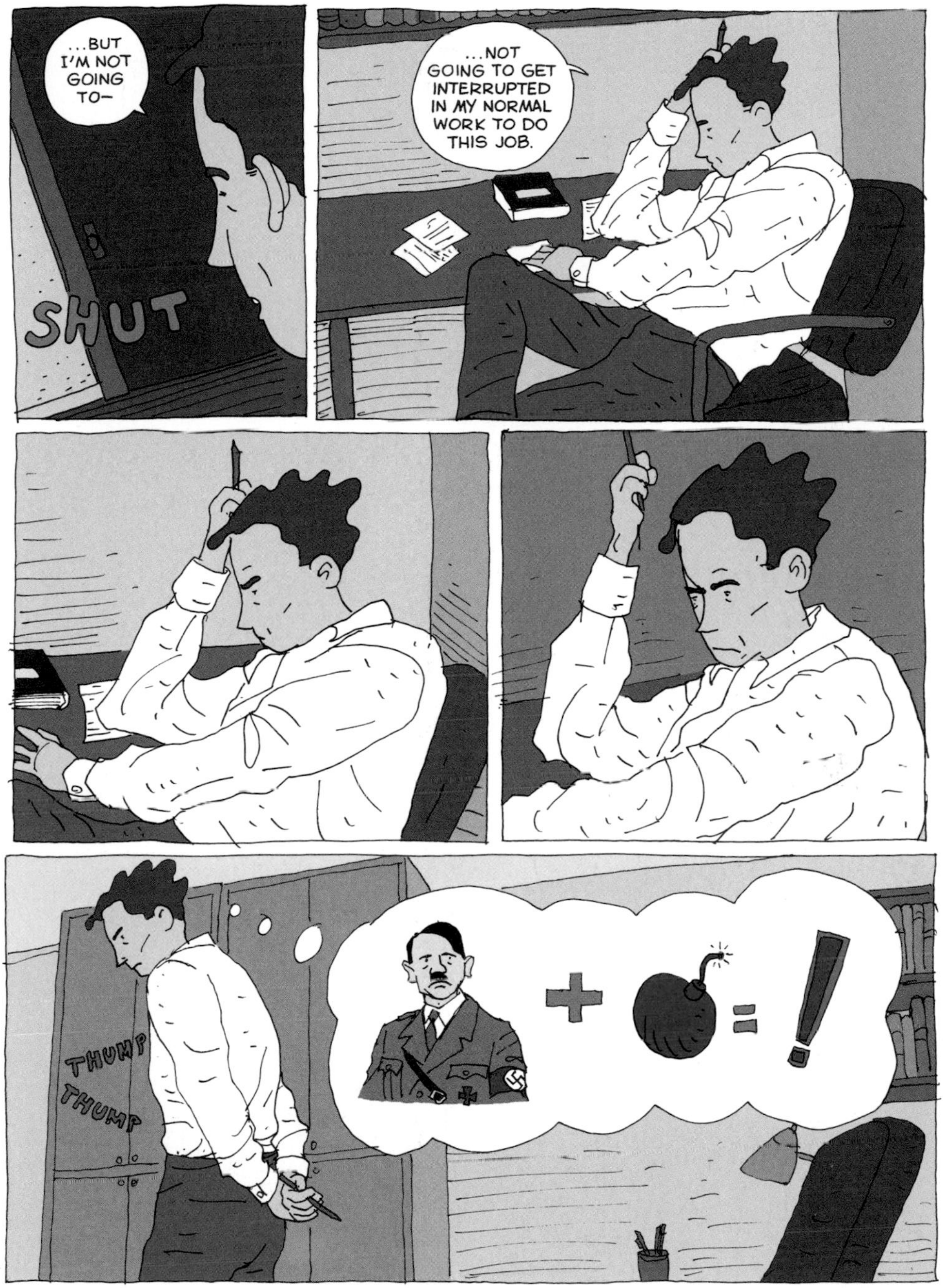
...BUT I'M NOT GOING TO—
SHUT
...NOT GOING TO GET INTERRUPTED IN MY NORMAL WORK TO DO THIS JOB.
THUMP
THUMP
+
=
!

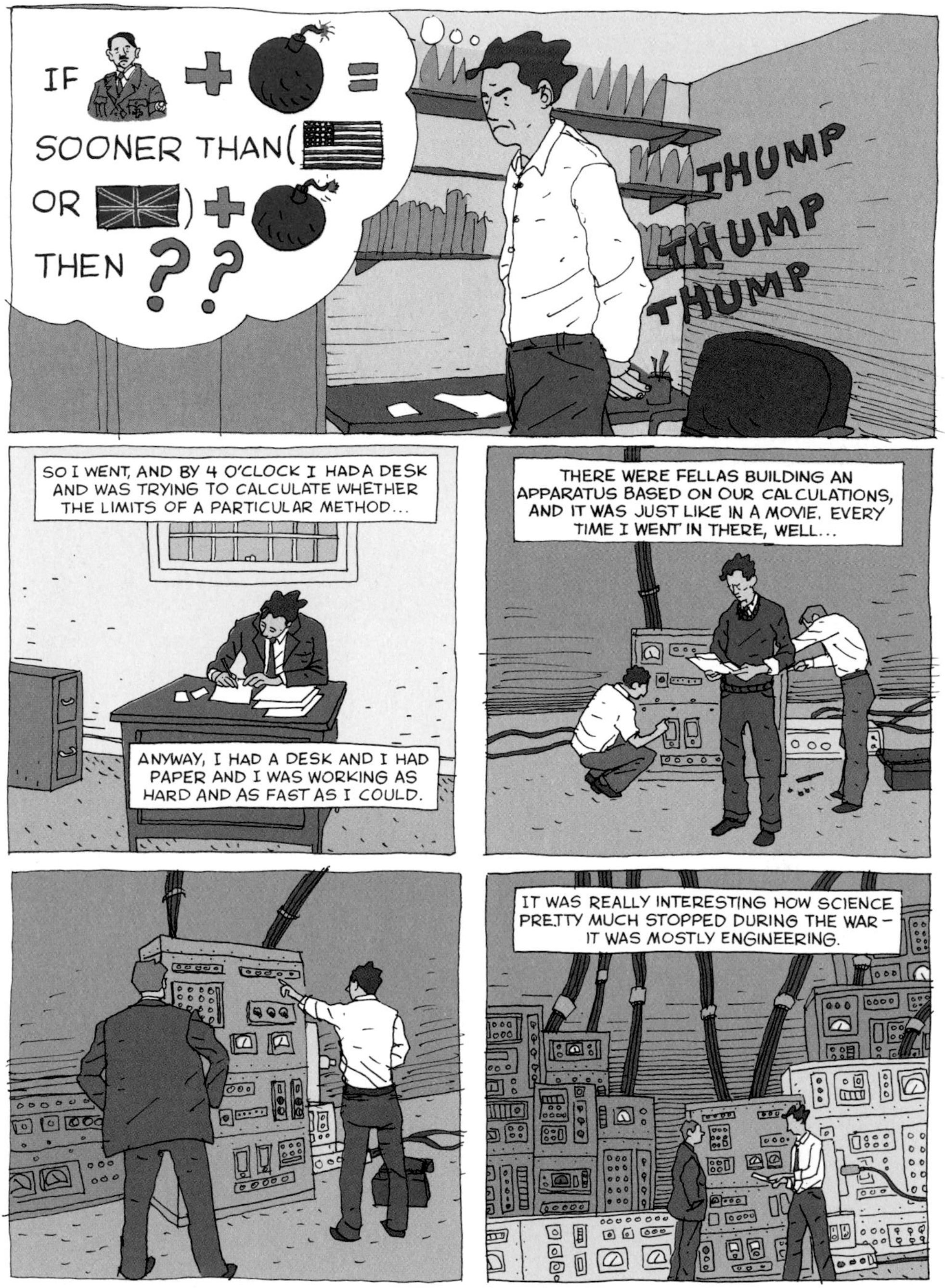
IF + =
SOONER THAN(
OR) +
THEN ??
THUMP
THUMP
THUMP
SO I WENT, AND BY 4 O'CLOCK I HAD A DESK AND WAS TRYING TO CALCULATE WHETHER THE LIMITS OF A PARTICULAR METHOD...
ANYWAY, I HAD A DESK AND I HAD PAPER AND I WAS WORKING AS HARD AND AS FAST AS I COULD.
THERE WERE FELLAS BUILDING AN APPARATUS BASED ON OUR CALCULATIONS, AND IT WAS JUST LIKE IN A MOVIE. EVERY TIME I WENT IN THERE, WELL...
IT WAS REALLY INTERESTING HOW SCIENCE PRETTY MUCH STOPPED DURING THE WAR – IT WAS MOSTLY ENGINEERING.

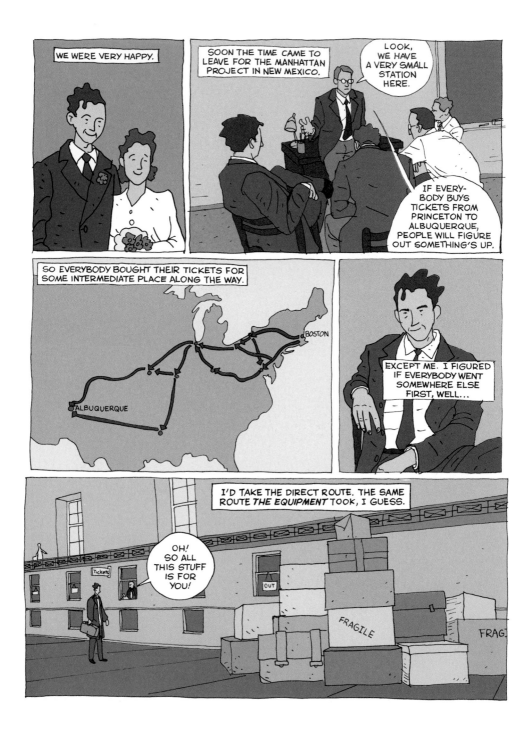

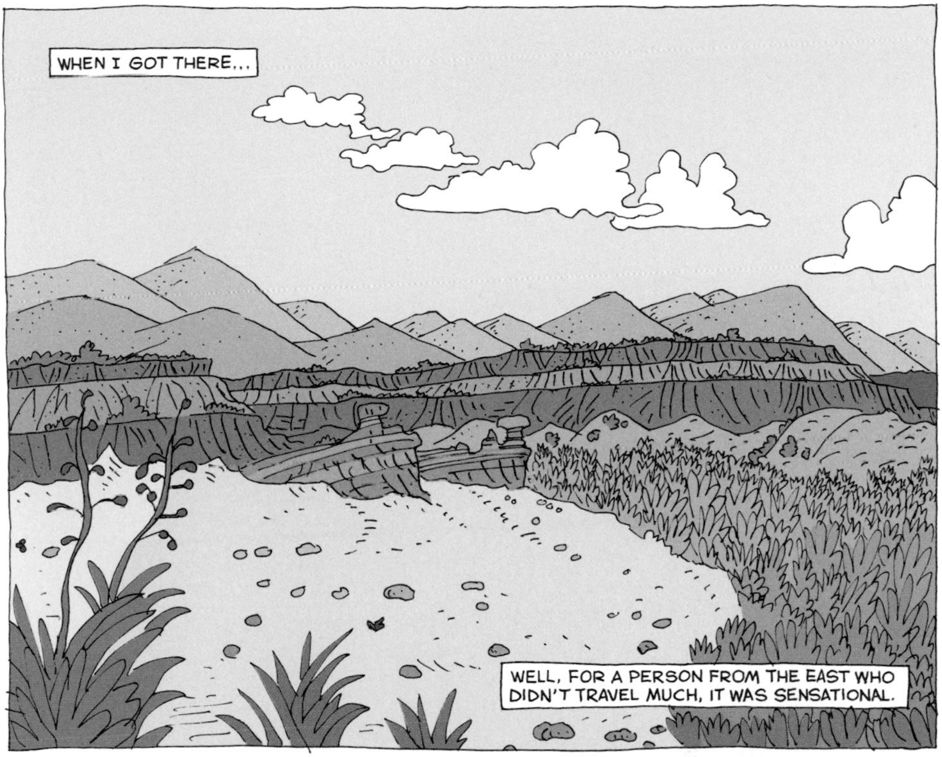
WHEN I GOT THERE...
WELL, FOR A PERSON FROM THE EAST WHO DIDN'T TRAVEL MUCH, IT WAS SENSATIONAL.

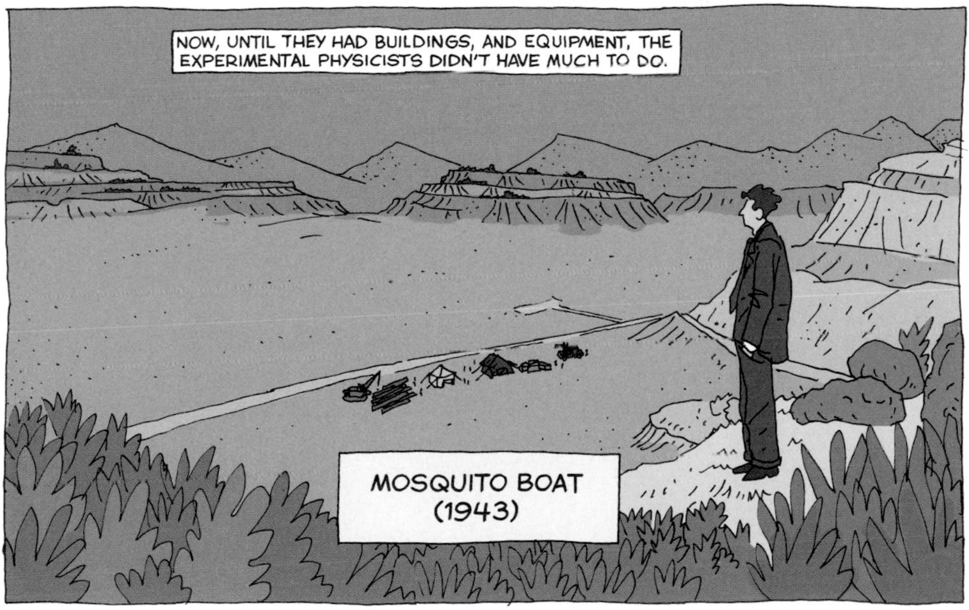
NOW, UNTIL THEY HAD BUILDINGS, AND EQUIPMENT, THE EXPERIMENTAL PHYSICISTS DIDN'T HAVE MUCH TO DO.
MOSQUITO BOAT (1943)

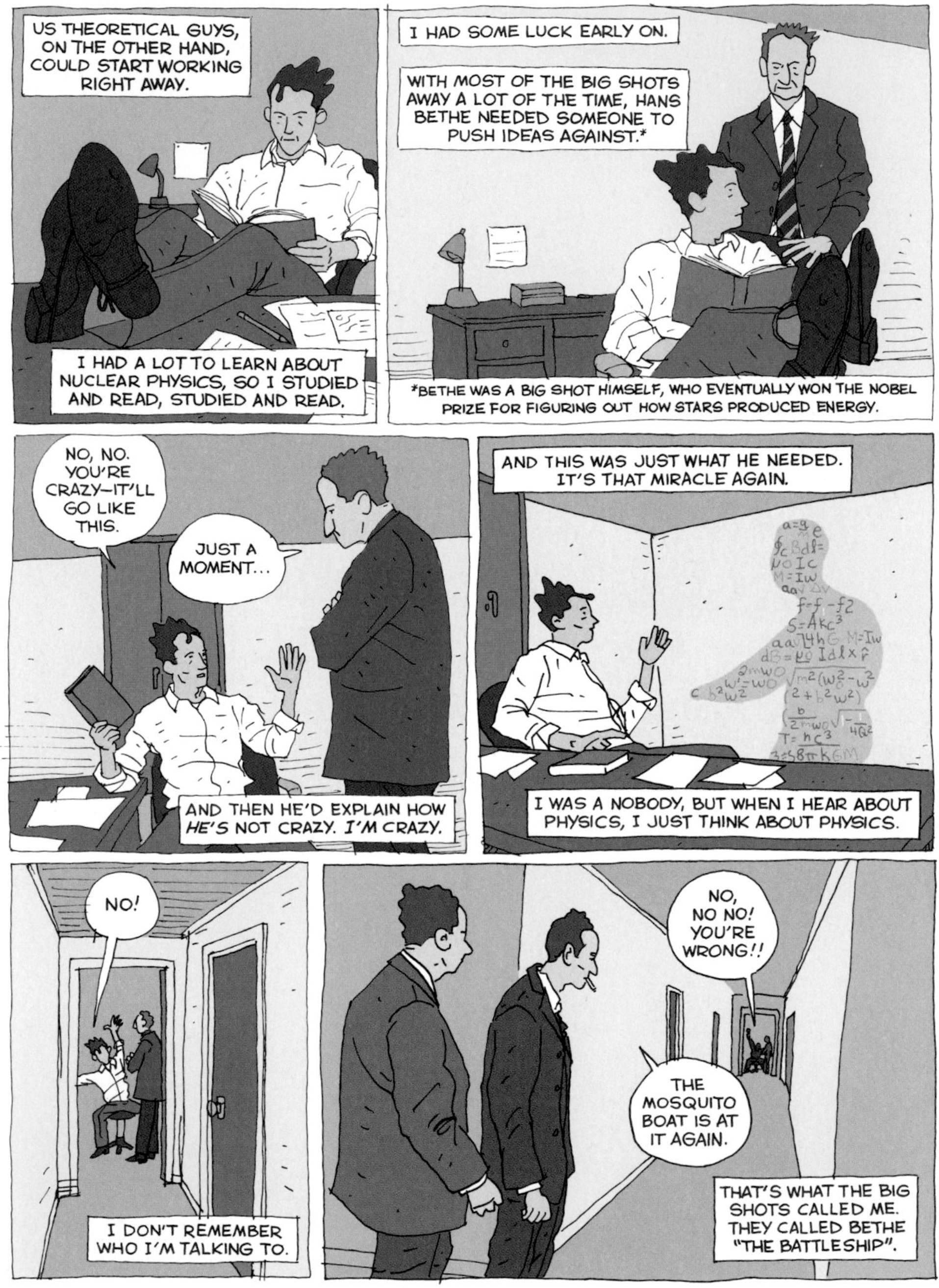
US THEORETICAL GUYS, ON THE OTHER HAND, COULD START WORKING RIGHT AWAY.
I HAD A LOT TO LEARN ABOUT NUCLEAR PHYSICS, SO I STUDIED AND READ, STUDIED AND READ.
I HAD SOME LUCK EARLY ON.
WITH MOST OF THE BIG SHOTS AWAY A LOT OF THE TIME, HANS BETHE NEEDED SOMEONE TO PUSH IDEAS AGAINST.*
*BETHE WAS A BIG SHOT HIMSELF, WHO EVENTUALLY WON THE NOBEL PRIZE FOR FIGURING OUT HOW STARS PRODUCED ENERGY.
NO, NO. YOU'RE CRAZY—IT'LL GO LIKE THIS.
JUST A MOMENT...
AND THEN HE'D EXPLAIN HOW *HE'S* NOT CRAZY. *I'M* CRAZY.
AND THIS WAS JUST WHAT HE NEEDED. IT'S THAT MIRACLE AGAIN.
I WAS A NOBODY, BUT WHEN I HEAR ABOUT PHYSICS, I JUST THINK ABOUT PHYSICS.
NO!
I DON'T REMEMBER WHO I'M TALKING TO.
NO, NO NO! YOU'RE WRONG!!
THE MOSQUITO BOAT IS AT IT AGAIN.
THAT'S WHAT THE BIG SHOTS CALLED ME. THEY CALLED BETHE "THE BATTLESHIP".

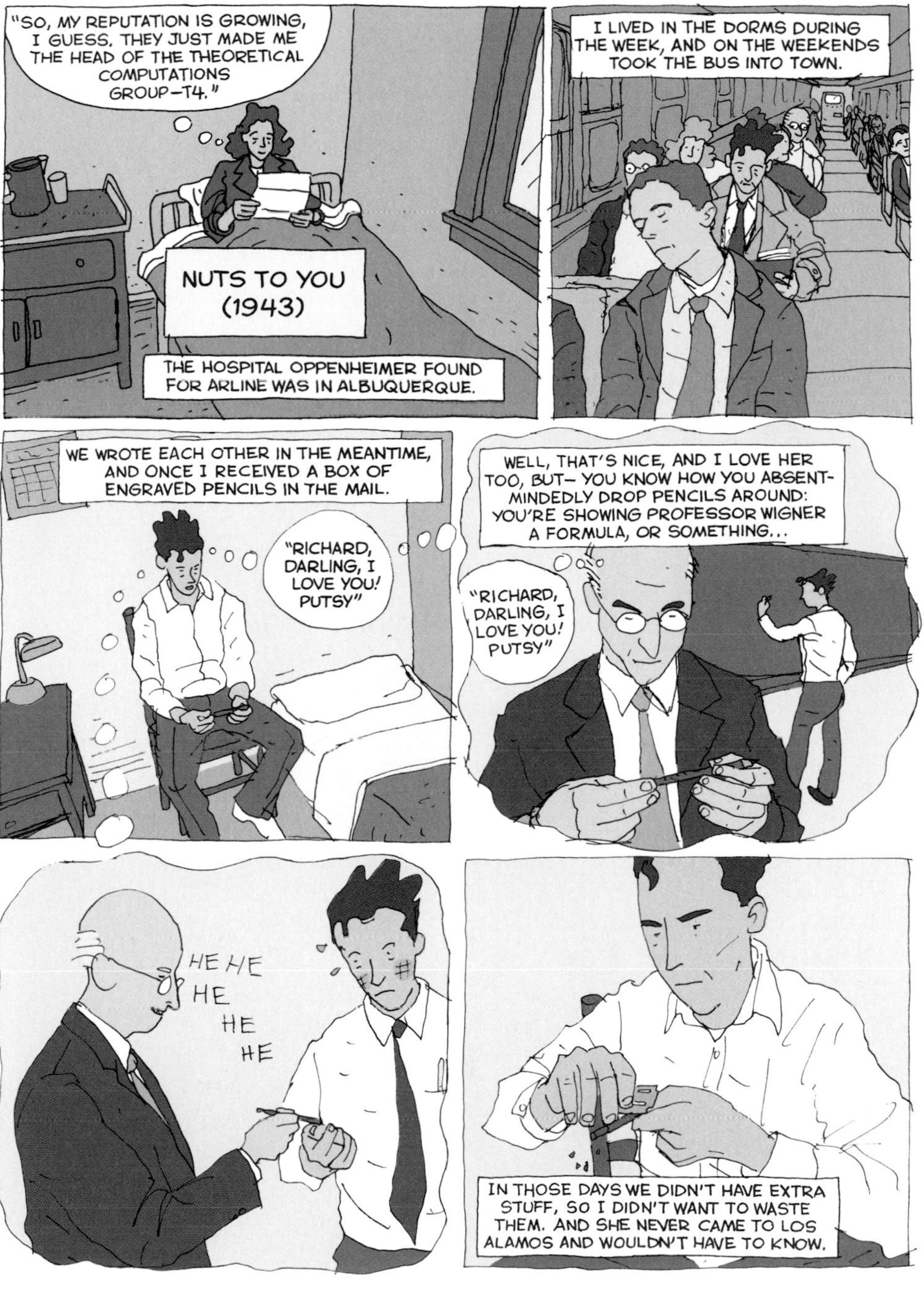
"SO, MY REPUTATION IS GROWING, I GUESS. THEY JUST MADE ME THE HEAD OF THE THEORETICAL COMPUTATIONS GROUP—T4."
NUTS TO YOU (1943)
THE HOSPITAL OPPENHEIMER FOUND FOR ARLINE WAS IN ALBUQUERQUE.
I LIVED IN THE DORMS DURING THE WEEK, AND ON THE WEEKENDS TOOK THE BUS INTO TOWN.
WE WROTE EACH OTHER IN THE MEANTIME, AND ONCE I RECEIVED A BOX OF ENGRAVED PENCILS IN THE MAIL.
"RICHARD, DARLING, I LOVE YOU! PUTSY"
WELL, THAT'S NICE, AND I LOVE HER TOO, BUT— YOU KNOW HOW YOU ABSENT-MINDEDLY DROP PENCILS AROUND: YOU'RE SHOWING PROFESSOR WIGNER A FORMULA, OR SOMETHING...
"RICHARD, DARLING, I LOVE YOU! PUTSY"
HE HE HE HE HE
IN THOSE DAYS WE DIDN'T HAVE EXTRA STUFF, SO I DIDN'T WANT TO WASTE THEM. AND SHE NEVER CAME TO LOS ALAMOS AND WOULDN'T HAVE TO KNOW.

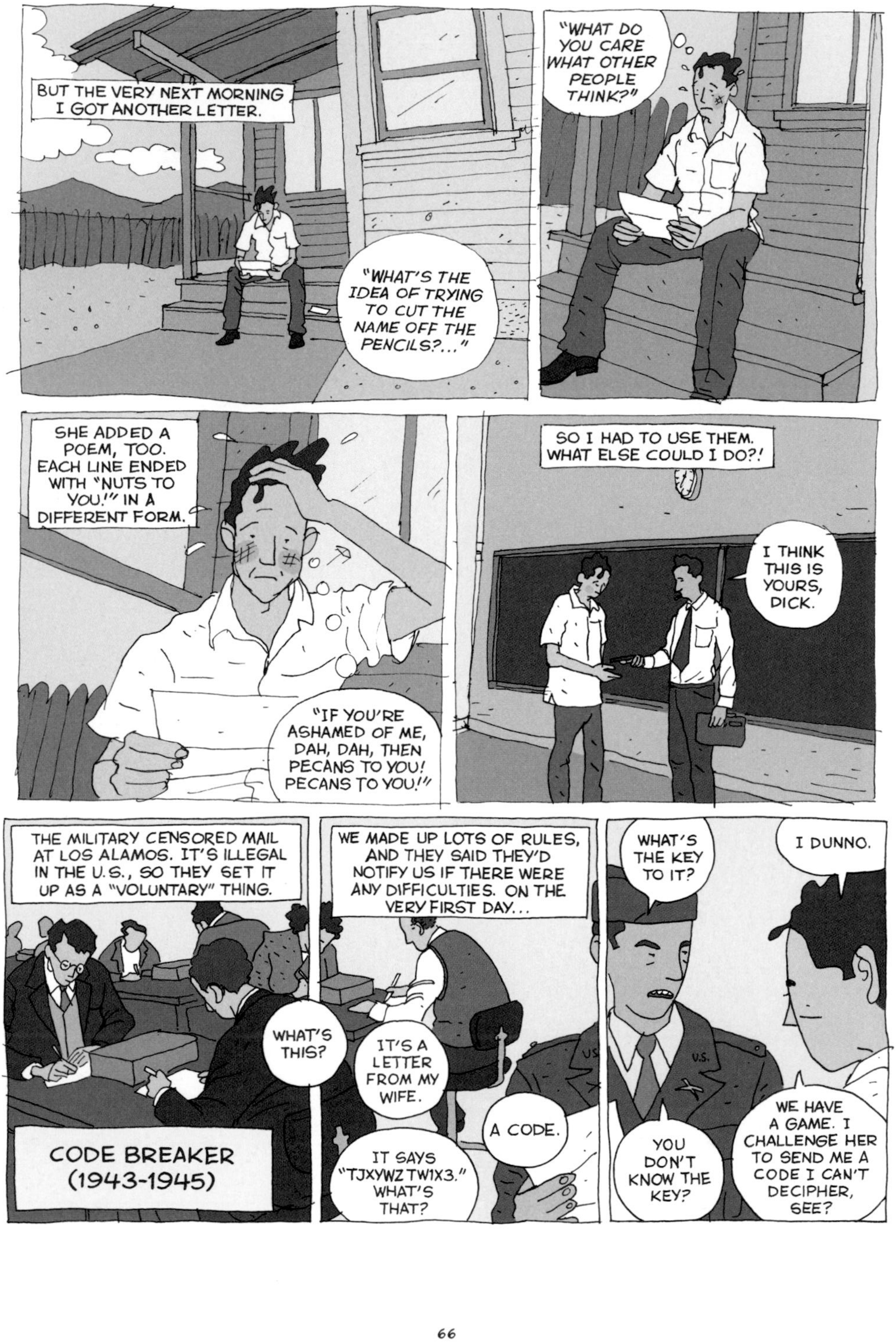
BUT THE VERY NEXT MORNING I GOT ANOTHER LETTER.
"WHAT'S THE IDEA OF TRYING TO CUT THE NAME OFF THE PENCILS?..."
"WHAT DO YOU CARE WHAT OTHER PEOPLE THINK?"
SHE ADDED A POEM, TOO. EACH LINE ENDED WITH "NUTS TO YOU!" IN A DIFFERENT FORM.
"IF YOU'RE ASHAMED OF ME, DAH, DAH, THEN PECANS TO YOU! PECANS TO YOU!"
SO I HAD TO USE THEM. WHAT ELSE COULD I DO?!
I THINK THIS IS YOURS, DICK.
THE MILITARY CENSORED MAIL AT LOS ALAMOS. IT'S ILLEGAL IN THE U.S., SO THEY SET IT UP AS A "VOLUNTARY" THING.
CODE BREAKER (1943-1945)
WE MADE UP LOTS OF RULES, AND THEY SAID THEY'D NOTIFY US IF THERE WERE ANY DIFFICULTIES. ON THE VERY FIRST DAY...
WHAT'S THIS?
IT'S A LETTER FROM MY WIFE.
IT SAYS "TJXYWZ TW1X3." WHAT'S THAT?
A CODE.
WHAT'S THE KEY TO IT?
I DUNNO.
YOU DON'T KNOW THE KEY?
WE HAVE A GAME. I CHALLENGE HER TO SEND ME A CODE I CAN'T DECIPHER, SEE?

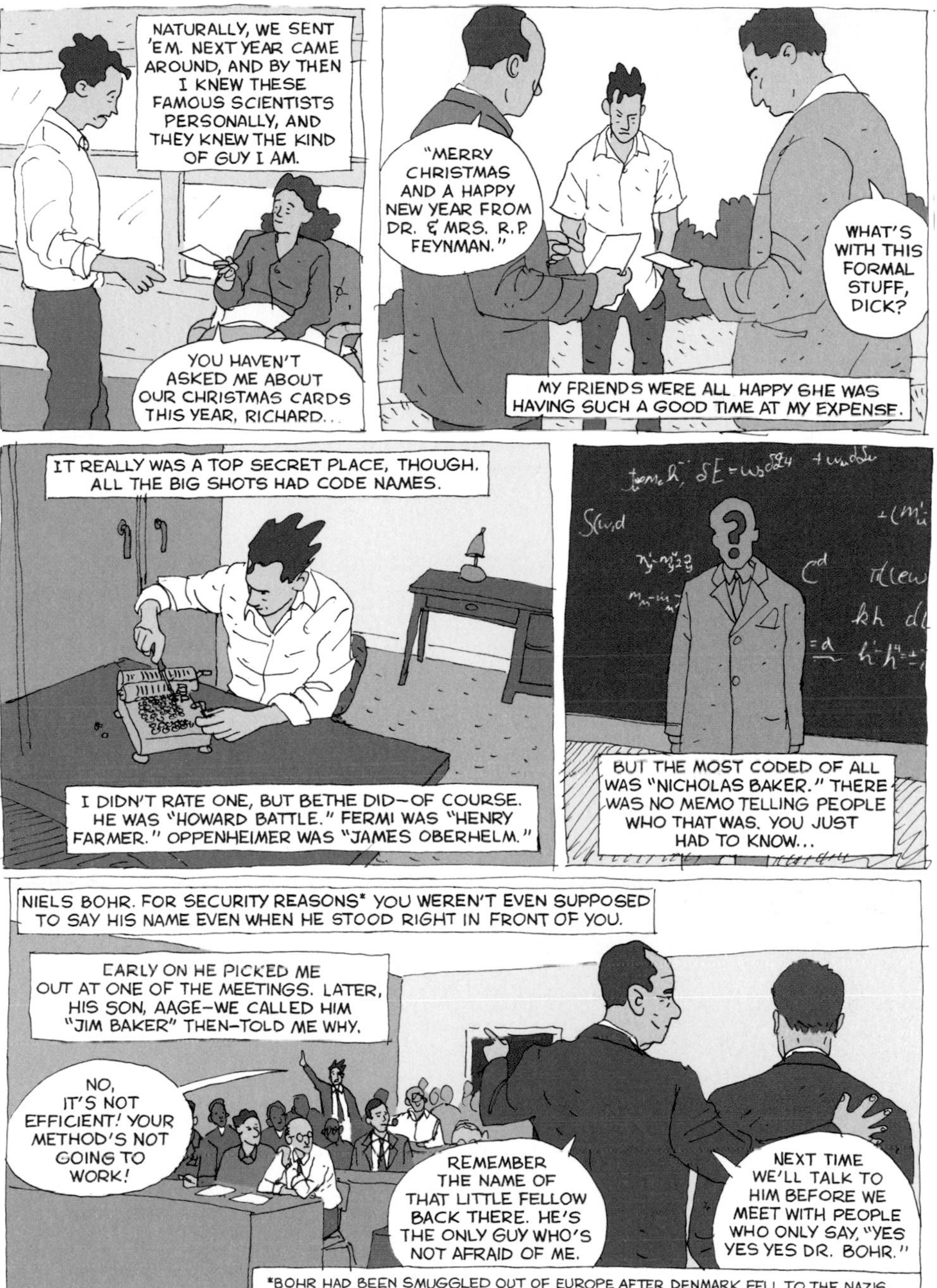
NATURALLY, WE SENT 'EM. NEXT YEAR CAME AROUND, AND BY THEN I KNEW THESE FAMOUS SCIENTISTS PERSONALLY, AND THEY KNEW THE KIND OF GUY I AM.
YOU HAVEN'T ASKED ME ABOUT OUR CHRISTMAS CARDS THIS YEAR, RICHARD...
"MERRY CHRISTMAS AND A HAPPY NEW YEAR FROM DR. & MRS. R.P. FEYNMAN."
WHAT'S WITH THIS FORMAL STUFF, DICK?
MY FRIENDS WERE ALL HAPPY SHE WAS HAVING SUCH A GOOD TIME AT MY EXPENSE.
IT REALLY WAS A TOP SECRET PLACE, THOUGH. ALL THE BIG SHOTS HAD CODE NAMES.
I DIDN'T RATE ONE, BUT BETHE DID—OF COURSE. HE WAS "HOWARD BATTLE." FERMI WAS "HENRY FARMER." OPPENHEIMER WAS "JAMES OBERHELM."
BUT THE MOST CODED OF ALL WAS "NICHOLAS BAKER." THERE WAS NO MEMO TELLING PEOPLE WHO THAT WAS. YOU JUST HAD TO KNOW...
NIELS BOHR. FOR SECURITY REASONS* YOU WEREN'T EVEN SUPPOSED TO SAY HIS NAME EVEN WHEN HE STOOD RIGHT IN FRONT OF YOU.
EARLY ON HE PICKED ME OUT AT ONE OF THE MEETINGS. LATER, HIS SON, AAGE—WE CALLED HIM "JIM BAKER" THEN—TOLD ME WHY.
NO, IT'S NOT EFFICIENT! YOUR METHOD'S NOT GOING TO WORK!
REMEMBER THE NAME OF THAT LITTLE FELLOW BACK THERE. HE'S THE ONLY GUY WHO'S NOT AFRAID OF ME.
NEXT TIME WE'LL TALK TO HIM BEFORE WE MEET WITH PEOPLE WHO ONLY SAY, "YES YES YES DR. BOHR."
*BOHR HAD BEEN SMUGGLED OUT OF EUROPE AFTER DENMARK FELL TO THE NAZIS.

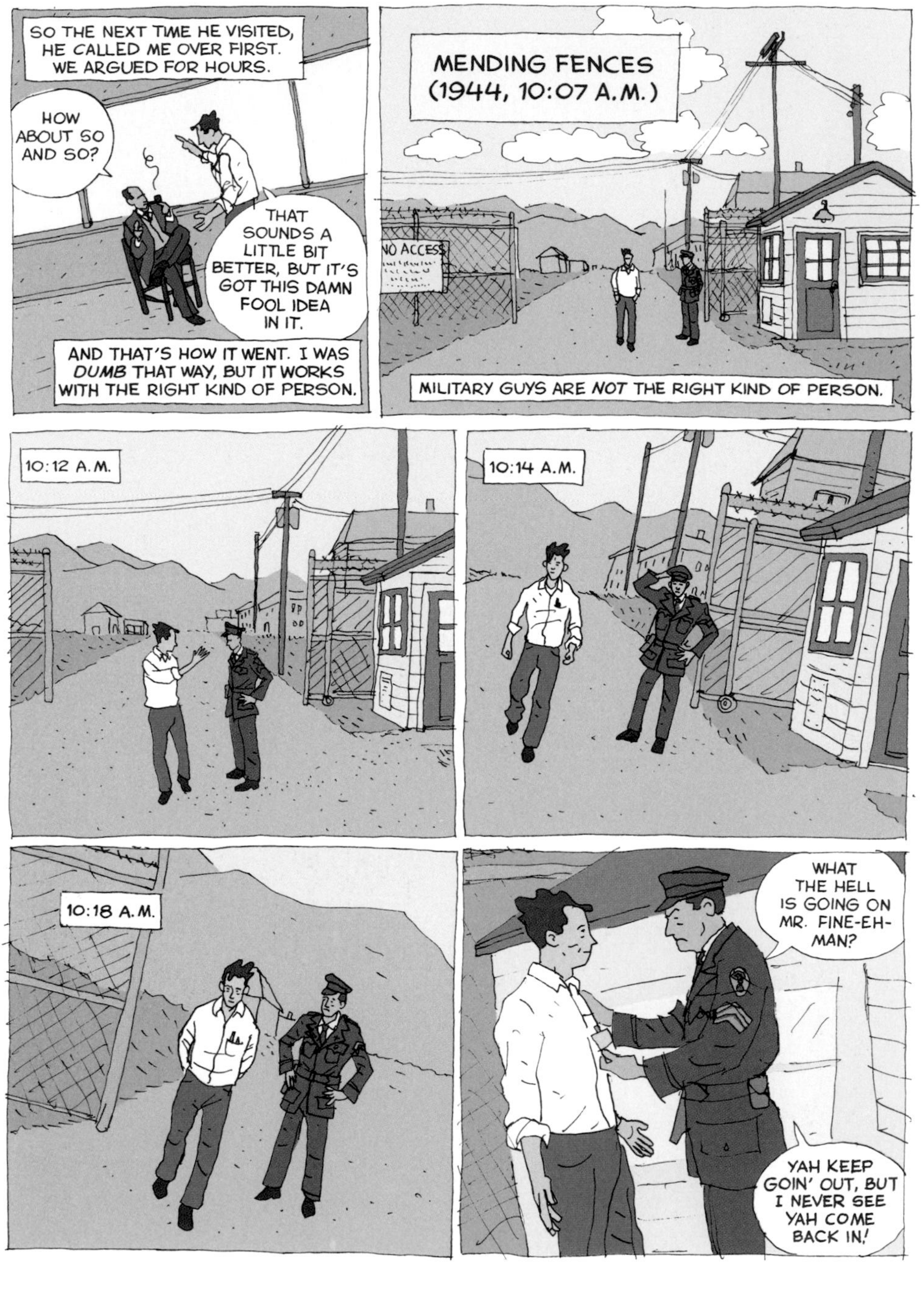
SO THE NEXT TIME HE VISITED, HE CALLED ME OVER FIRST. WE ARGUED FOR HOURS.
HOW ABOUT SO AND SO?
THAT SOUNDS A LITTLE BIT BETTER, BUT IT'S GOT THIS DAMN FOOL IDEA IN IT.
AND THAT'S HOW IT WENT. I WAS DUMB THAT WAY, BUT IT WORKS WITH THE RIGHT KIND OF PERSON.
MENDING FENCES (1944, 10:07 A.M.)
NO ACCESS
MILITARY GUYS ARE NOT THE RIGHT KIND OF PERSON.
10:12 A.M.
10:14 A.M.
10:18 A.M.
WHAT THE HELL IS GOING ON MR. FINE-EH-MAN?
YAH KEEP GOIN' OUT, BUT I NEVER SEE YAH COME BACK IN!

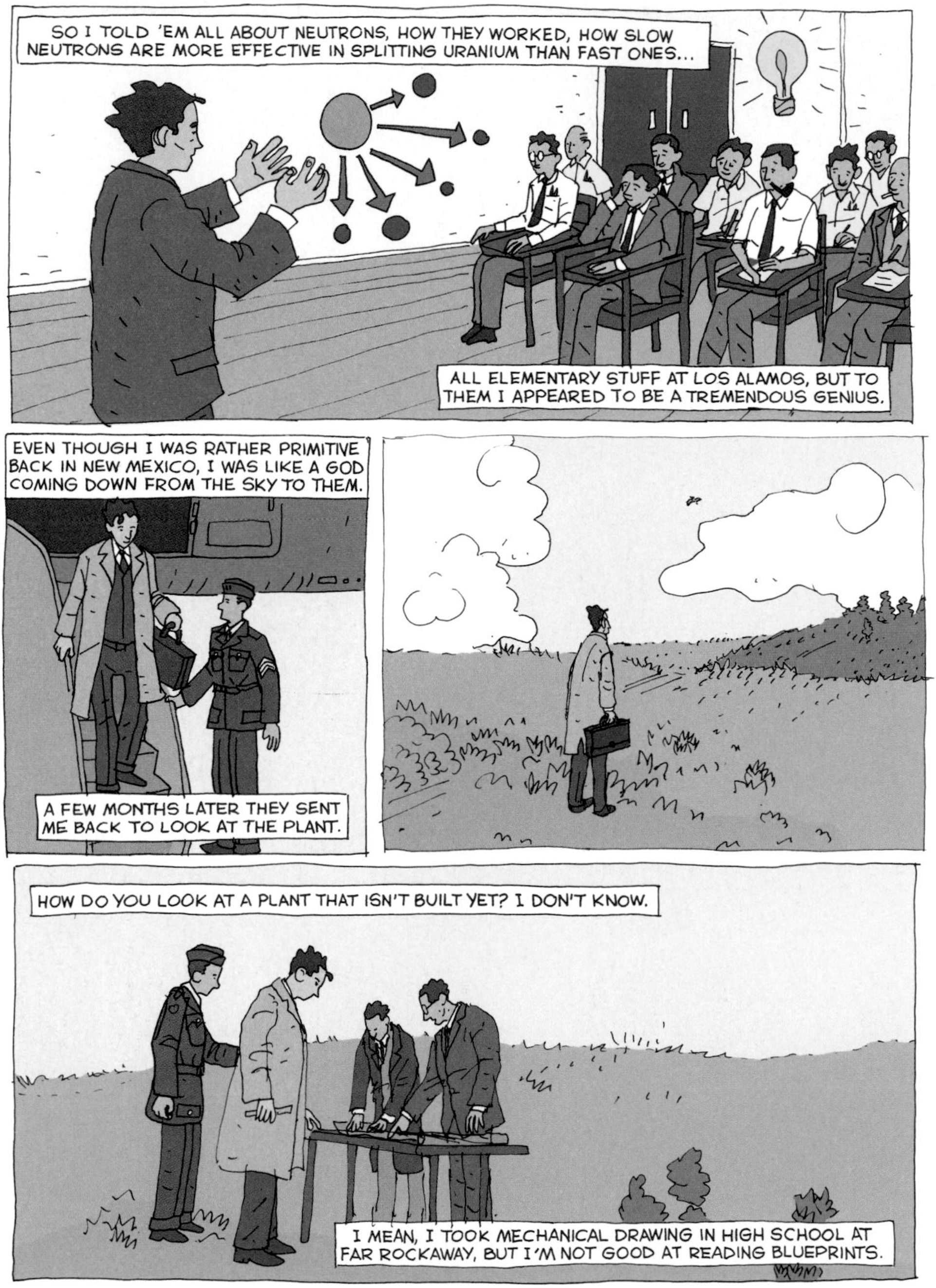

SO I TOLD 'EM ALL ABOUT NEUTRONS, HOW THEY WORKED, HOW SLOW NEUTRONS ARE MORE EFFECTIVE IN SPLITTING URANIUM THAN FAST ONES...
ALL ELEMENTARY STUFF AT LOS ALAMOS, BUT TO THEM I APPEARED TO BE A TREMENDOUS GENIUS.
EVEN THOUGH I WAS RATHER PRIMITIVE BACK IN NEW MEXICO, I WAS LIKE A GOD COMING DOWN FROM THE SKY TO THEM.
A FEW MONTHS LATER THEY SENT ME BACK TO LOOK AT THE PLANT.
HOW DO YOU LOOK AT A PLANT THAT ISN'T BUILT YET? I DON'T KNOW.
I MEAN, I TOOK MECHANICAL DRAWING IN HIGH SCHOOL AT FAR ROCKAWAY, BUT I'M NOT GOOD AT READING BLUEPRINTS.

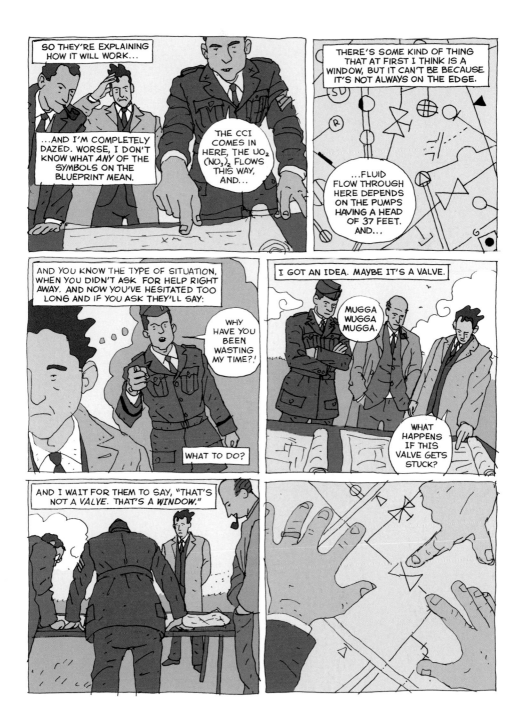

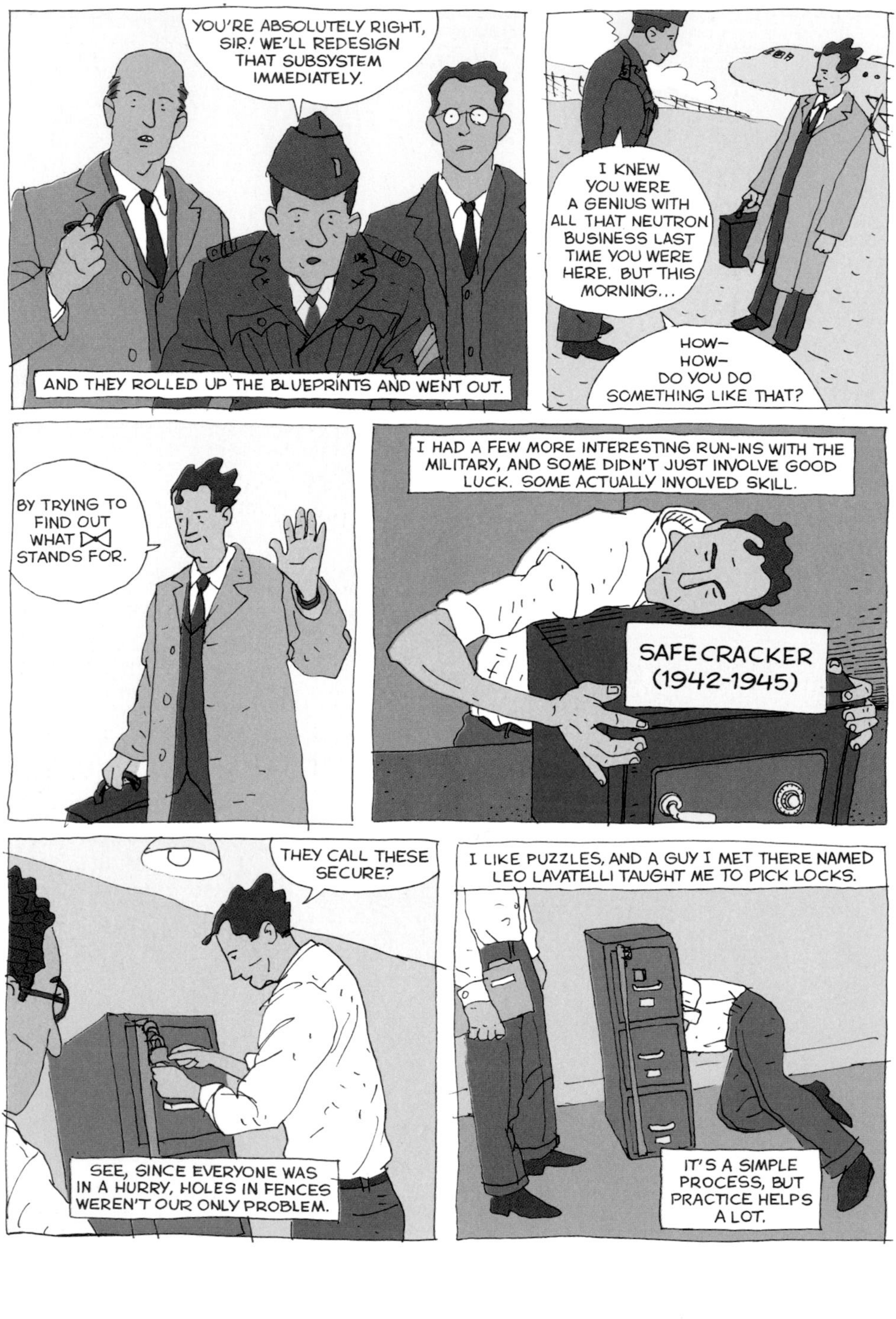
YOU'RE ABSOLUTELY RIGHT, SIR! WE'LL REDESIGN THAT SUBSYSTEM IMMEDIATELY.
AND THEY ROLLED UP THE BLUEPRINTS AND WENT OUT.
I KNEW YOU WERE A GENIUS WITH ALL THAT NEUTRON BUSINESS LAST TIME YOU WERE HERE. BUT THIS MORNING...
HOW— HOW— DO YOU DO SOMETHING LIKE THAT?
BY TRYING TO FIND OUT WHAT ⋈ STANDS FOR.
I HAD A FEW MORE INTERESTING RUN-INS WITH THE MILITARY, AND SOME DIDN'T JUST INVOLVE GOOD LUCK. SOME ACTUALLY INVOLVED SKILL.
SAFECRACKER (1942-1945)
THEY CALL THESE SECURE?
SEE, SINCE EVERYONE WAS IN A HURRY, HOLES IN FENCES WEREN'T OUR ONLY PROBLEM.
I LIKE PUZZLES, AND A GUY I MET THERE NAMED LEO LAVATELLI TAUGHT ME TO PICK LOCKS.
IT'S A SIMPLE PROCESS, BUT PRACTICE HELPS A LOT.

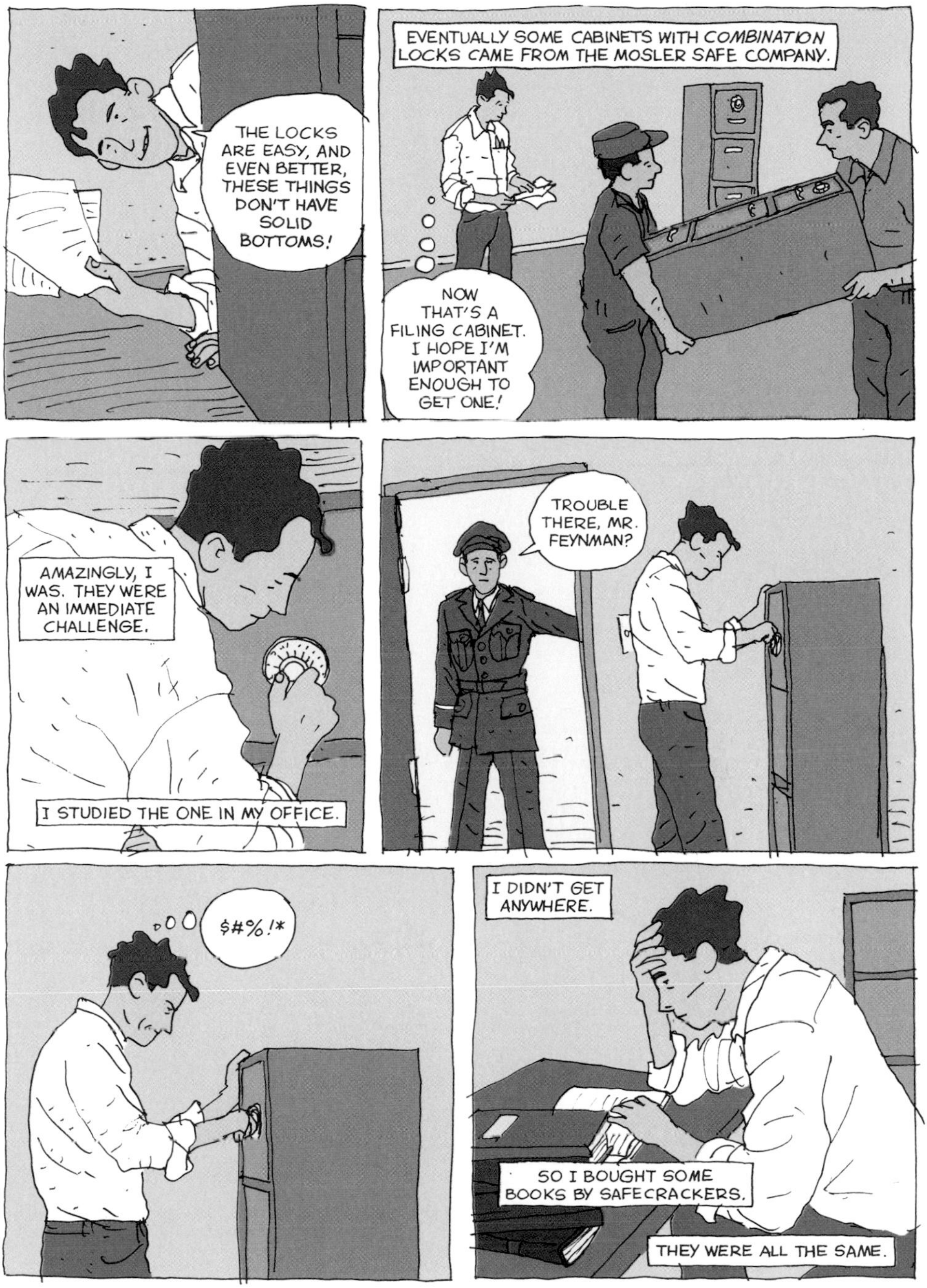
THE LOCKS ARE EASY, AND EVEN BETTER, THESE THINGS DON'T HAVE SOLID BOTTOMS!
EVENTUALLY SOME CABINETS WITH COMBINATION LOCKS CAME FROM THE MOSLER SAFE COMPANY.
NOW THAT'S A FILING CABINET. I HOPE I'M IMPORTANT ENOUGH TO GET ONE!
AMAZINGLY, I WAS. THEY WERE AN IMMEDIATE CHALLENGE.
I STUDIED THE ONE IN MY OFFICE.
TROUBLE THERE, MR. FEYNMAN?
$#%!*
I DIDN'T GET ANYWHERE.
SO I BOUGHT SOME BOOKS BY SAFECRACKERS.
THEY WERE ALL THE SAME.

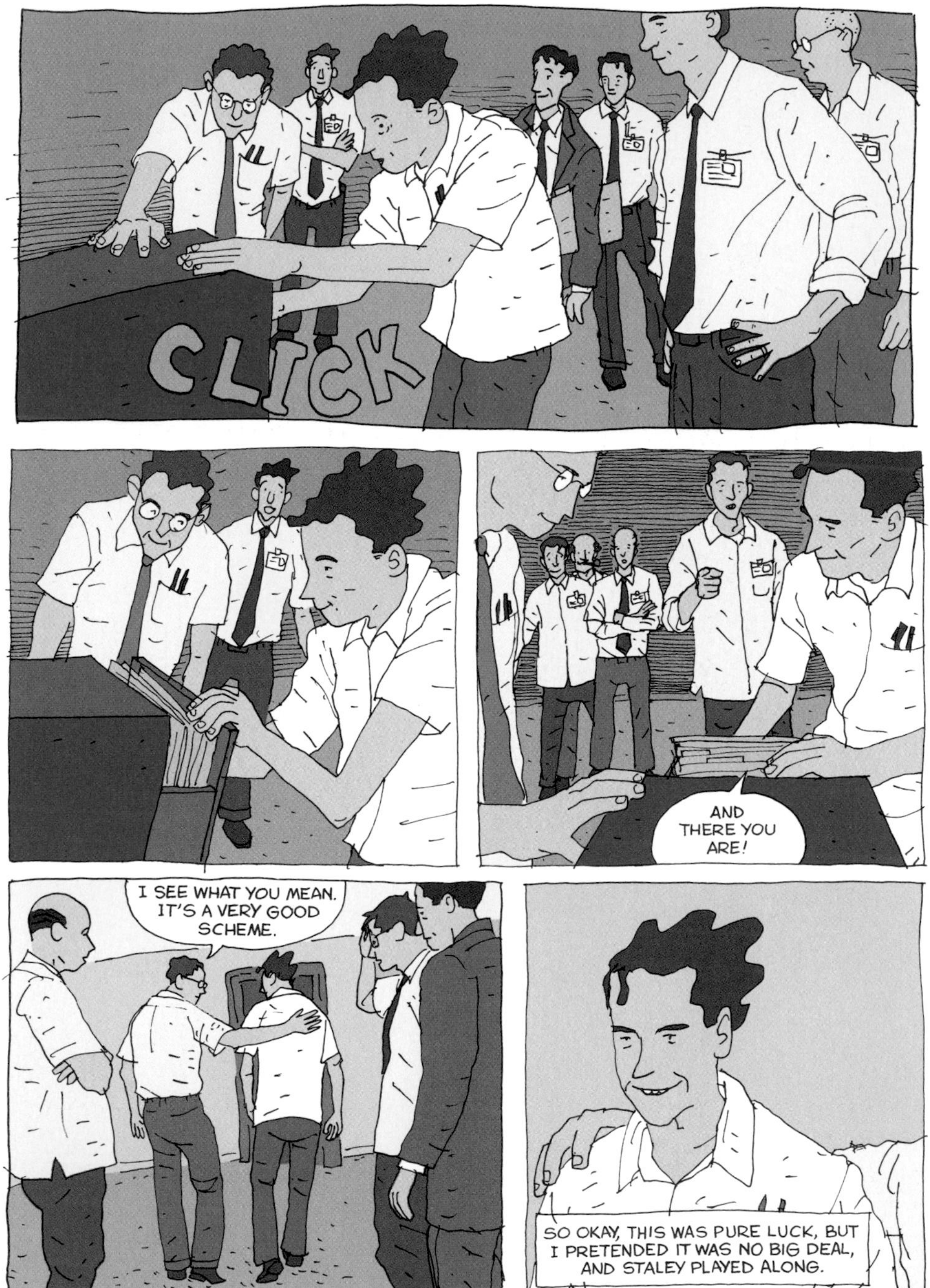
CLICK
AND THERE YOU ARE!
I SEE WHAT YOU MEAN. IT'S A VERY GOOD SCHEME.
SO OKAY, THIS WAS PURE LUCK, BUT I PRETENDED IT WAS NO BIG DEAL, AND STALEY PLAYED ALONG.

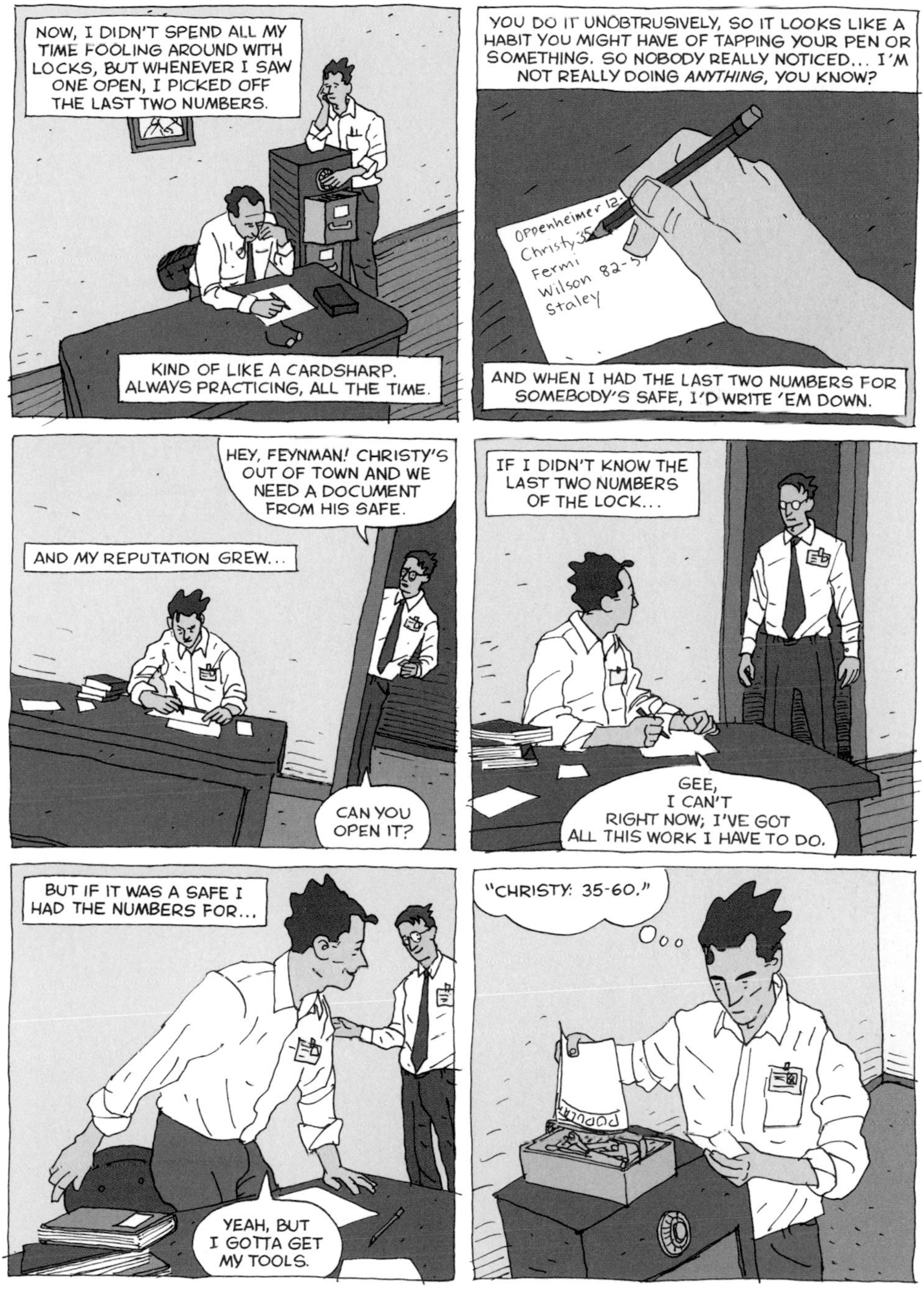
NOW, I DIDN'T SPEND ALL MY TIME FOOLING AROUND WITH LOCKS, BUT WHENEVER I SAW ONE OPEN, I PICKED OFF THE LAST TWO NUMBERS.
KIND OF LIKE A CARDSHARP. ALWAYS PRACTICING, ALL THE TIME.
YOU DO IT UNOBTRUSIVELY, SO IT LOOKS LIKE A HABIT YOU MIGHT HAVE OF TAPPING YOUR PEN OR SOMETHING. SO NOBODY REALLY NOTICED... I'M NOT REALLY DOING *ANYTHING*, YOU KNOW?
Oppenheimer 12-
Christy 35
Fermi
Wilson 82-5
Staley
AND WHEN I HAD THE LAST TWO NUMBERS FOR SOMEBODY'S SAFE, I'D WRITE 'EM DOWN.
AND MY REPUTATION GREW...
HEY, FEYNMAN! CHRISTY'S OUT OF TOWN AND WE NEED A DOCUMENT FROM HIS SAFE.
CAN YOU OPEN IT?
IF I DIDN'T KNOW THE LAST TWO NUMBERS OF THE LOCK...
GEE, I CAN'T RIGHT NOW; I'VE GOT ALL THIS WORK I HAVE TO DO.
BUT IF IT WAS A SAFE I HAD THE NUMBERS FOR...
YEAH, BUT I GOTTA GET MY TOOLS.
"CHRISTY: 35-60."

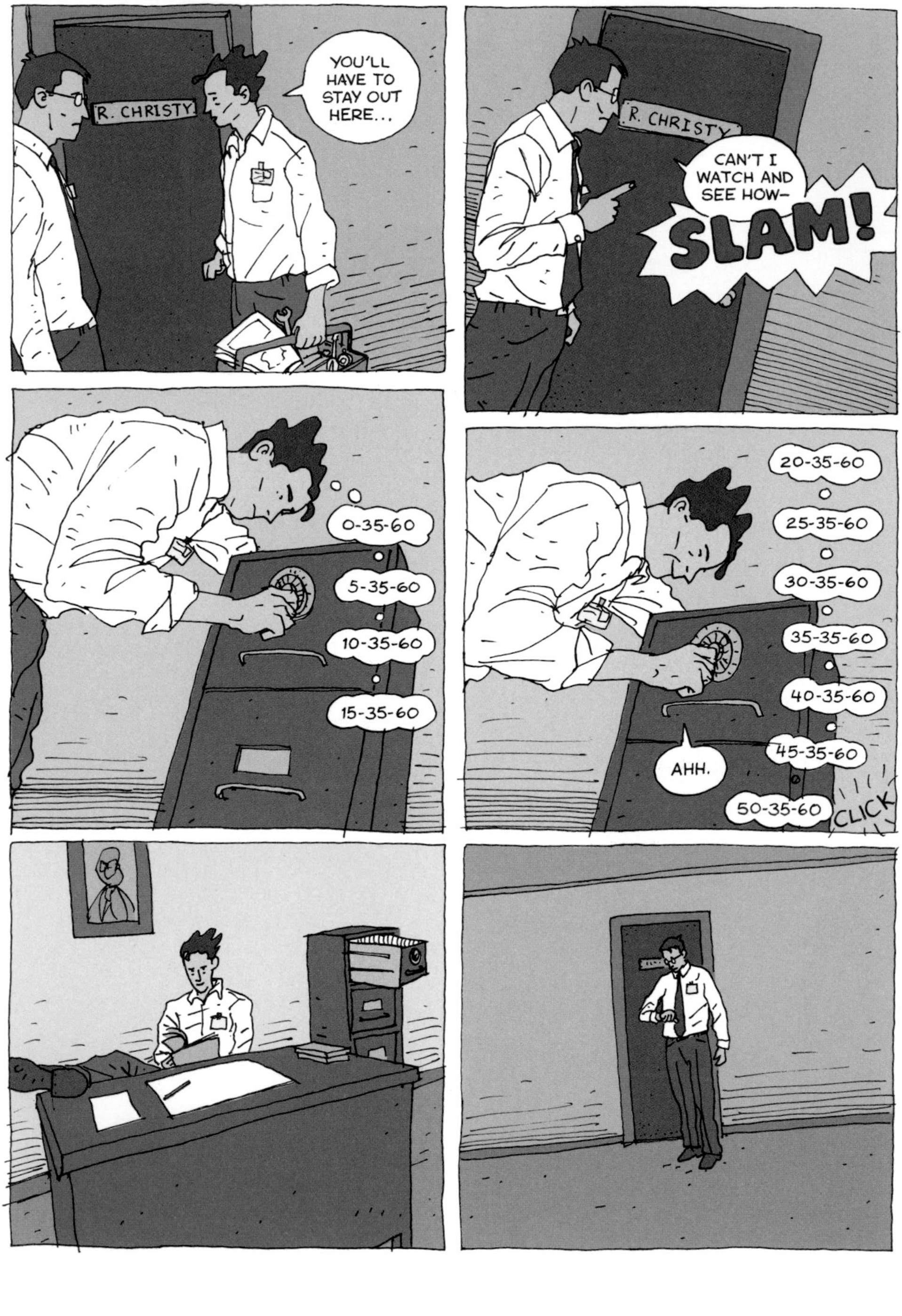
R. CHRISTY
YOU'LL HAVE TO STAY OUT HERE...
R. CHRISTY
CAN'T I WATCH AND SEE HOW–
SLAM!
0-35-60
5-35-60
10-35-60
15-35-60
20-35-60
25-35-60
30-35-60
35-35-60
40-35-60
45-35-60
AHH.
50-35-60
CLICK

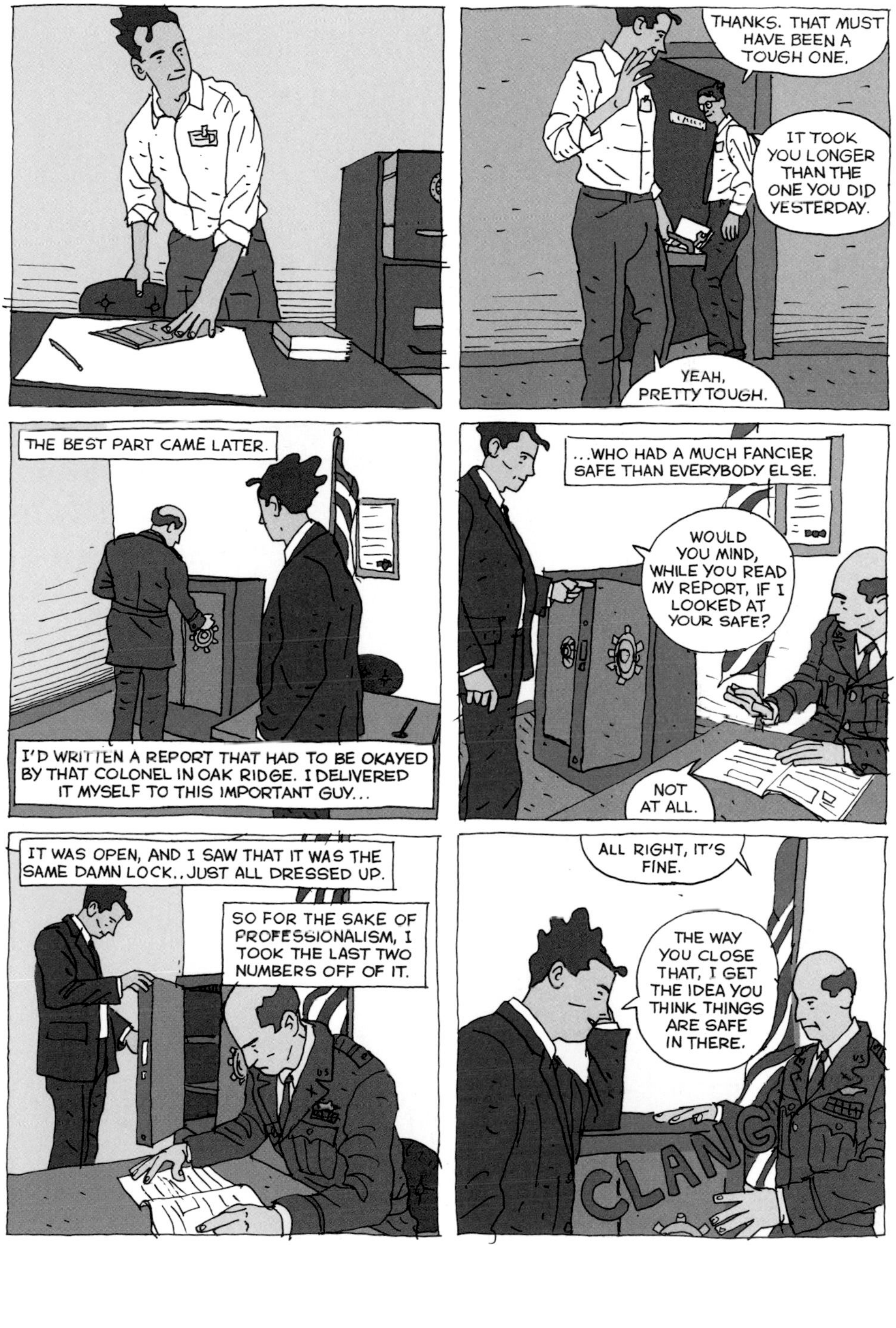
THANKS. THAT MUST HAVE BEEN A TOUGH ONE.
IT TOOK YOU LONGER THAN THE ONE YOU DID YESTERDAY.
YEAH, PRETTY TOUGH.
THE BEST PART CAME LATER.
I'D WRITTEN A REPORT THAT HAD TO BE OKAYED BY THAT COLONEL IN OAK RIDGE. I DELIVERED IT MYSELF TO THIS IMPORTANT GUY...
...WHO HAD A MUCH FANCIER SAFE THAN EVERYBODY ELSE.
WOULD YOU MIND, WHILE YOU READ MY REPORT, IF I LOOKED AT YOUR SAFE?
NOT AT ALL.
IT WAS OPEN, AND I SAW THAT IT WAS THE SAME DAMN LOCK.. JUST ALL DRESSED UP.
SO FOR THE SAKE OF PROFESSIONALISM, I TOOK THE LAST TWO NUMBERS OFF OF IT.
ALL RIGHT, IT'S FINE.
THE WAY YOU CLOSE THAT, I GET THE IDEA YOU THINK THINGS ARE SAFE IN THERE.
CLANG

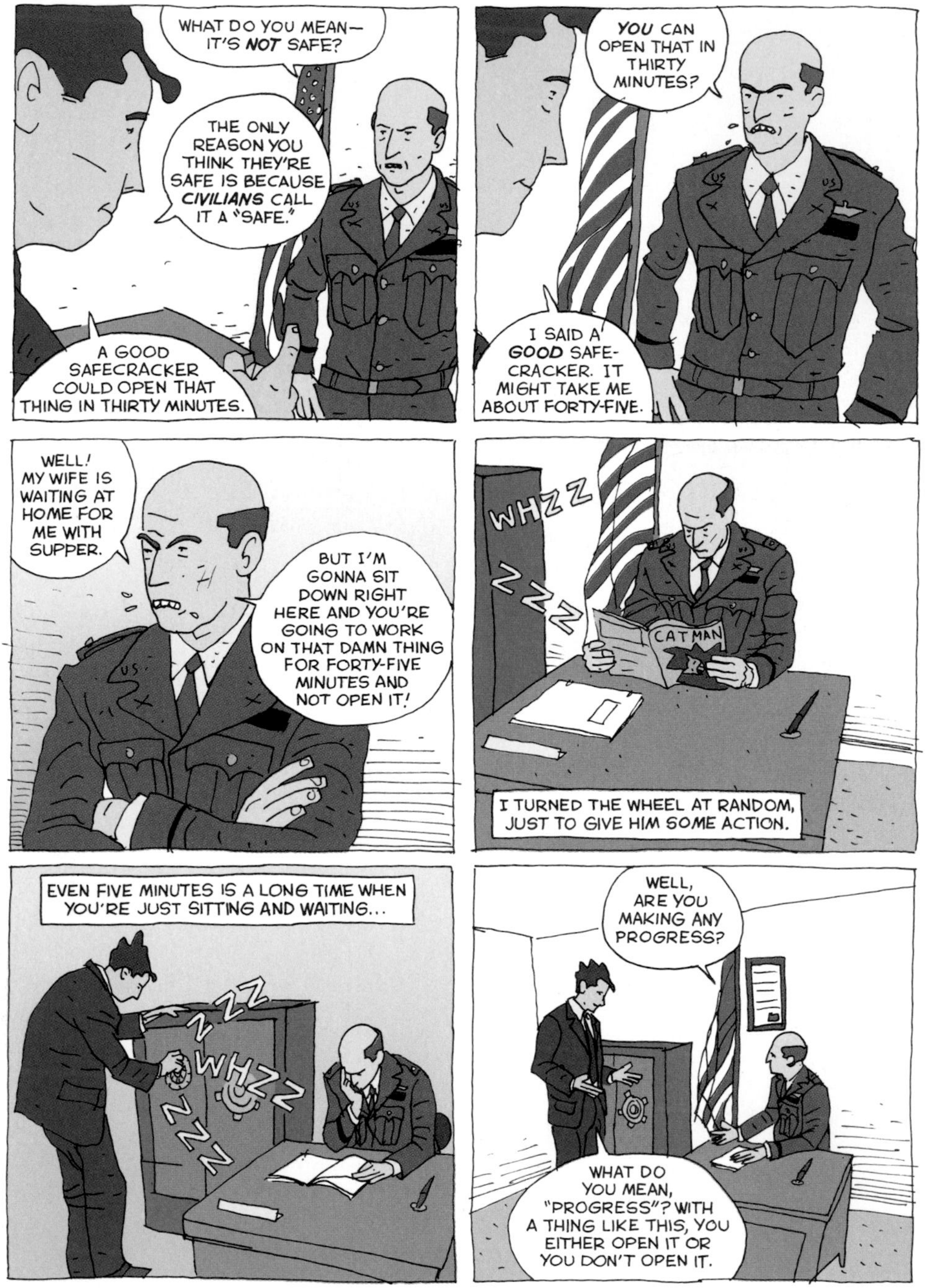
WHAT DO YOU MEAN— IT'S **NOT** SAFE?
THE ONLY REASON YOU THINK THEY'RE SAFE IS BECAUSE **CIVILIANS** CALL IT A "SAFE."
A GOOD SAFECRACKER COULD OPEN THAT THING IN THIRTY MINUTES.
YOU CAN OPEN THAT IN THIRTY MINUTES?
I SAID A **GOOD** SAFE-CRACKER. IT MIGHT TAKE ME ABOUT FORTY-FIVE.
WELL! MY WIFE IS WAITING AT HOME FOR ME WITH SUPPER.
BUT I'M GONNA SIT DOWN RIGHT HERE AND YOU'RE GOING TO WORK ON THAT DAMN THING FOR FORTY-FIVE MINUTES AND NOT OPEN IT!
WHZZ
ZZZ
CATMAN
I TURNED THE WHEEL AT RANDOM, JUST TO GIVE HIM SOME ACTION.
EVEN FIVE MINUTES IS A LONG TIME WHEN YOU'RE JUST SITTING AND WAITING...
ZZ
WHZZ
ZZZ
WELL, ARE YOU MAKING ANY PROGRESS?
WHAT DO YOU MEAN, "PROGRESS"? WITH A THING LIKE THIS, YOU EITHER OPEN IT OR YOU DON'T OPEN IT.

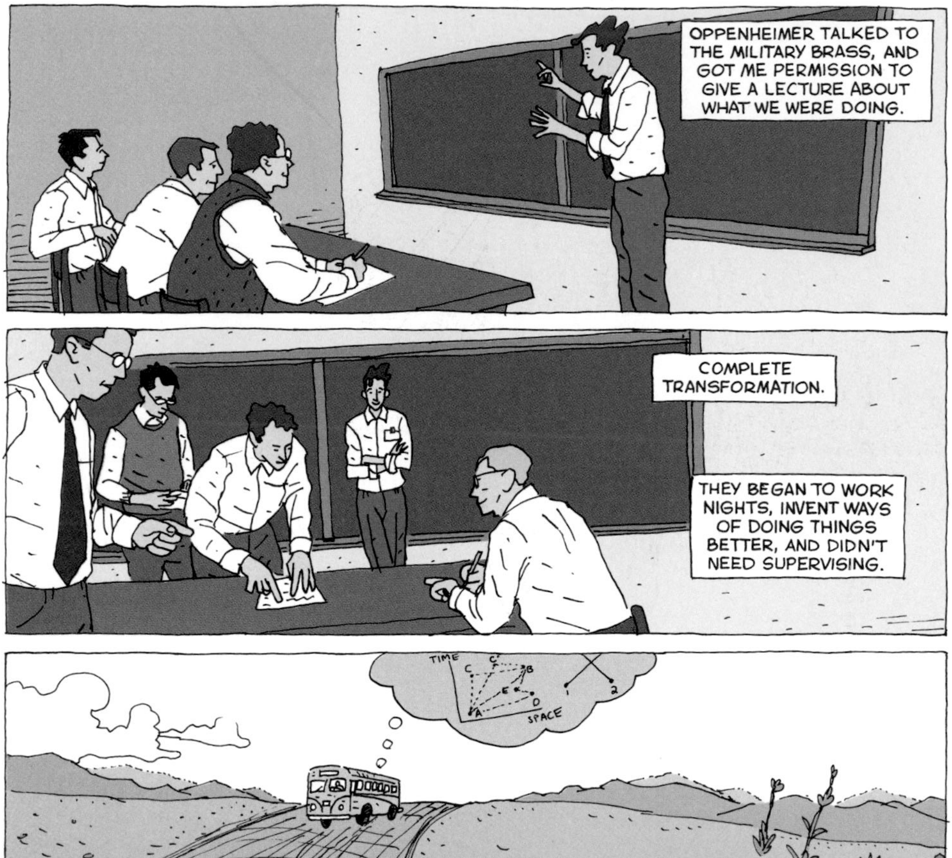
OPPENHEIMER TALKED TO THE MILITARY BRASS, AND GOT ME PERMISSION TO GIVE A LECTURE ABOUT WHAT WE WERE DOING.
COMPLETE TRANSFORMATION.
THEY BEGAN TO WORK NIGHTS, INVENT WAYS OF DOING THINGS BETTER, AND DIDN'T NEED SUPERVISING.
TIME
SPACE
WHICH WAS GOOD, BECAUSE I WAS STILL TRAVELING TO ALBUQUERQUE ALL THE TIME.
OVER THERE, I DIDN'T ALWAYS COME OUT ON TOP.
NO. THAT ONE'S WRONG.
ONCE WHEN I VISITED, ARLINE WAS PRACTICING CHINESE CALLIGRAPHY. I THOUGHT IT WAS LOVELY, BUT...
WHAT DO YOU MEAN, "WRONG"? IT'S ONLY A HUMAN CONVENTION.

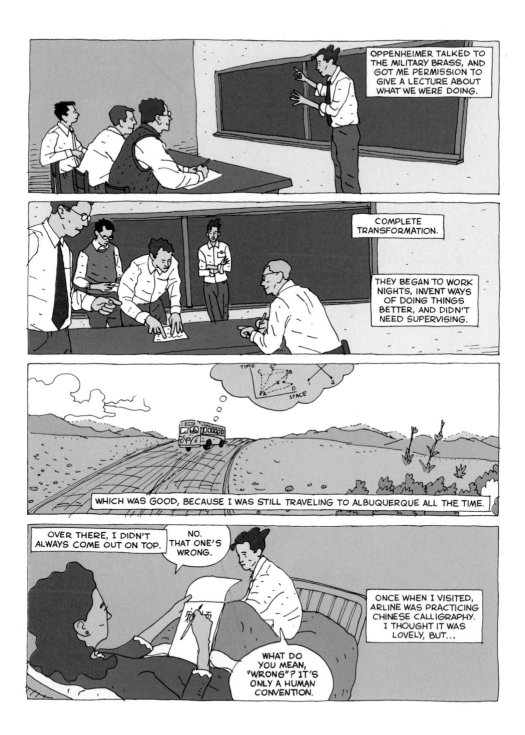

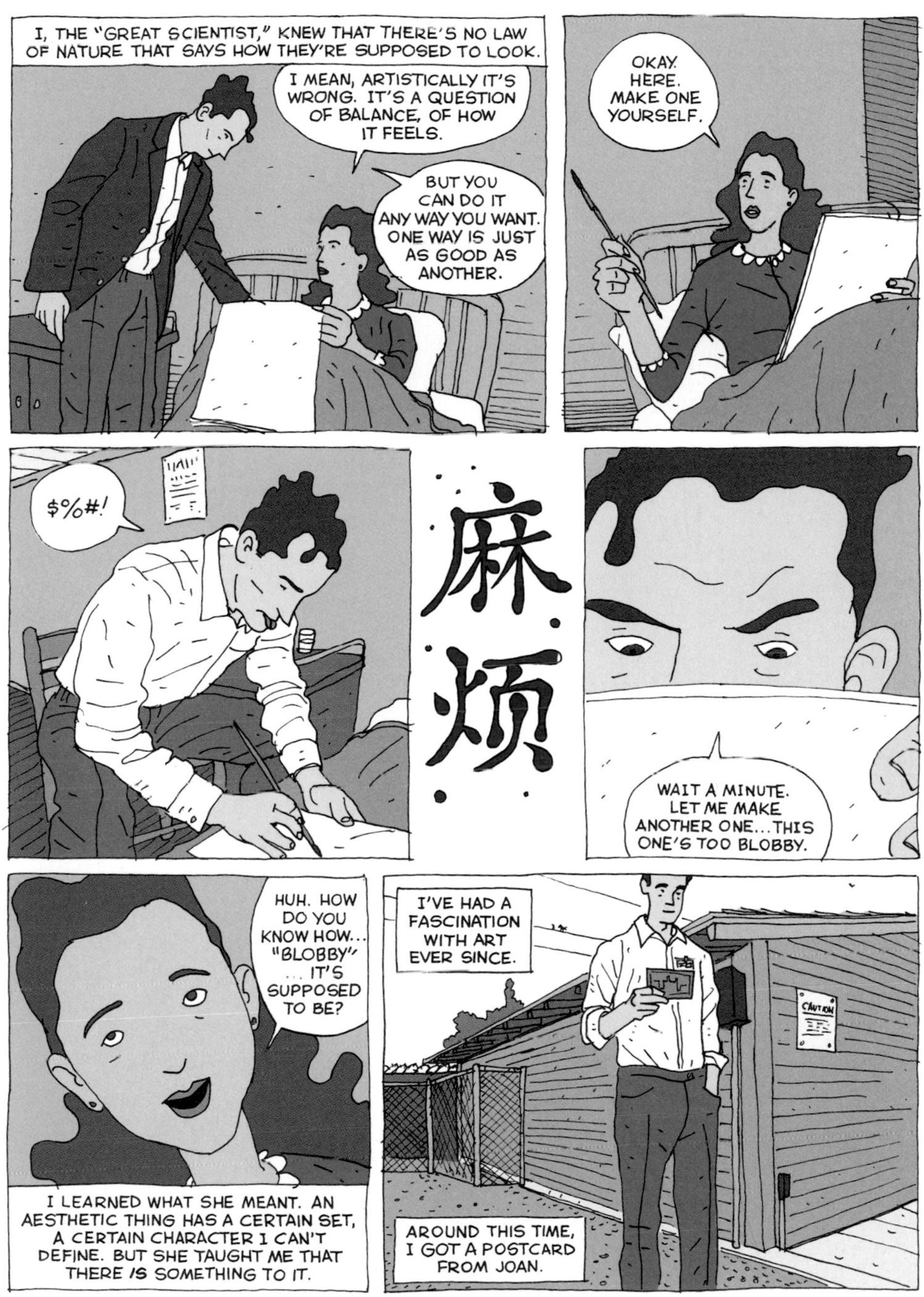
I, THE "GREAT SCIENTIST," KNEW THAT THERE'S NO LAW OF NATURE THAT SAYS HOW THEY'RE SUPPOSED TO LOOK.
I MEAN, ARTISTICALLY IT'S WRONG. IT'S A QUESTION OF BALANCE, OF HOW IT FEELS.
BUT YOU CAN DO IT ANY WAY YOU WANT. ONE WAY IS JUST AS GOOD AS ANOTHER.
OKAY. HERE. MAKE ONE YOURSELF.
$%#!
麻烦
WAIT A MINUTE. LET ME MAKE ANOTHER ONE... THIS ONE'S TOO BLOBBY.
HUH. HOW DO YOU KNOW HOW... "BLOBBY" ... IT'S SUPPOSED TO BE?
I LEARNED WHAT SHE MEANT. AN AESTHETIC THING HAS A CERTAIN SET, A CERTAIN CHARACTER I CAN'T DEFINE. BUT SHE TAUGHT ME THAT THERE IS SOMETHING TO IT.
I'VE HAD A FASCINATION WITH ART EVER SINCE.
CAUTION
AROUND THIS TIME, I GOT A POSTCARD FROM JOAN.

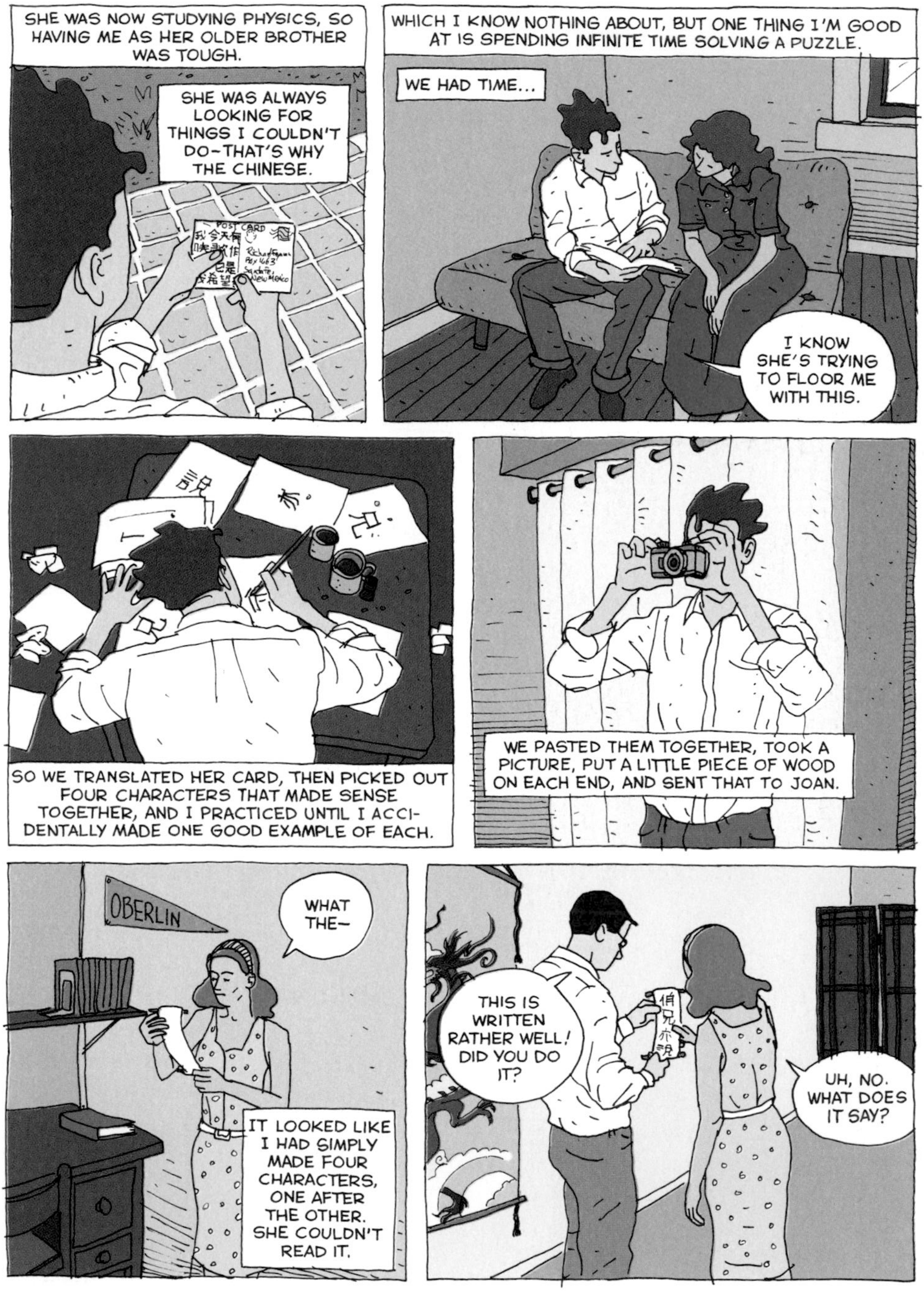
SHE WAS NOW STUDYING PHYSICS, SO HAVING ME AS HER OLDER BROTHER WAS TOUGH.
SHE WAS ALWAYS LOOKING FOR THINGS I COULDN'T DO–THAT'S WHY THE CHINESE.
WHICH I KNOW NOTHING ABOUT, BUT ONE THING I'M GOOD AT IS SPENDING INFINITE TIME SOLVING A PUZZLE.
WE HAD TIME...
I KNOW SHE'S TRYING TO FLOOR ME WITH THIS.
SO WE TRANSLATED HER CARD, THEN PICKED OUT FOUR CHARACTERS THAT MADE SENSE TOGETHER, AND I PRACTICED UNTIL I ACCIDENTALLY MADE ONE GOOD EXAMPLE OF EACH.
WE PASTED THEM TOGETHER, TOOK A PICTURE, PUT A LITTLE PIECE OF WOOD ON EACH END, AND SENT THAT TO JOAN.
OBERLIN
WHAT THE–
IT LOOKED LIKE I HAD SIMPLY MADE FOUR CHARACTERS, ONE AFTER THE OTHER. SHE COULDN'T READ IT.
THIS IS WRITTEN RATHER WELL! DID YOU DO IT?
UH, NO. WHAT DOES IT SAY?

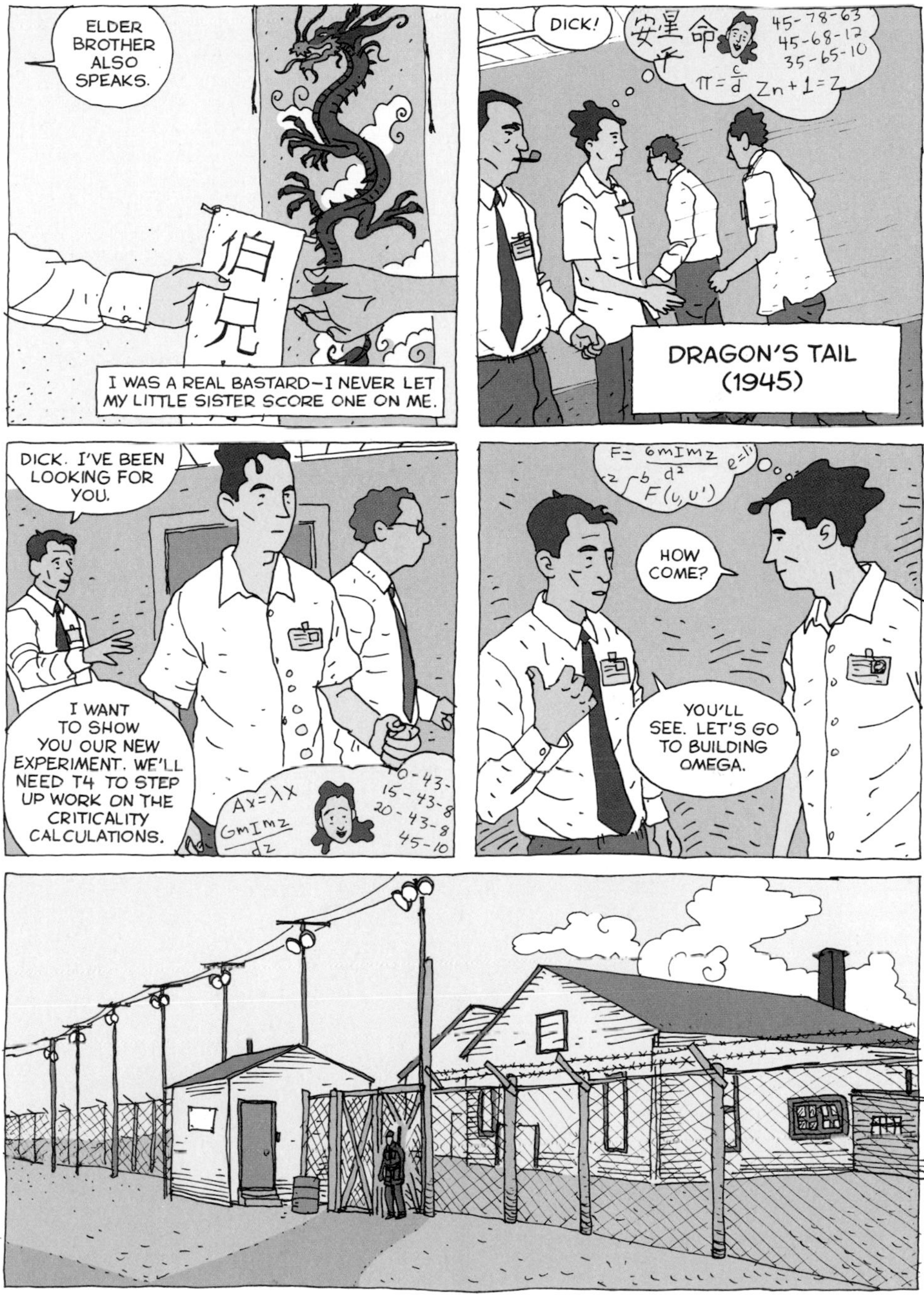
ELDER BROTHER ALSO SPEAKS.
I WAS A REAL BASTARD—I NEVER LET MY LITTLE SISTER SCORE ONE ON ME.
DICK!
DRAGON'S TAIL (1945)
DICK. I'VE BEEN LOOKING FOR YOU.
I WANT TO SHOW YOU OUR NEW EXPERIMENT. WE'LL NEED T4 TO STEP UP WORK ON THE CRITICALITY CALCULATIONS.
HOW COME?
YOU'LL SEE. LET'S GO TO BUILDING OMEGA.

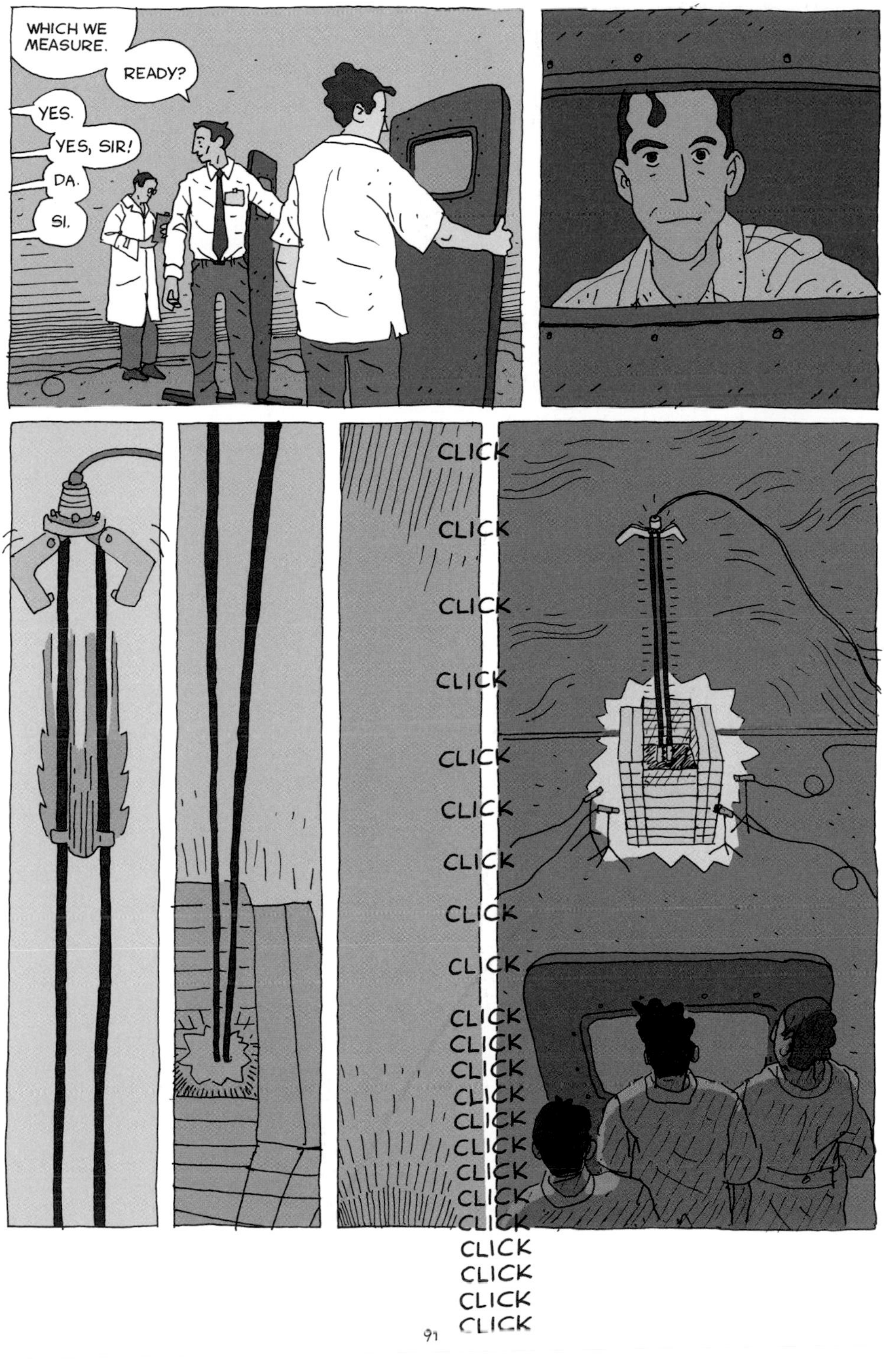
WHICH WE MEASURE.
READY?
YES.
YES, SIR!
DA.
SI.
CLICK
CLICK
CLICK
CLICK
CLICK
CLICK
CLICK
CLICK
CLICK
CLICK
CLICK
CLICK
CLICK
CLICK
CLICK
CLICK
CLICK
CLICK
CLICK
CLICK
CLICK
CLICK

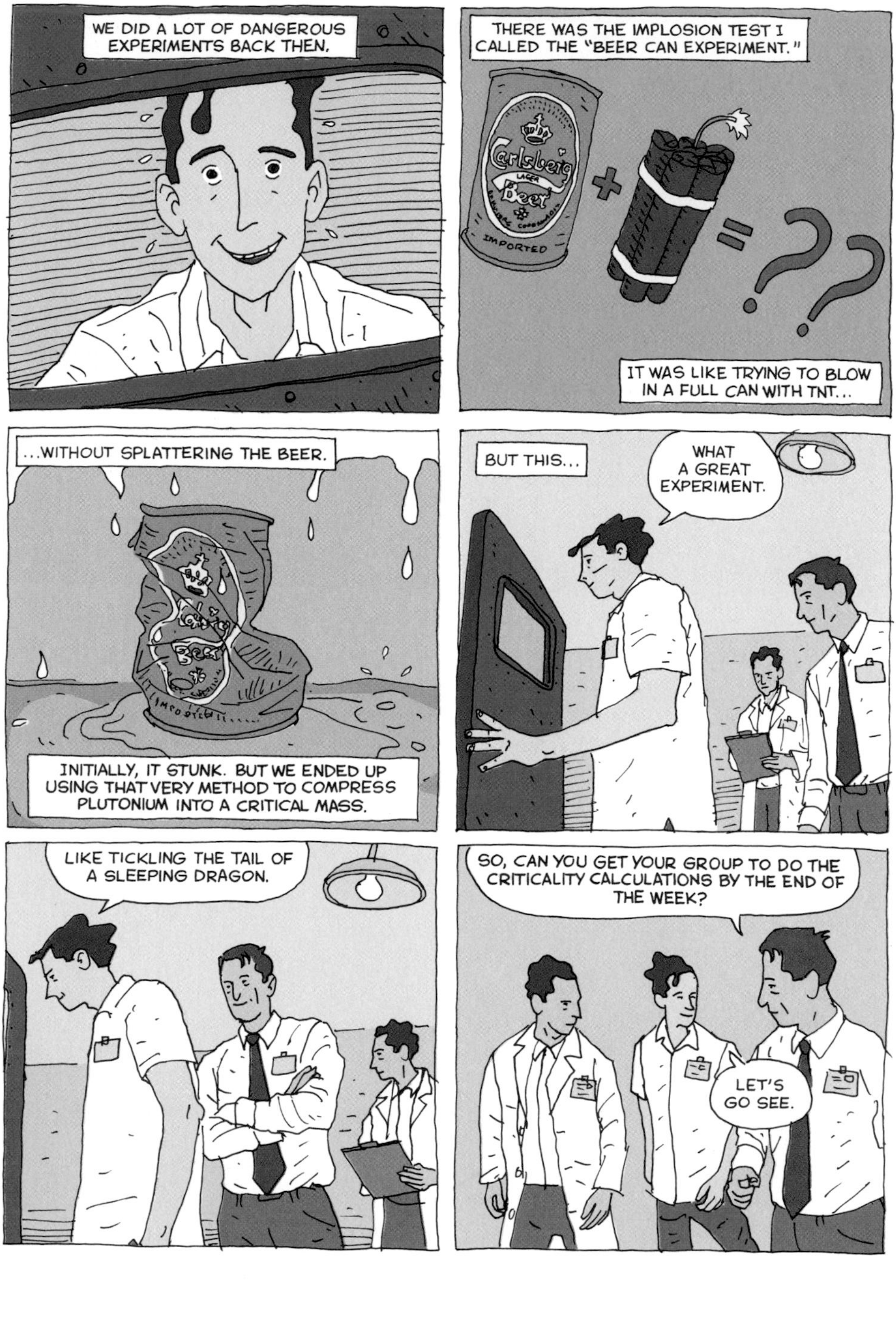
WE DID A LOT OF DANGEROUS EXPERIMENTS BACK THEN.
THERE WAS THE IMPLOSION TEST I CALLED THE "BEER CAN EXPERIMENT."
Carlsberg LAGER Beer
IMPORTED
+ = ??
IT WAS LIKE TRYING TO BLOW IN A FULL CAN WITH TNT...
...WITHOUT SPLATTERING THE BEER.
INITIALLY, IT STUNK. BUT WE ENDED UP USING THAT VERY METHOD TO COMPRESS PLUTONIUM INTO A CRITICAL MASS.
BUT THIS...
WHAT A GREAT EXPERIMENT.
LIKE TICKLING THE TAIL OF A SLEEPING DRAGON.
SO, CAN YOU GET YOUR GROUP TO DO THE CRITICALITY CALCULATIONS BY THE END OF THE WEEK?
LET'S GO SEE.

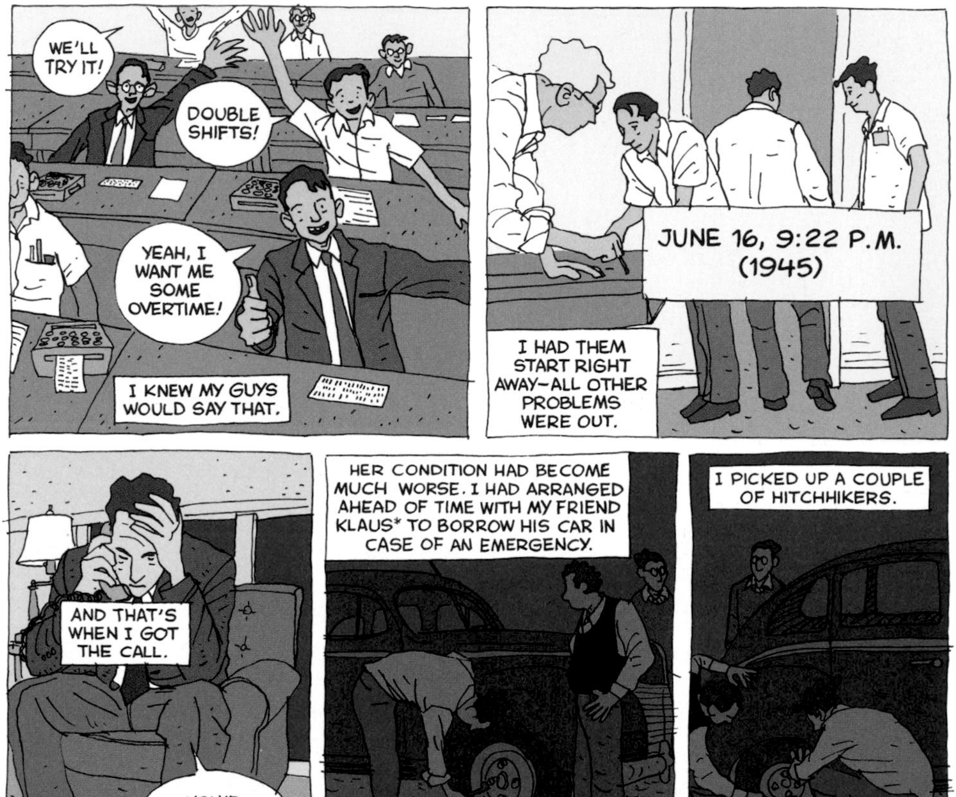
WE'LL TRY IT!
DOUBLE SHIFTS!
YEAH, I WANT ME SOME OVERTIME!
I KNEW MY GUYS WOULD SAY THAT.
JUNE 16, 9:22 P.M. (1945)
I HAD THEM START RIGHT AWAY–ALL OTHER PROBLEMS WERE OUT.
AND THAT'S WHEN I GOT THE CALL.
YOU'D BETTER COME DOWN HERE RIGHT AWAY.
HER CONDITION HAD BECOME MUCH WORSE. I HAD ARRANGED AHEAD OF TIME WITH MY FRIEND KLAUS* TO BORROW HIS CAR IN CASE OF AN EMERGENCY.
I PICKED UP A COUPLE OF HITCHHIKERS.
YOU KNOW, TO HELP ME IN CASE SOMETHING HAPPENED.
WE HITCHHIKED MOST OF THE WAY.
66

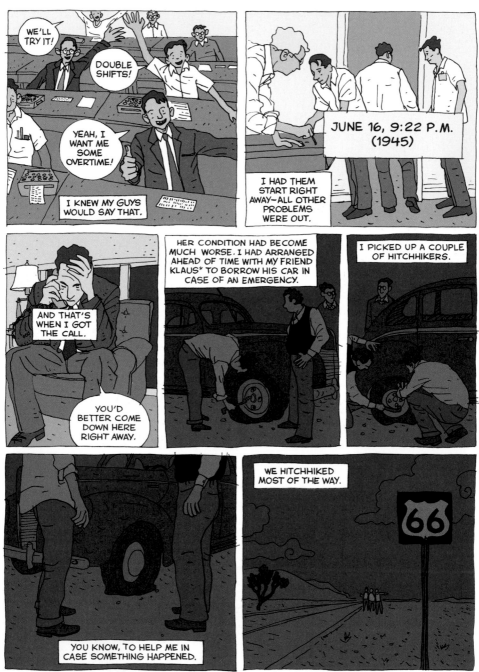

* KLAUS FUCHS TURNED OUT TO BE A RUSSIAN SPY, AND HE'D USED THIS SAME CAR TO TAKE SECRETS OUT OF LOS ALAMOS. BUT NOBODY KNEW THAT THEN.

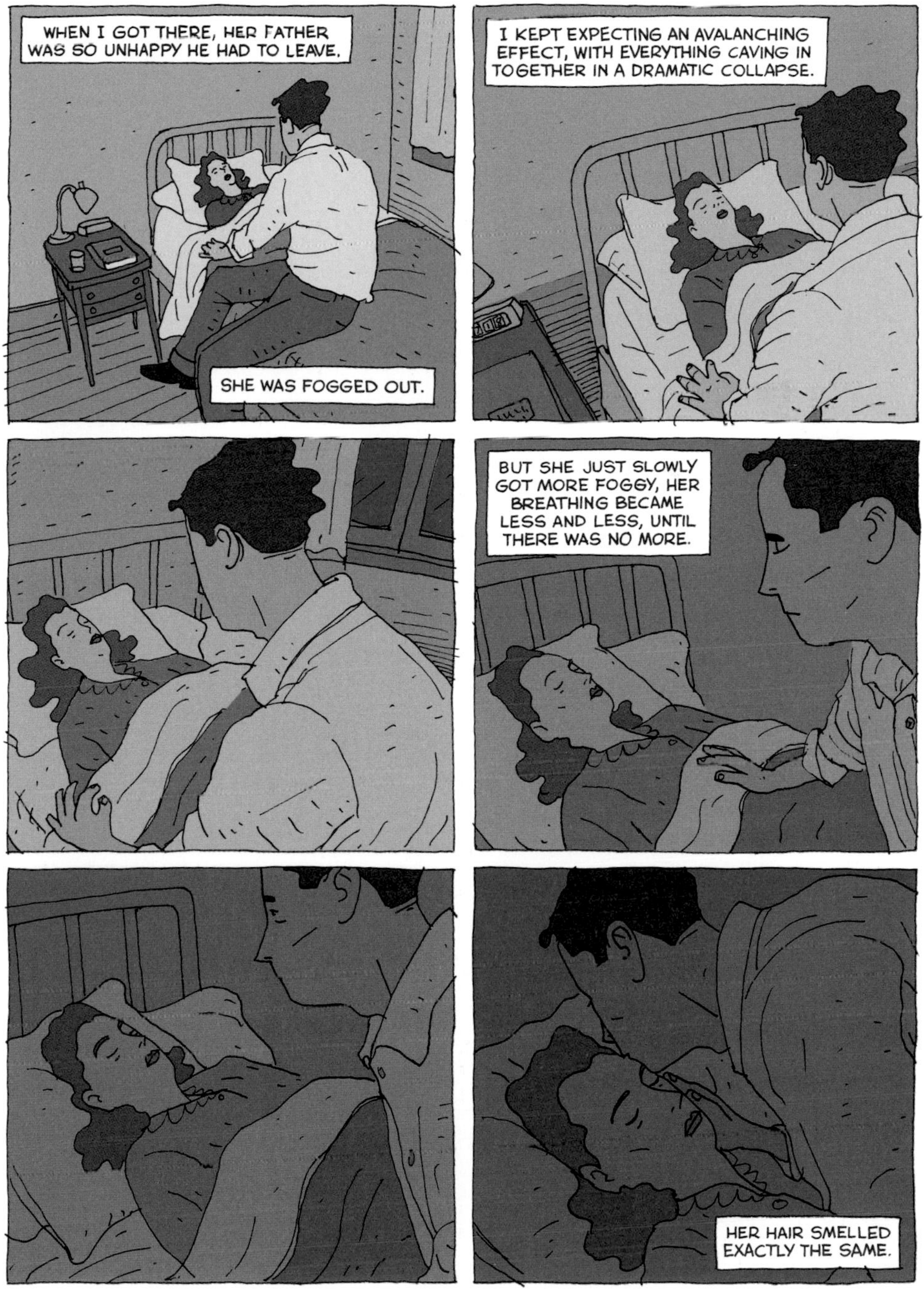
WHEN I GOT THERE, HER FATHER WAS SO UNHAPPY HE HAD TO LEAVE.
SHE WAS FOGGED OUT.
I KEPT EXPECTING AN AVALANCHING EFFECT, WITH EVERYTHING CAVING IN TOGETHER IN A DRAMATIC COLLAPSE.
BUT SHE JUST SLOWLY GOT MORE FOGGY, HER BREATHING BECAME LESS AND LESS, UNTIL THERE WAS NO MORE.
HER HAIR SMELLED EXACTLY THE SAME.

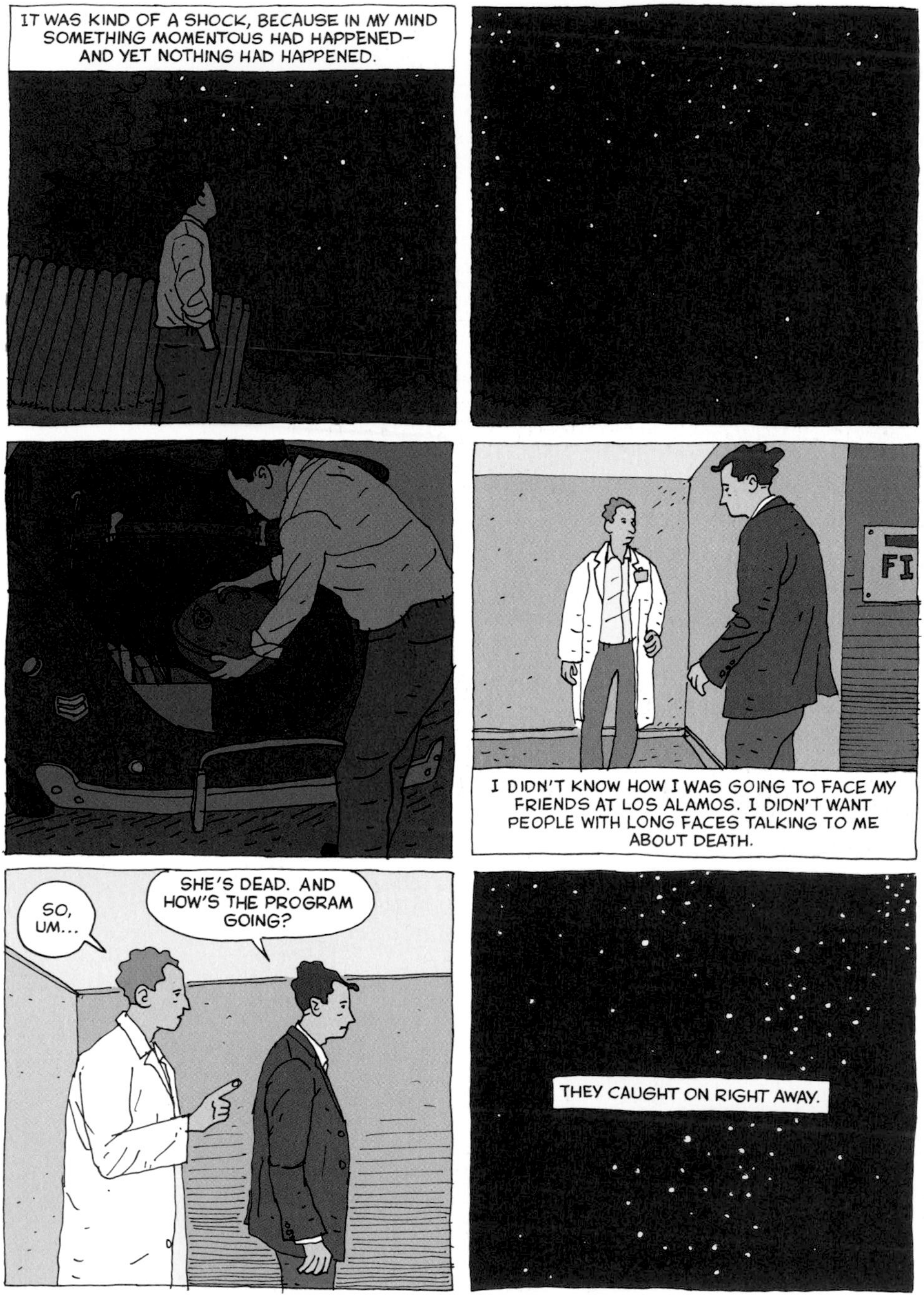
IT WAS KIND OF A SHOCK, BECAUSE IN MY MIND SOMETHING MOMENTOUS HAD HAPPENED—AND YET NOTHING HAD HAPPENED.
FI
I DIDN'T KNOW HOW I WAS GOING TO FACE MY FRIENDS AT LOS ALAMOS. I DIDN'T WANT PEOPLE WITH LONG FACES TALKING TO ME ABOUT DEATH.
SO, UM...
SHE'S DEAD. AND HOW'S THE PROGRAM GOING?
THEY CAUGHT ON RIGHT AWAY.

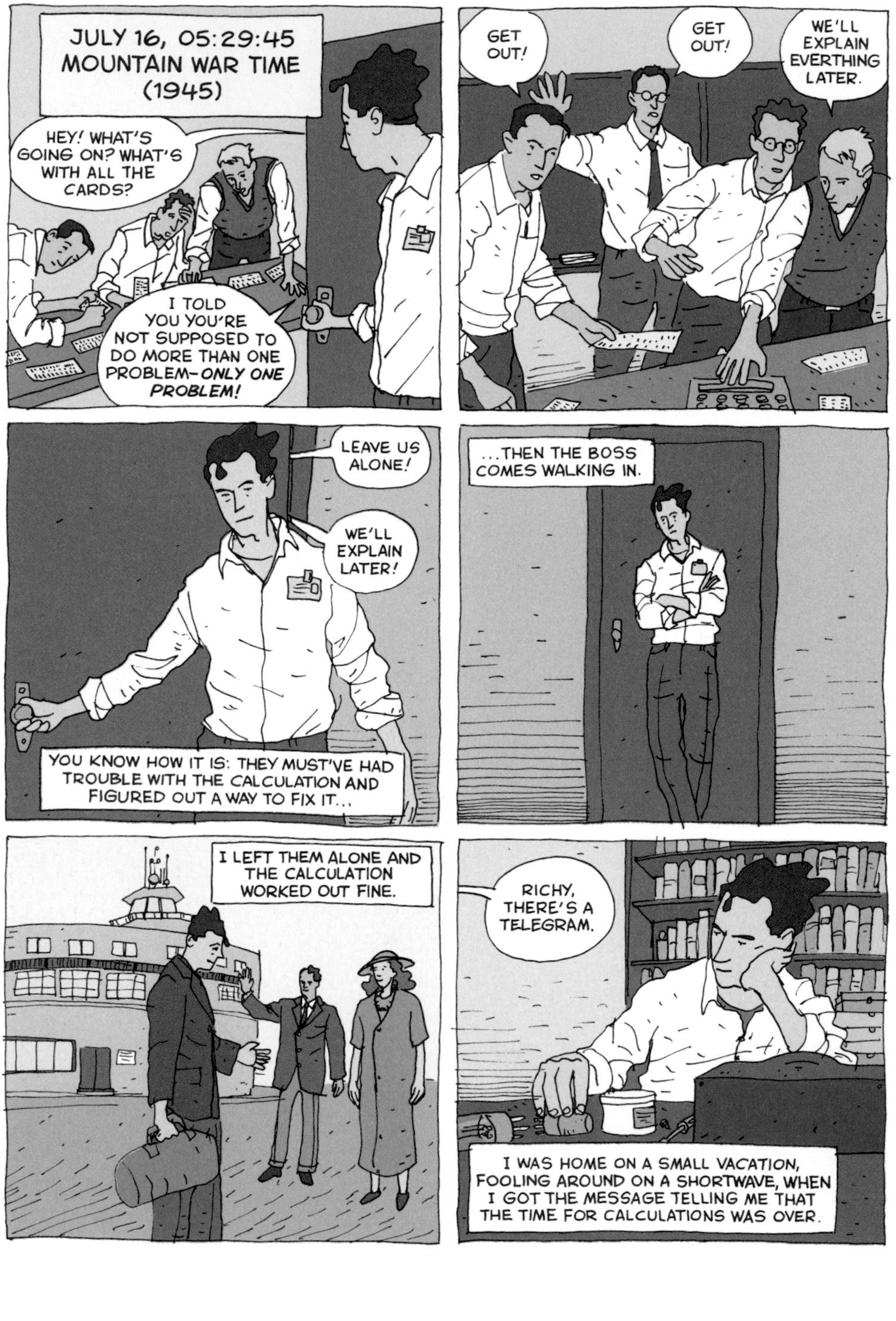
JULY 16, 05:29:45 MOUNTAIN WAR TIME (1945)
HEY! WHAT'S GOING ON? WHAT'S WITH ALL THE CARDS?
I TOLD YOU YOU'RE NOT SUPPOSED TO DO MORE THAN ONE PROBLEM–*ONLY ONE PROBLEM!*
GET OUT!
GET OUT!
WE'LL EXPLAIN EVERTHING LATER.
LEAVE US ALONE!
WE'LL EXPLAIN LATER!
YOU KNOW HOW IT IS: THEY MUST'VE HAD TROUBLE WITH THE CALCULATION AND FIGURED OUT A WAY TO FIX IT...
...THEN THE BOSS COMES WALKING IN.
I LEFT THEM ALONE AND THE CALCULATION WORKED OUT FINE.
RICHY, THERE'S A TELEGRAM.
I WAS HOME ON A SMALL VACATION, FOOLING AROUND ON A SHORTWAVE, WHEN I GOT THE MESSAGE TELLING ME THAT THE TIME FOR CALCULATIONS WAS OVER.

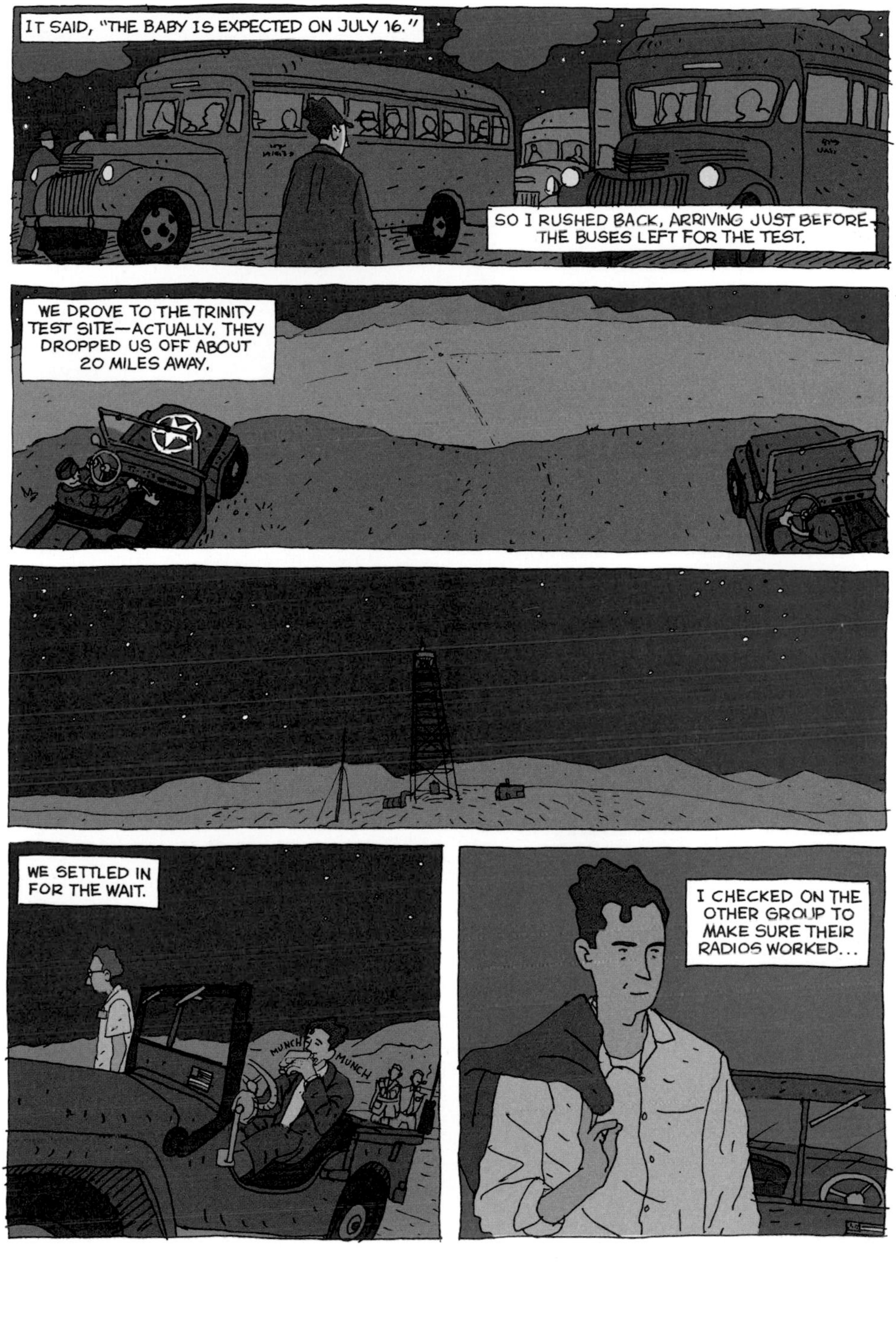
IT SAID, "THE BABY IS EXPECTED ON JULY 16."
SO I RUSHED BACK, ARRIVING JUST BEFORE THE BUSES LEFT FOR THE TEST.
WE DROVE TO THE TRINITY TEST SITE—ACTUALLY, THEY DROPPED US OFF ABOUT 20 MILES AWAY.
WE SETTLED IN FOR THE WAIT.
MUNCH
MUNCH
I CHECKED ON THE OTHER GROUP TO MAKE SURE THEIR RADIOS WORKED...

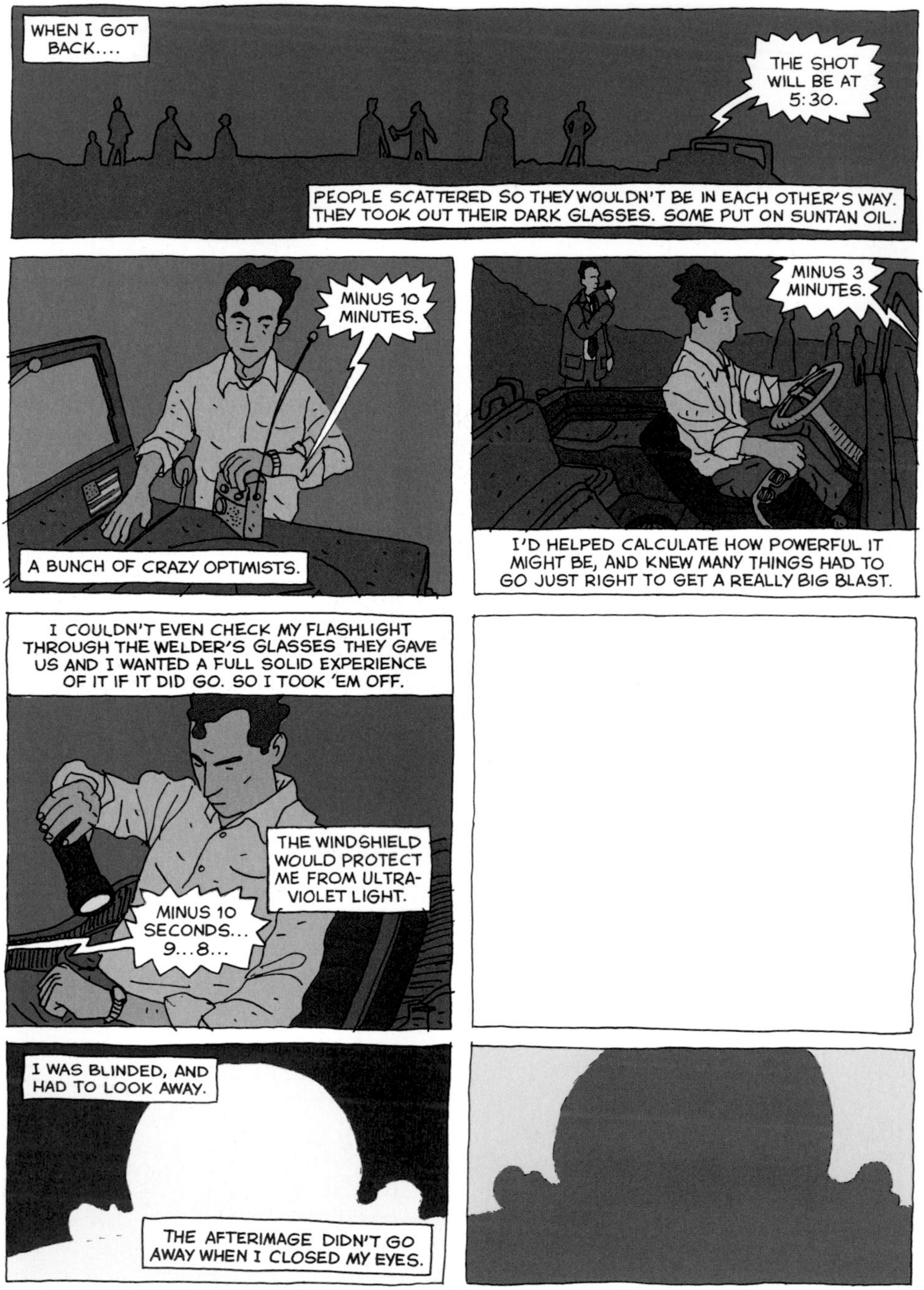
WHEN I GOT BACK....
THE SHOT WILL BE AT 5:30.
PEOPLE SCATTERED SO THEY WOULDN'T BE IN EACH OTHER'S WAY. THEY TOOK OUT THEIR DARK GLASSES. SOME PUT ON SUNTAN OIL.
MINUS 10 MINUTES.
A BUNCH OF CRAZY OPTIMISTS.
MINUS 3 MINUTES.
I'D HELPED CALCULATE HOW POWERFUL IT MIGHT BE, AND KNEW MANY THINGS HAD TO GO JUST RIGHT TO GET A REALLY BIG BLAST.
I COULDN'T EVEN CHECK MY FLASHLIGHT THROUGH THE WELDER'S GLASSES THEY GAVE US AND I WANTED A FULL SOLID EXPERIENCE OF IT IF IT DID GO. SO I TOOK 'EM OFF.
THE WINDSHIELD WOULD PROTECT ME FROM ULTRA-VIOLET LIGHT.
MINUS 10 SECONDS... 9...8...
I WAS BLINDED, AND HAD TO LOOK AWAY.
THE AFTERIMAGE DIDN'T GO AWAY WHEN I CLOSED MY EYES.

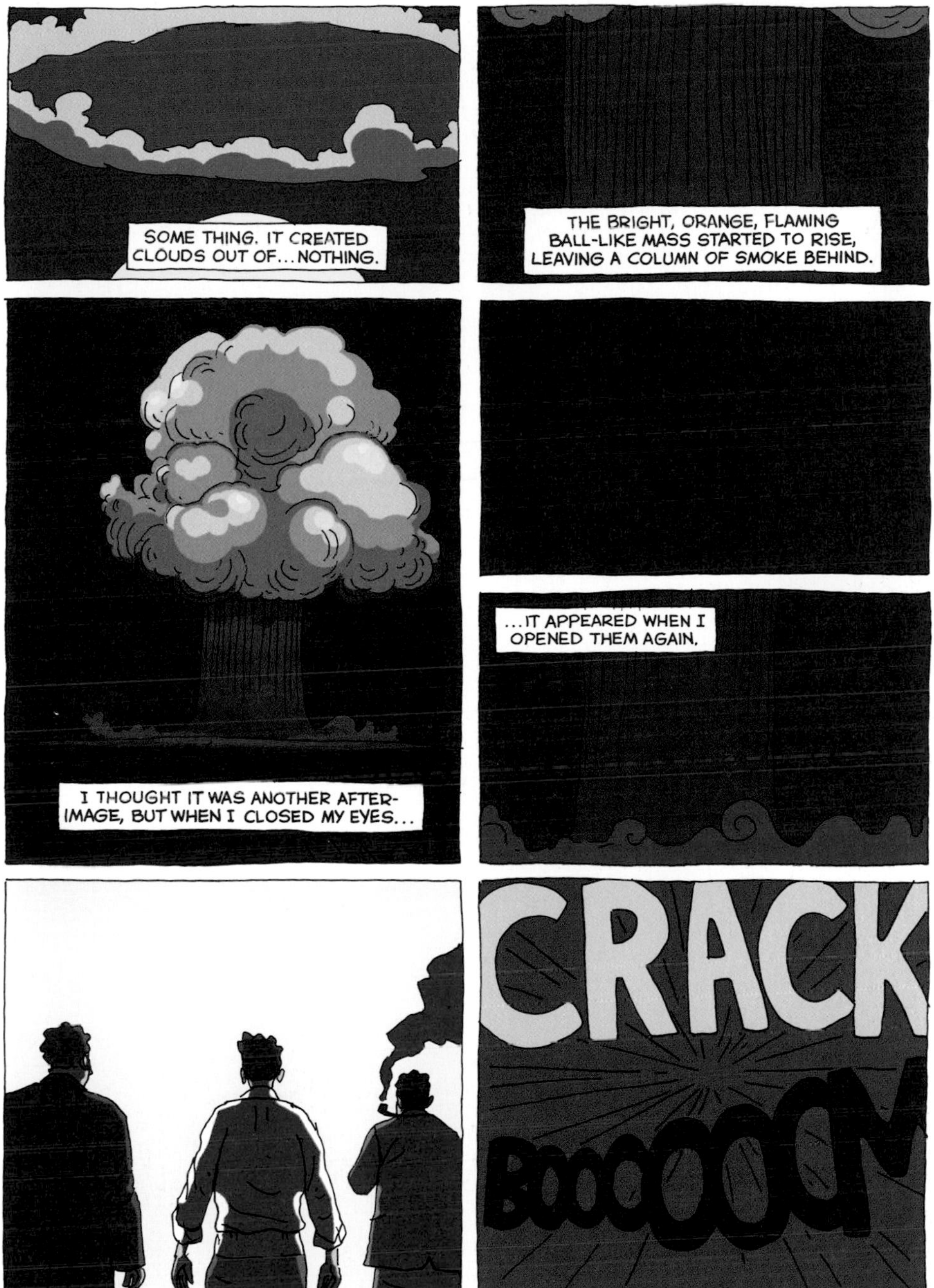
SOME THING. IT CREATED CLOUDS OUT OF... NOTHING.
THE BRIGHT, ORANGE, FLAMING BALL-LIKE MASS STARTED TO RISE, LEAVING A COLUMN OF SMOKE BEHIND.
I THOUGHT IT WAS ANOTHER AFTER-IMAGE, BUT WHEN I CLOSED MY EYES...
...IT APPEARED WHEN I OPENED THEM AGAIN.
CRACK

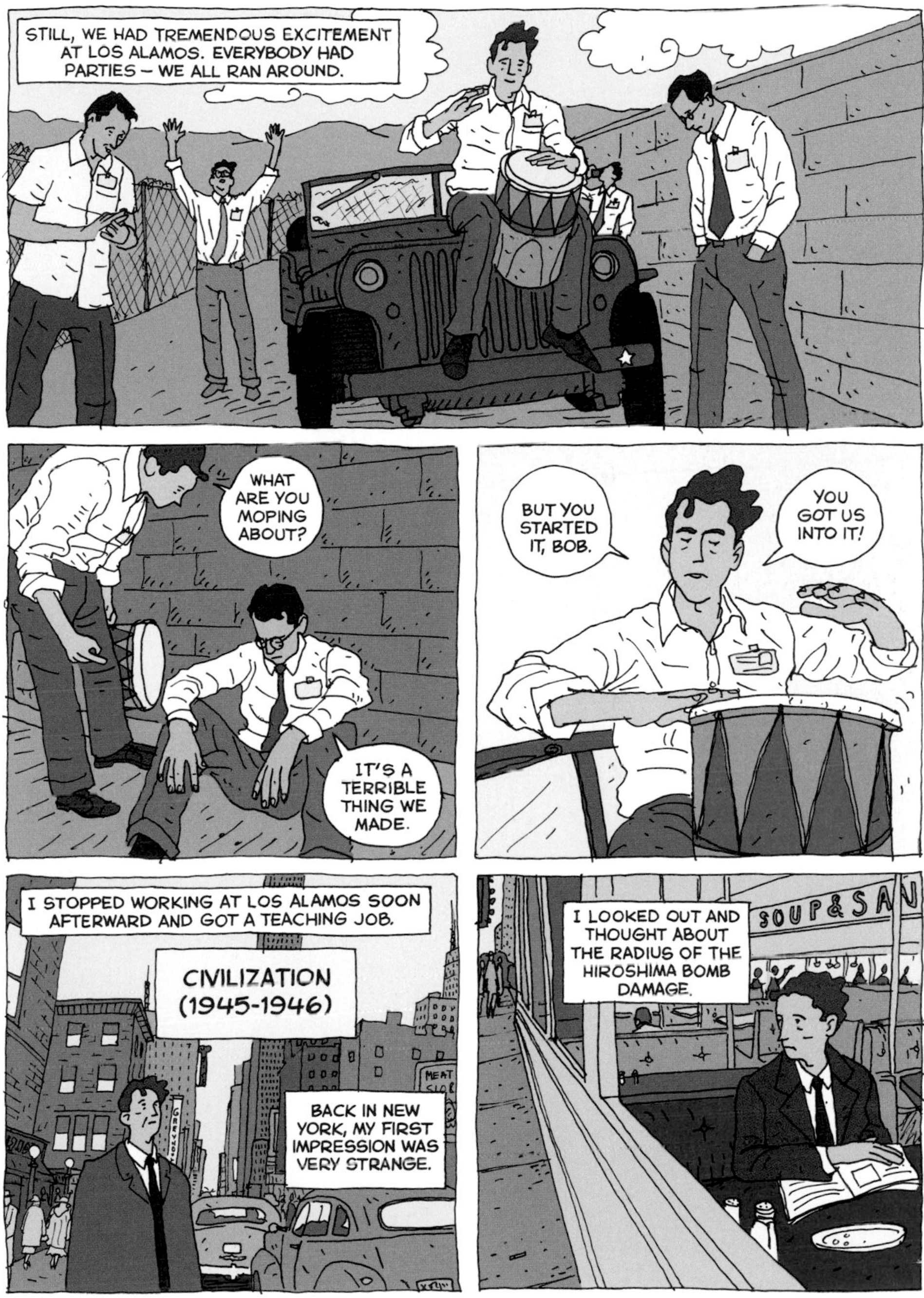
STILL, WE HAD TREMENDOUS EXCITEMENT AT LOS ALAMOS. EVERYBODY HAD PARTIES – WE ALL RAN AROUND.
WHAT ARE YOU MOPING ABOUT?
IT'S A TERRIBLE THING WE MADE.
BUT YOU STARTED IT, BOB.
YOU GOT US INTO IT!
I STOPPED WORKING AT LOS ALAMOS SOON AFTERWARD AND GOT A TEACHING JOB.
CIVILIZATION (1945-1946)
BACK IN NEW YORK, MY FIRST IMPRESSION WAS VERY STRANGE.
I LOOKED OUT AND THOUGHT ABOUT THE RADIUS OF THE HIROSHIMA BOMB DAMAGE.
SOUP&SAN

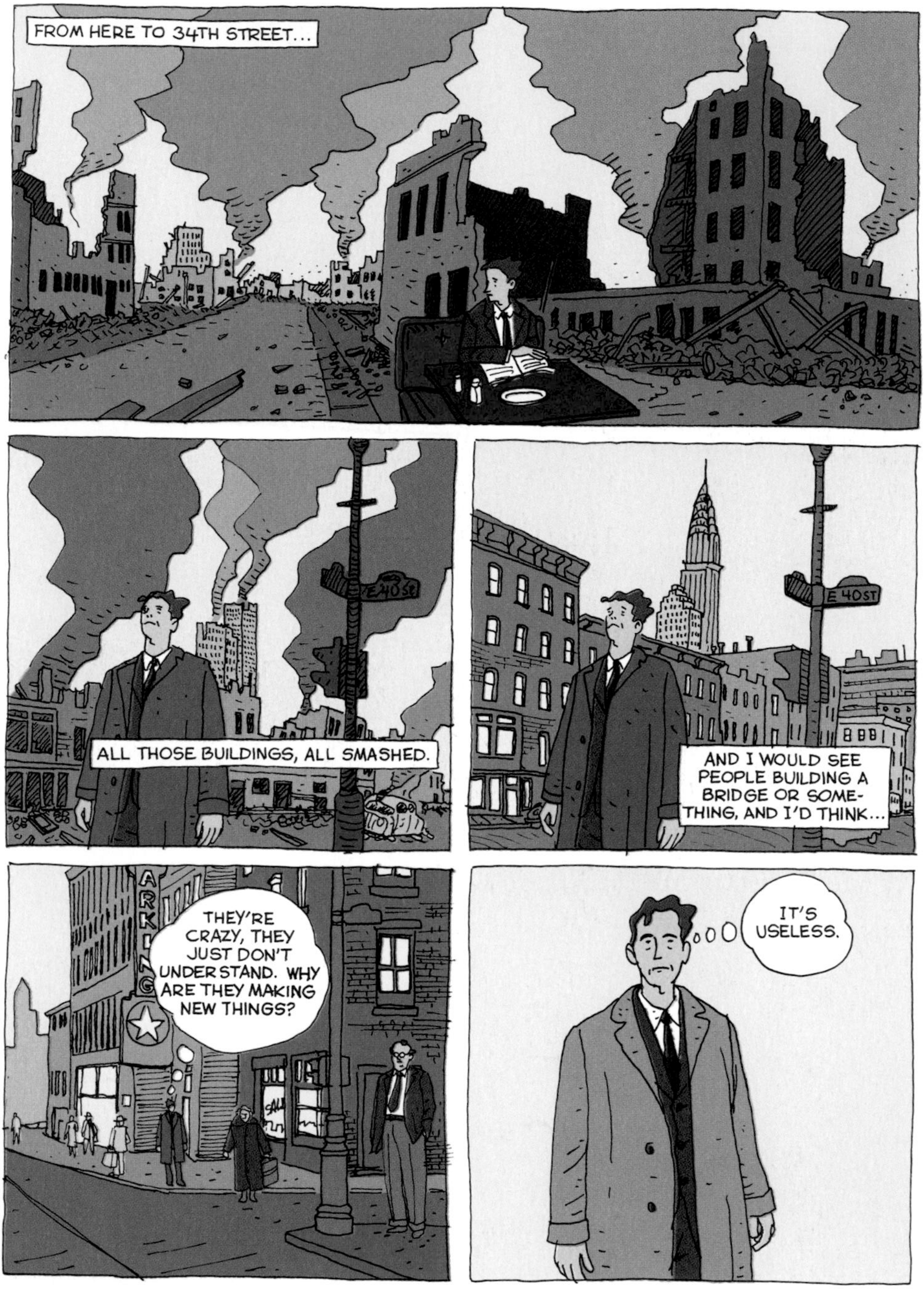
FROM HERE TO 34TH STREET...
ALL THOSE BUILDINGS, ALL SMASHED.
E 40 St
E 40 ST
AND I WOULD SEE PEOPLE BUILDING A BRIDGE OR SOMETHING, AND I'D THINK...
THEY'RE CRAZY, THEY JUST DON'T UNDERSTAND. WHY ARE THEY MAKING NEW THINGS?
IT'S USELESS.

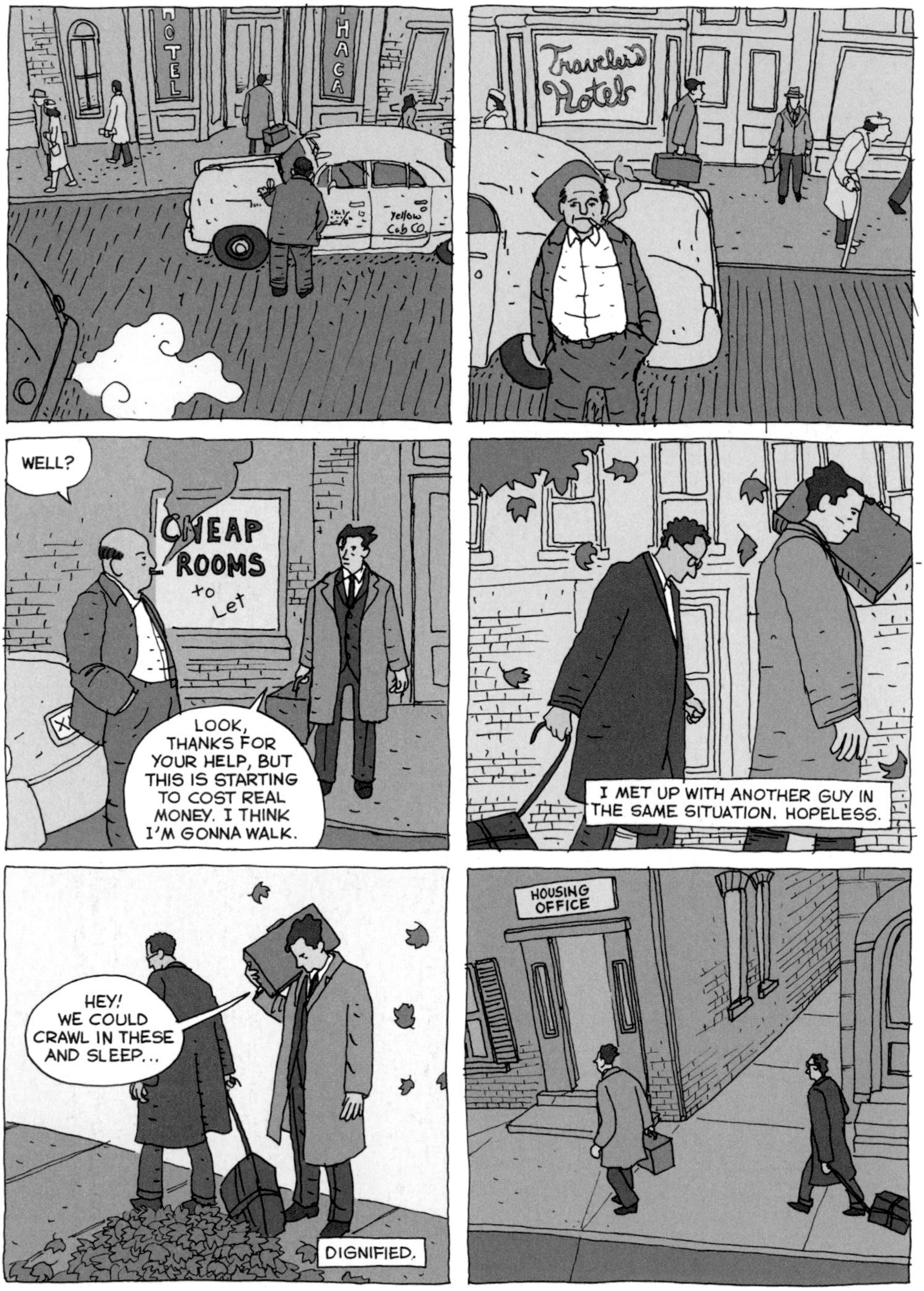
HOTEL
ITHACA
Yellow Cab CO
Traveler's Hotel
WELL?
CHEAP ROOMS to Let
LOOK, THANKS FOR YOUR HELP, BUT THIS IS STARTING TO COST REAL MONEY. I THINK I'M GONNA WALK.
I MET UP WITH ANOTHER GUY IN THE SAME SITUATION. HOPELESS.
HEY! WE COULD CRAWL IN THESE AND SLEEP...
DIGNIFIED.
HOUSING OFFICE

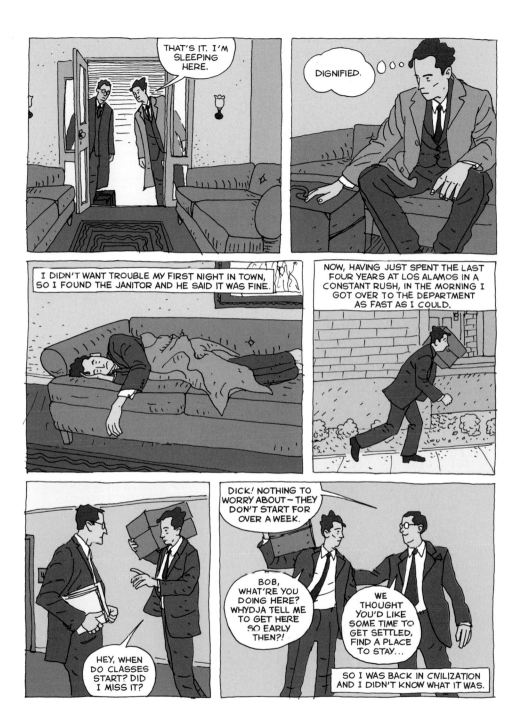

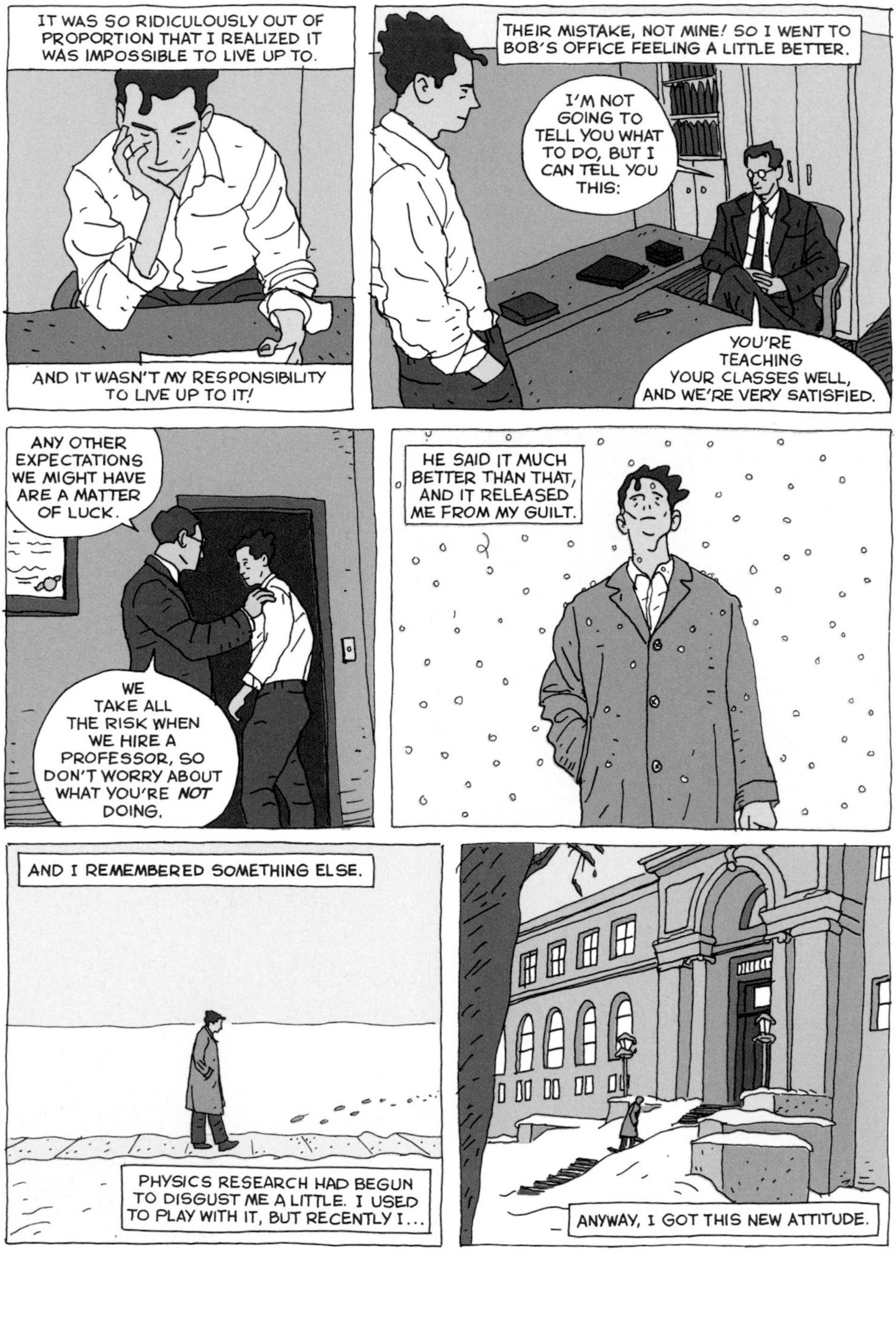
IT WAS SO RIDICULOUSLY OUT OF PROPORTION THAT I REALIZED IT WAS IMPOSSIBLE TO LIVE UP TO.
AND IT WASN'T MY RESPONSIBILITY TO LIVE UP TO IT!
THEIR MISTAKE, NOT MINE! SO I WENT TO BOB'S OFFICE FEELING A LITTLE BETTER.
I'M NOT GOING TO TELL YOU WHAT TO DO, BUT I CAN TELL YOU THIS:
YOU'RE TEACHING YOUR CLASSES WELL, AND WE'RE VERY SATISFIED.
ANY OTHER EXPECTATIONS WE MIGHT HAVE ARE A MATTER OF LUCK.
WE TAKE ALL THE RISK WHEN WE HIRE A PROFESSOR, SO DON'T WORRY ABOUT WHAT YOU'RE *NOT* DOING.
HE SAID IT MUCH BETTER THAN THAT, AND IT RELEASED ME FROM MY GUILT.
AND I REMEMBERED SOMETHING ELSE.
PHYSICS RESEARCH HAD BEGUN TO DISGUST ME A LITTLE. I USED TO PLAY WITH IT, BUT RECENTLY I...
ANYWAY, I GOT THIS NEW ATTITUDE.

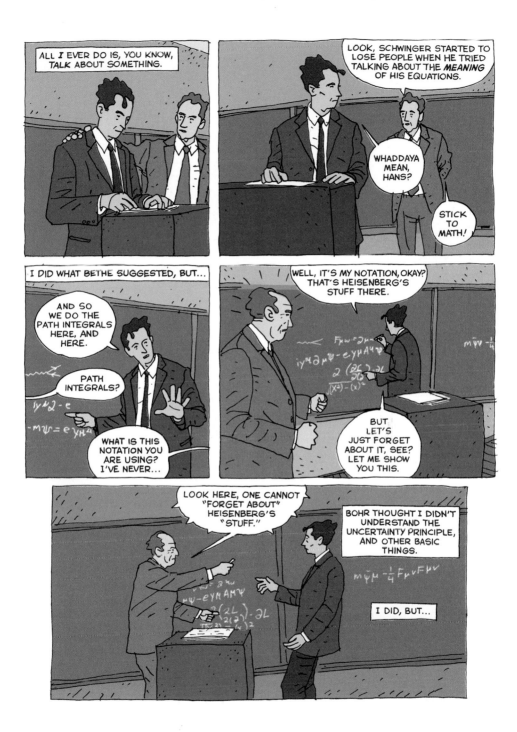

A VOICE FROM
THE DEEP
(1948)

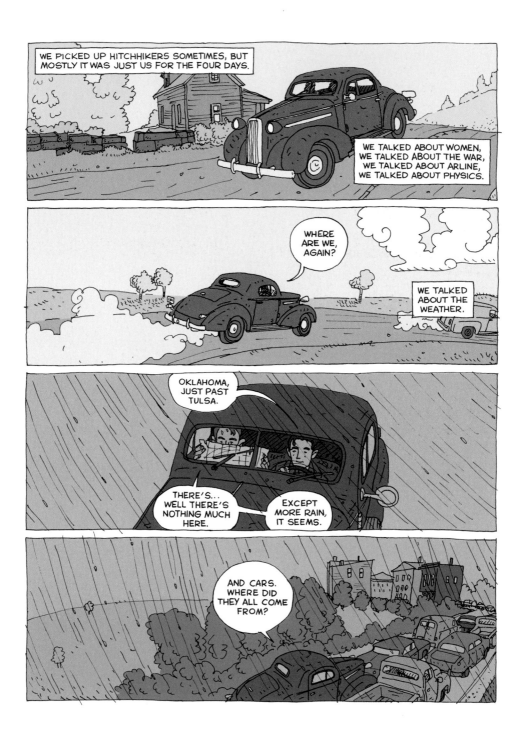

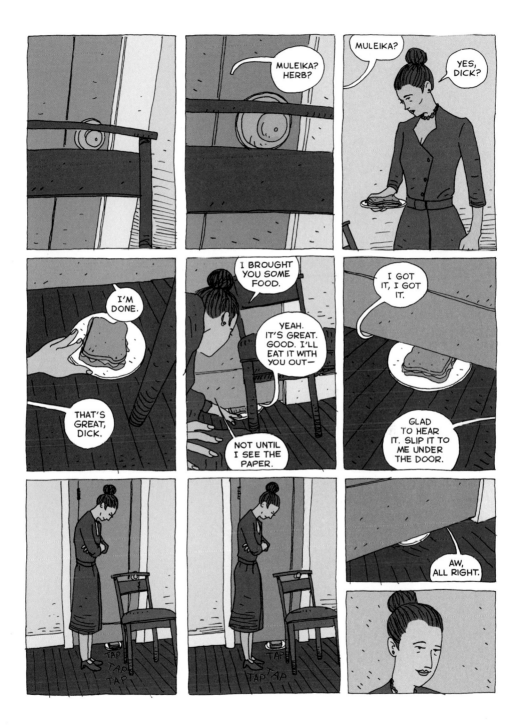

131

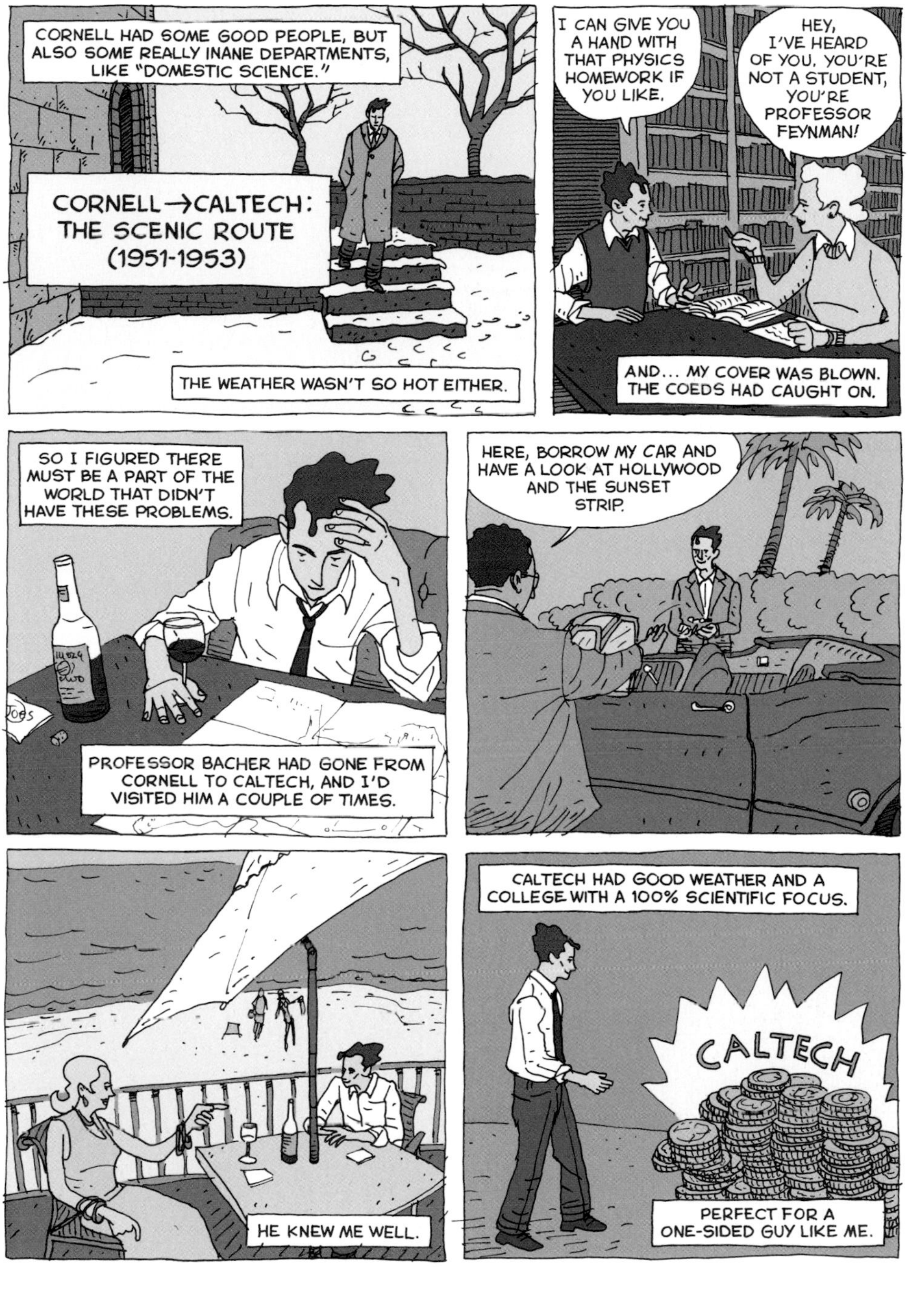
CORNELL HAD SOME GOOD PEOPLE, BUT ALSO SOME REALLY INANE DEPARTMENTS, LIKE "DOMESTIC SCIENCE."
CORNELL→CALTECH: THE SCENIC ROUTE (1951-1953)
THE WEATHER WASN'T SO HOT EITHER.
I CAN GIVE YOU A HAND WITH THAT PHYSICS HOMEWORK IF YOU LIKE.
HEY, I'VE HEARD OF YOU. YOU'RE NOT A STUDENT, YOU'RE PROFESSOR FEYNMAN!
AND... MY COVER WAS BLOWN. THE COEDS HAD CAUGHT ON.
SO I FIGURED THERE MUST BE A PART OF THE WORLD THAT DIDN'T HAVE THESE PROBLEMS.
PROFESSOR BACHER HAD GONE FROM CORNELL TO CALTECH, AND I'D VISITED HIM A COUPLE OF TIMES.
HERE, BORROW MY CAR AND HAVE A LOOK AT HOLLYWOOD AND THE SUNSET STRIP.
HE KNEW ME WELL.
CALTECH HAD GOOD WEATHER AND A COLLEGE WITH A 100% SCIENTIFIC FOCUS.
CALTECH
PERFECT FOR A ONE-SIDED GUY LIKE ME.

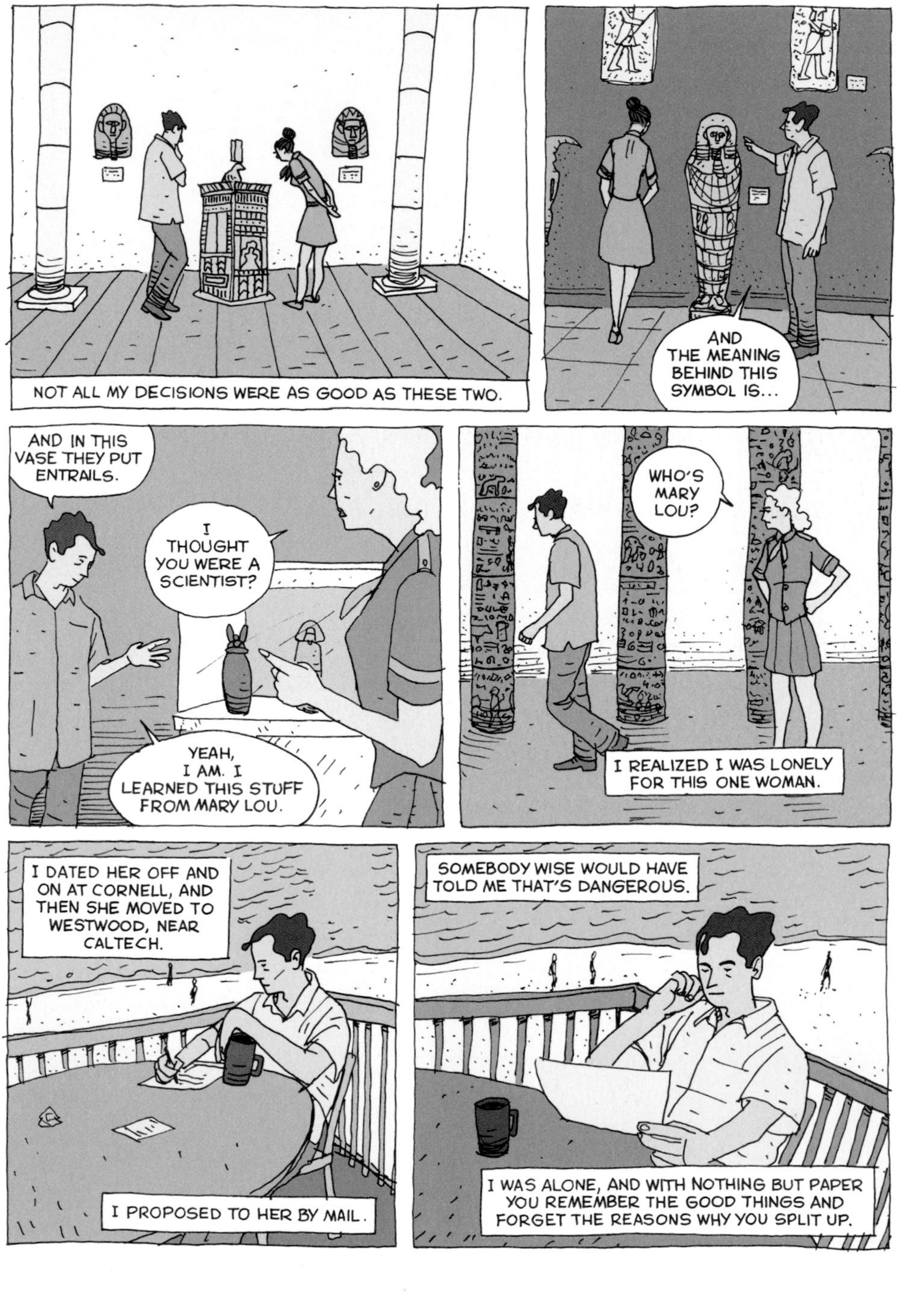
NOT ALL MY DECISIONS WERE AS GOOD AS THESE TWO.
AND THE MEANING BEHIND THIS SYMBOL IS...
AND IN THIS VASE THEY PUT ENTRAILS.
I THOUGHT YOU WERE A SCIENTIST?
YEAH, I AM. I LEARNED THIS STUFF FROM MARY LOU.
WHO'S MARY LOU?
I REALIZED I WAS LONELY FOR THIS ONE WOMAN.
I DATED HER OFF AND ON AT CORNELL, AND THEN SHE MOVED TO WESTWOOD, NEAR CALTECH.
I PROPOSED TO HER BY MAIL.
SOMEBODY WISE WOULD HAVE TOLD ME THAT'S DANGEROUS.
I WAS ALONE, AND WITH NOTHING BUT PAPER YOU REMEMBER THE GOOD THINGS AND FORGET THE REASONS WHY YOU SPLIT UP.

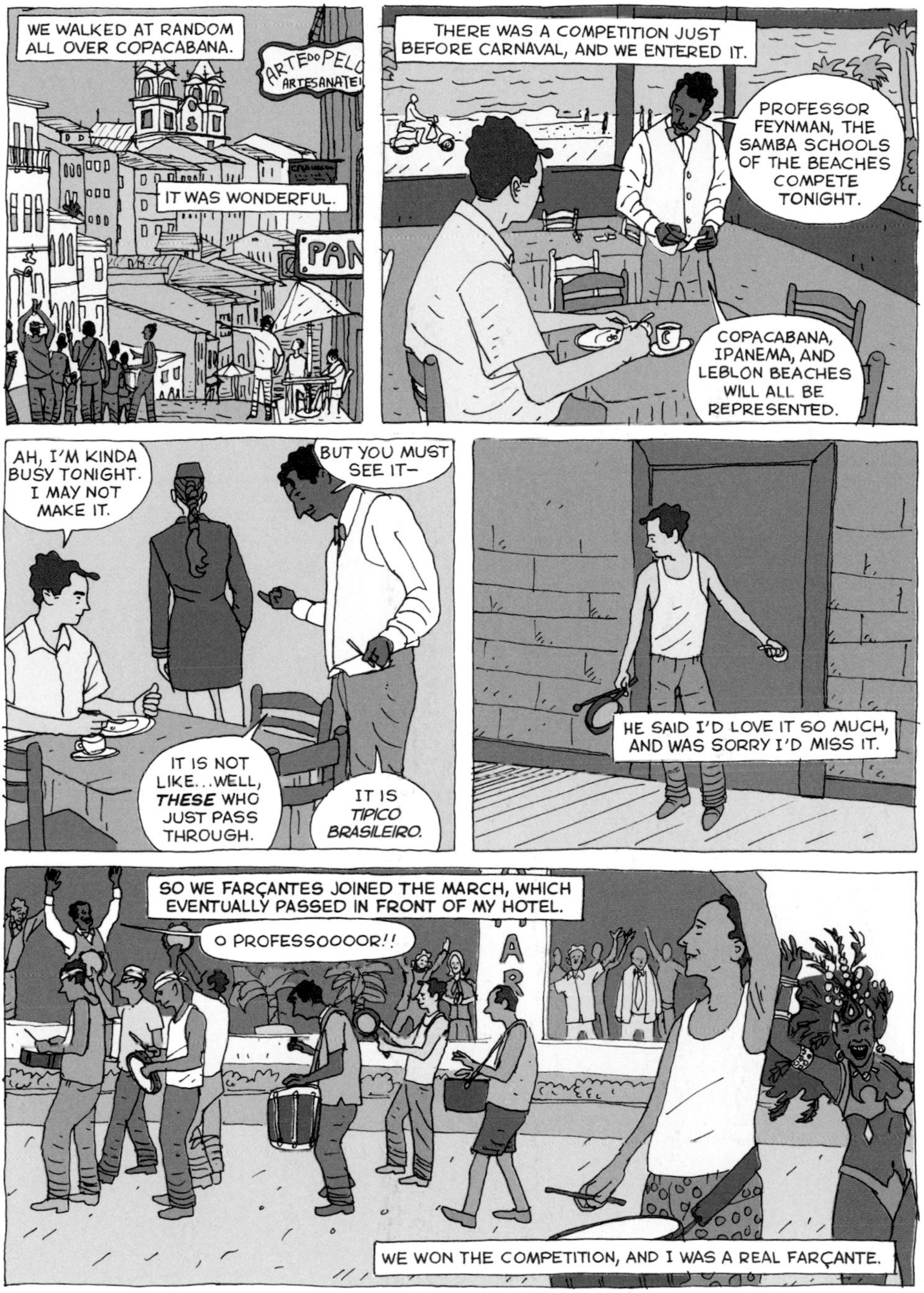
WE WALKED AT RANDOM ALL OVER COPACABANA.
ARTE DO PELO
ARTESANATE!
IT WAS WONDERFUL.
PAN
THERE WAS A COMPETITION JUST BEFORE CARNAVAL, AND WE ENTERED IT.
PROFESSOR FEYNMAN, THE SAMBA SCHOOLS OF THE BEACHES COMPETE TONIGHT.
COPACABANA, IPANEMA, AND LEBLON BEACHES WILL ALL BE REPRESENTED.
AH, I'M KINDA BUSY TONIGHT. I MAY NOT MAKE IT.
BUT YOU MUST SEE IT–
IT IS NOT LIKE...WELL, *THESE* WHO JUST PASS THROUGH.
IT IS *TIPICO BRASILEIRO.*
HE SAID I'D LOVE IT SO MUCH, AND WAS SORRY I'D MISS IT.
SO WE FARÇANTES JOINED THE MARCH, WHICH EVENTUALLY PASSED IN FRONT OF MY HOTEL.
O PROFESSOOOOR!!
A
R
WE WON THE COMPETITION, AND I WAS A REAL FARÇANTE.

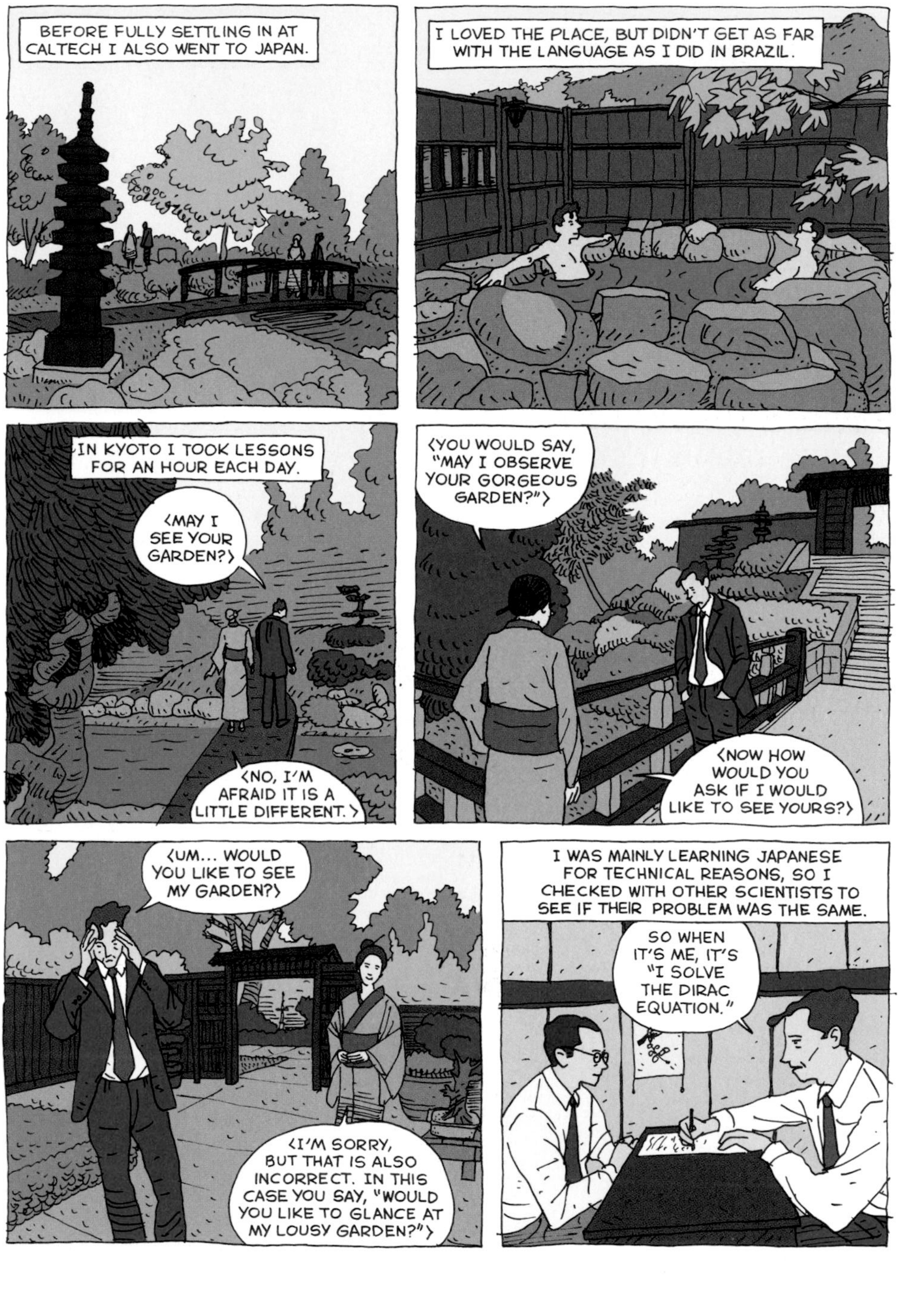

BEFORE FULLY SETTLING IN AT CALTECH I ALSO WENT TO JAPAN.
I LOVED THE PLACE, BUT DIDN'T GET AS FAR WITH THE LANGUAGE AS I DID IN BRAZIL.
IN KYOTO I TOOK LESSONS FOR AN HOUR EACH DAY.
⟨MAY I SEE YOUR GARDEN?⟩
⟨NO, I'M AFRAID IT IS A LITTLE DIFFERENT.⟩
⟨YOU WOULD SAY, "MAY I OBSERVE YOUR GORGEOUS GARDEN?"⟩
⟨NOW HOW WOULD YOU ASK IF I WOULD LIKE TO SEE YOURS?⟩
⟨UM... WOULD YOU LIKE TO SEE MY GARDEN?⟩
⟨I'M SORRY, BUT THAT IS ALSO INCORRECT. IN THIS CASE YOU SAY, "WOULD YOU LIKE TO GLANCE AT MY LOUSY GARDEN?"⟩
I WAS MAINLY LEARNING JAPANESE FOR TECHNICAL REASONS, SO I CHECKED WITH OTHER SCIENTISTS TO SEE IF THEIR PROBLEM WAS THE SAME.
SO WHEN IT'S ME, IT'S "I SOLVE THE DIRAC EQUATION."

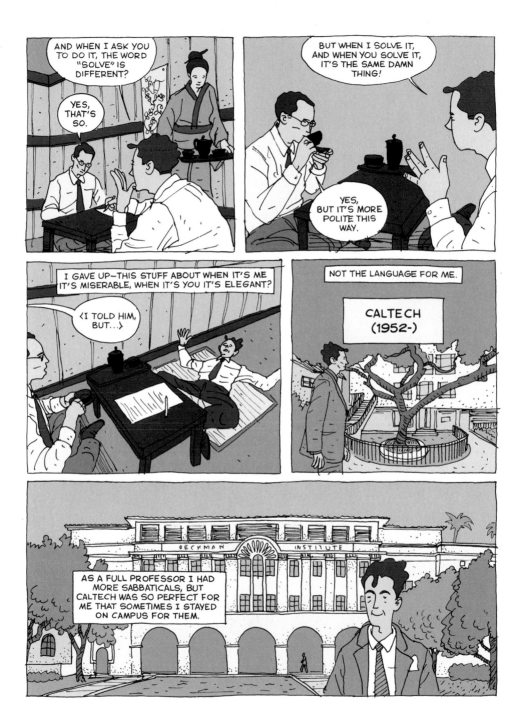

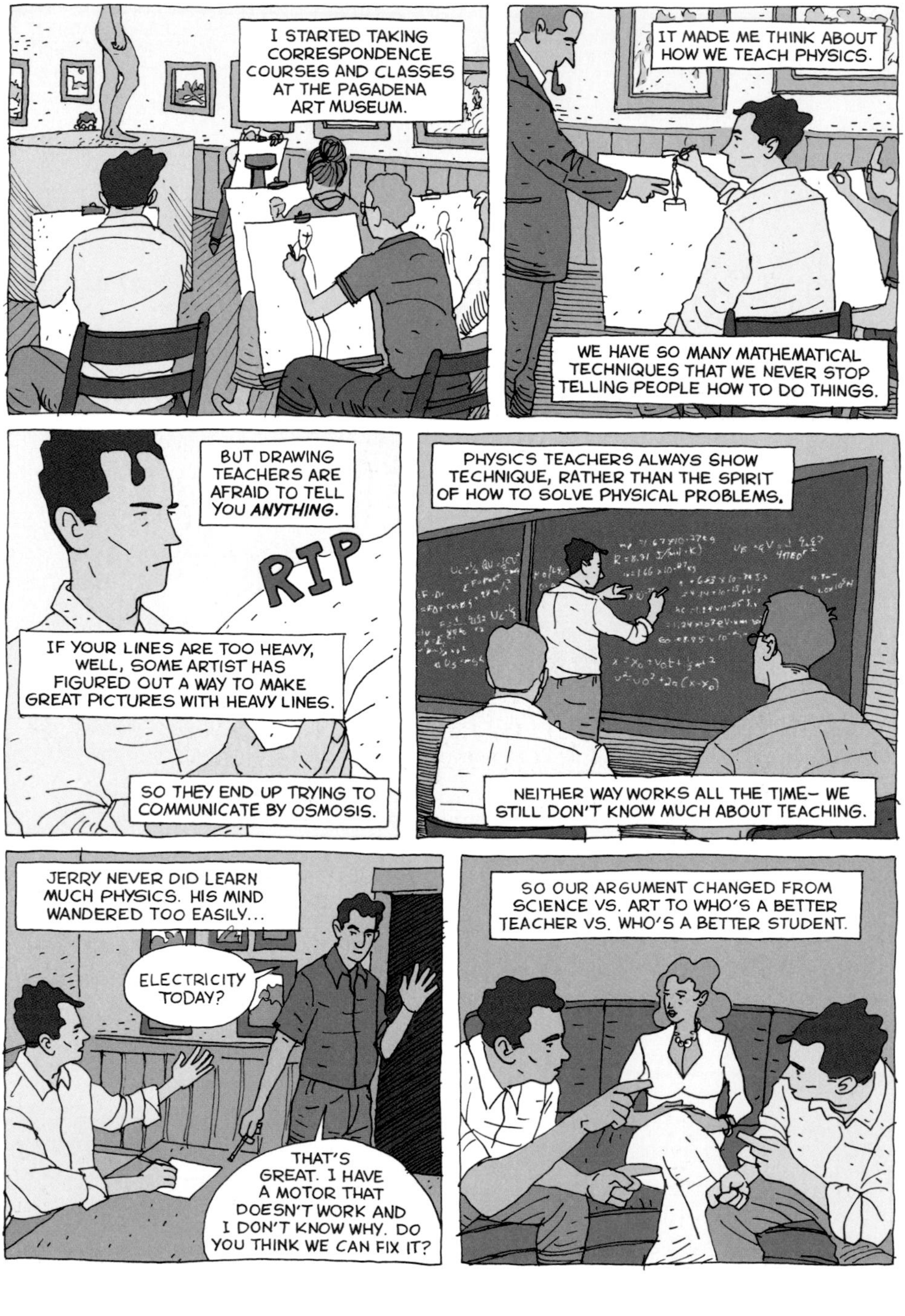

I STARTED TAKING CORRESPONDENCE COURSES AND CLASSES AT THE PASADENA ART MUSEUM.
IT MADE ME THINK ABOUT HOW WE TEACH PHYSICS.
WE HAVE SO MANY MATHEMATICAL TECHNIQUES THAT WE NEVER STOP TELLING PEOPLE HOW TO DO THINGS.
BUT DRAWING TEACHERS ARE AFRAID TO TELL YOU *ANYTHING*.
RIP
IF YOUR LINES ARE TOO HEAVY, WELL, SOME ARTIST HAS FIGURED OUT A WAY TO MAKE GREAT PICTURES WITH HEAVY LINES.
SO THEY END UP TRYING TO COMMUNICATE BY OSMOSIS.
PHYSICS TEACHERS ALWAYS SHOW TECHNIQUE, RATHER THAN THE SPIRIT OF HOW TO SOLVE PHYSICAL PROBLEMS.
NEITHER WAY WORKS ALL THE TIME– WE STILL DON'T KNOW MUCH ABOUT TEACHING.
JERRY NEVER DID LEARN MUCH PHYSICS. HIS MIND WANDERED TOO EASILY...
ELECTRICITY TODAY?
THAT'S GREAT. I HAVE A MOTOR THAT DOESN'T WORK AND I DON'T KNOW WHY. DO YOU THINK WE CAN FIX IT?
SO OUR ARGUMENT CHANGED FROM SCIENCE VS. ART TO WHO'S A BETTER TEACHER VS. WHO'S A BETTER STUDENT.

HELIUM AND THE θ-t PUZZLE AND V-A VECTOR LAW OF WEAK INTERACTION (1954 - 1957)

TEACHING, LEARNING, DISCOVERY. ALL MYSTERIES!

I WORKED OUT THE THEORY OF HELIUM, ONCE.

IT'S PSYCHOLOGICALLY FUNNY—I CAN REMEMBER THE COLOR OF THE PAPER I WAS WRITING ON AND THE ROOM AND EVERYTHING ELSE.

BUT I ALSO WONDER: WHAT WAS THE *PSYCHOLOGICAL* CONDITION?

I'D STRUGGLED AND STRUGGLED WITH HELIUM FOR TWO YEARS AND SUDDENLY SAW EVERYTHING. I LOOKED UP AND SAID...

WAIT. IT CAN'T BE THAT DIFFICULT. IT MUST BE VERY EASY. I'LL STAND BACK AND JUST TREAT IT VERY LIGHTLY.

I'LL JUST TAP IT.

BONK

BONK

AND THERE IT WAS! HOW MANY TIMES SINCE THEN, I'M WALKING ON THE BEACH AND I SAY...

NOW LOOK. IT CAN'T BE SO COMPLICATED. I'LL SIMPLY TAP IT AND TAP IT.

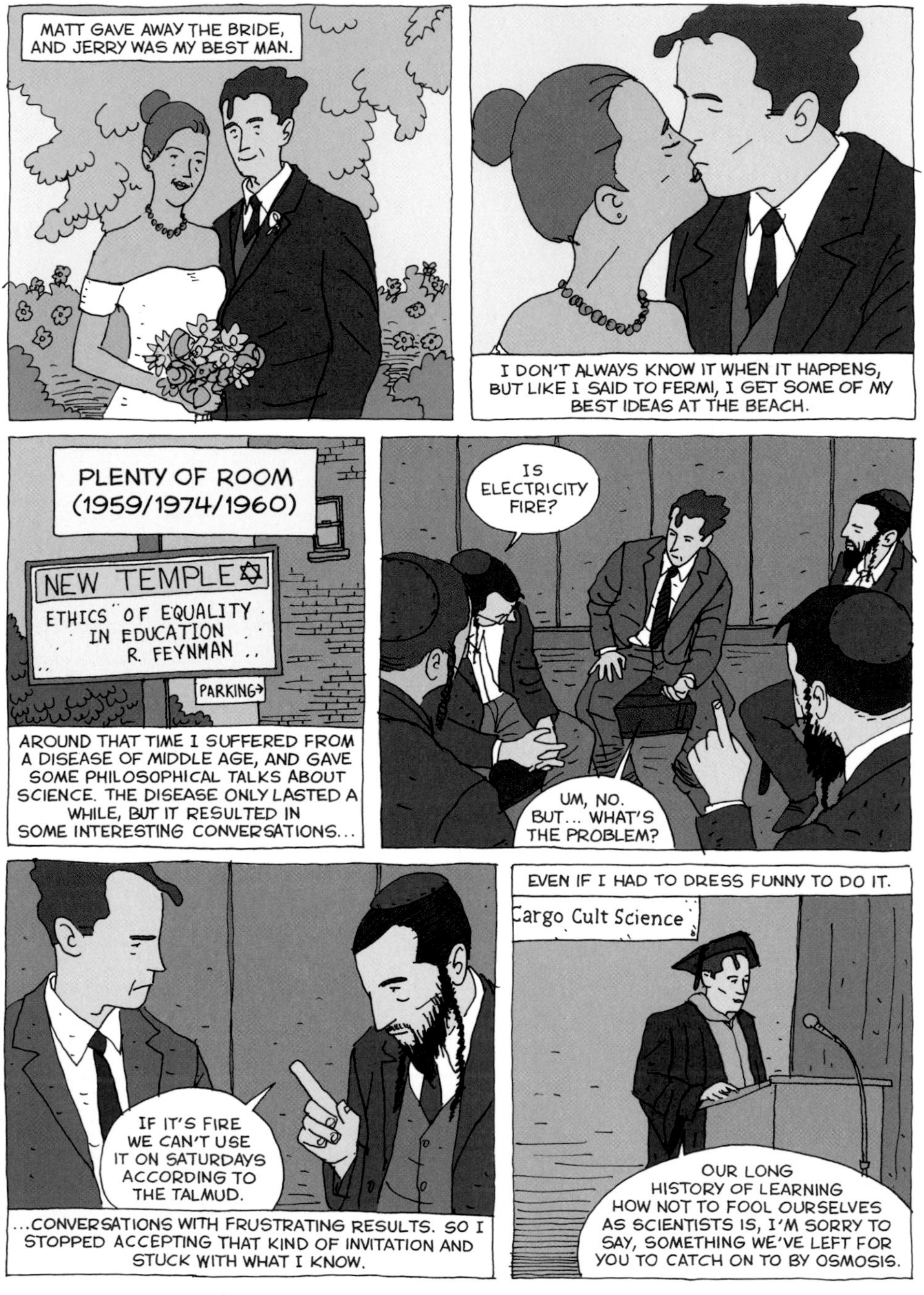
MATT GAVE AWAY THE BRIDE, AND JERRY WAS MY BEST MAN.
I DON'T ALWAYS KNOW IT WHEN IT HAPPENS, BUT LIKE I SAID TO FERMI, I GET SOME OF MY BEST IDEAS AT THE BEACH.
PLENTY OF ROOM (1959/1974/1960)
NEW TEMPLE
ETHICS OF EQUALITY IN EDUCATION R. FEYNMAN
PARKING→
AROUND THAT TIME I SUFFERED FROM A DISEASE OF MIDDLE AGE, AND GAVE SOME PHILOSOPHICAL TALKS ABOUT SCIENCE. THE DISEASE ONLY LASTED A WHILE, BUT IT RESULTED IN SOME INTERESTING CONVERSATIONS...
IS ELECTRICITY FIRE?
UM, NO. BUT... WHAT'S THE PROBLEM?
IF IT'S FIRE WE CAN'T USE IT ON SATURDAYS ACCORDING TO THE TALMUD.
...CONVERSATIONS WITH FRUSTRATING RESULTS. SO I STOPPED ACCEPTING THAT KIND OF INVITATION AND STUCK WITH WHAT I KNOW.
EVEN IF I HAD TO DRESS FUNNY TO DO IT.
Cargo Cult Science
OUR LONG HISTORY OF LEARNING HOW NOT TO FOOL OURSELVES AS SCIENTISTS IS, I'M SORRY TO SAY, SOMETHING WE'VE LEFT FOR YOU TO CATCH ON TO BY OSMOSIS.

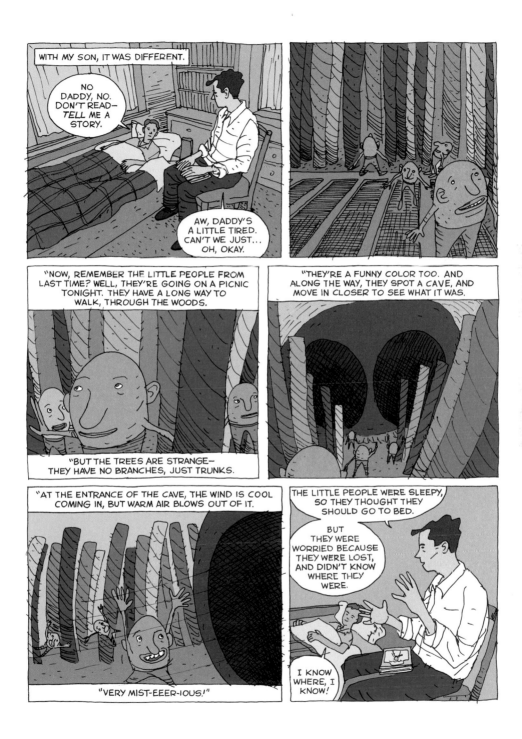

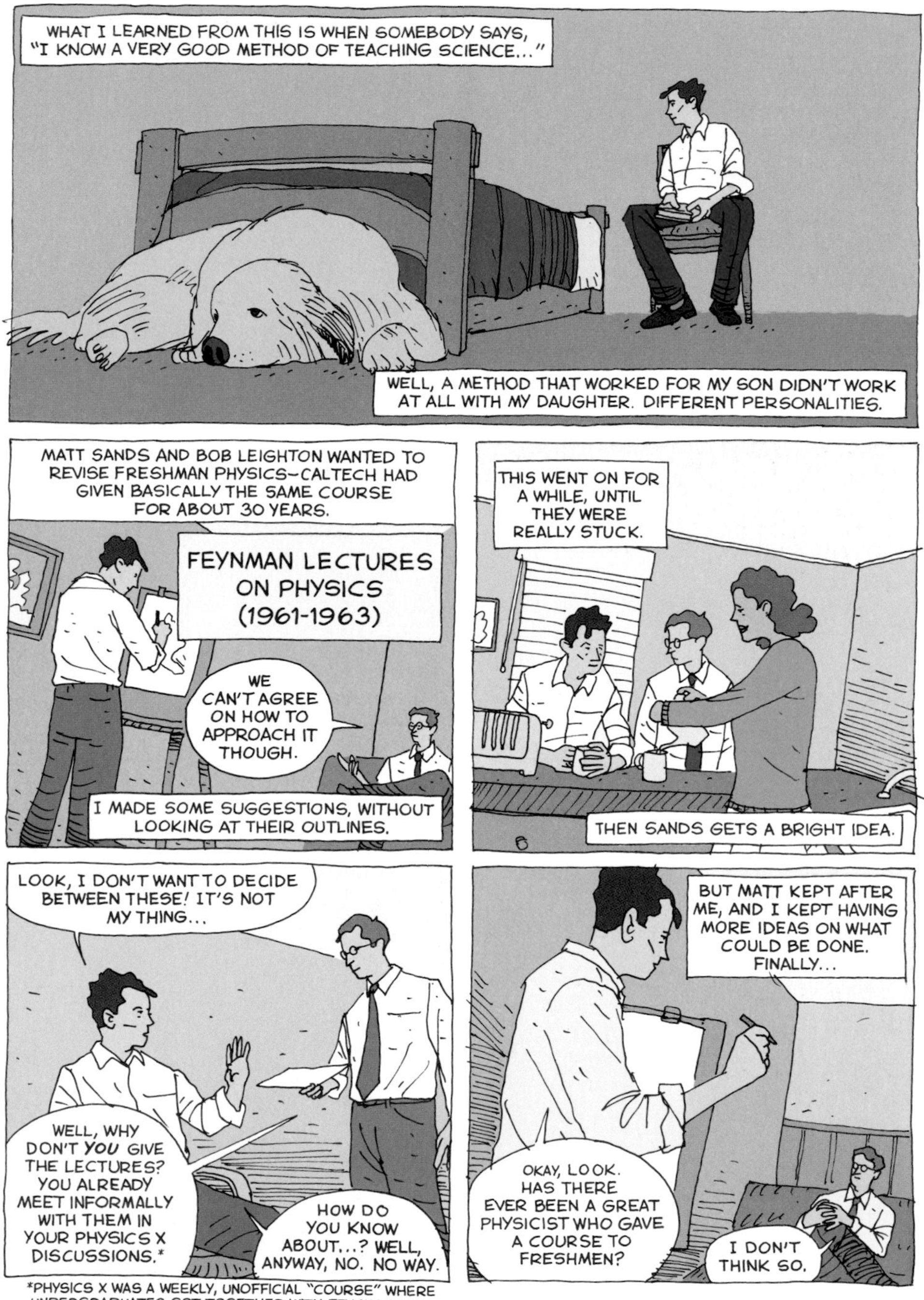
WHAT I LEARNED FROM THIS IS WHEN SOMEBODY SAYS, "I KNOW A VERY GOOD METHOD OF TEACHING SCIENCE..."
WELL, A METHOD THAT WORKED FOR MY SON DIDN'T WORK AT ALL WITH MY DAUGHTER. DIFFERENT PERSONALITIES.
MATT SANDS AND BOB LEIGHTON WANTED TO REVISE FRESHMAN PHYSICS—CALTECH HAD GIVEN BASICALLY THE SAME COURSE FOR ABOUT 30 YEARS.
FEYNMAN LECTURES ON PHYSICS (1961-1963)
WE CAN'T AGREE ON HOW TO APPROACH IT THOUGH.
I MADE SOME SUGGESTIONS, WITHOUT LOOKING AT THEIR OUTLINES.
THIS WENT ON FOR A WHILE, UNTIL THEY WERE REALLY STUCK.
THEN SANDS GETS A BRIGHT IDEA.
LOOK, I DON'T WANT TO DECIDE BETWEEN THESE! IT'S NOT MY THING...
WELL, WHY DON'T *YOU* GIVE THE LECTURES? YOU ALREADY MEET INFORMALLY WITH THEM IN YOUR PHYSICS X DISCUSSIONS.*
HOW DO YOU KNOW ABOUT...? WELL, ANYWAY, NO. NO WAY.
BUT MATT KEPT AFTER ME, AND I KEPT HAVING MORE IDEAS ON WHAT COULD BE DONE. FINALLY...
OKAY, LOOK. HAS THERE EVER BEEN A GREAT PHYSICIST WHO GAVE A COURSE TO FRESHMEN?
I DON'T THINK SO.

*PHYSICS X WAS A WEEKLY, UNOFFICIAL "COURSE" WHERE UNDERGRADUATES GOT TOGETHER WITH FEYNMAN AND ASKED HIM ANY (PHYSICS) QUESTIONS THEY WANTED.

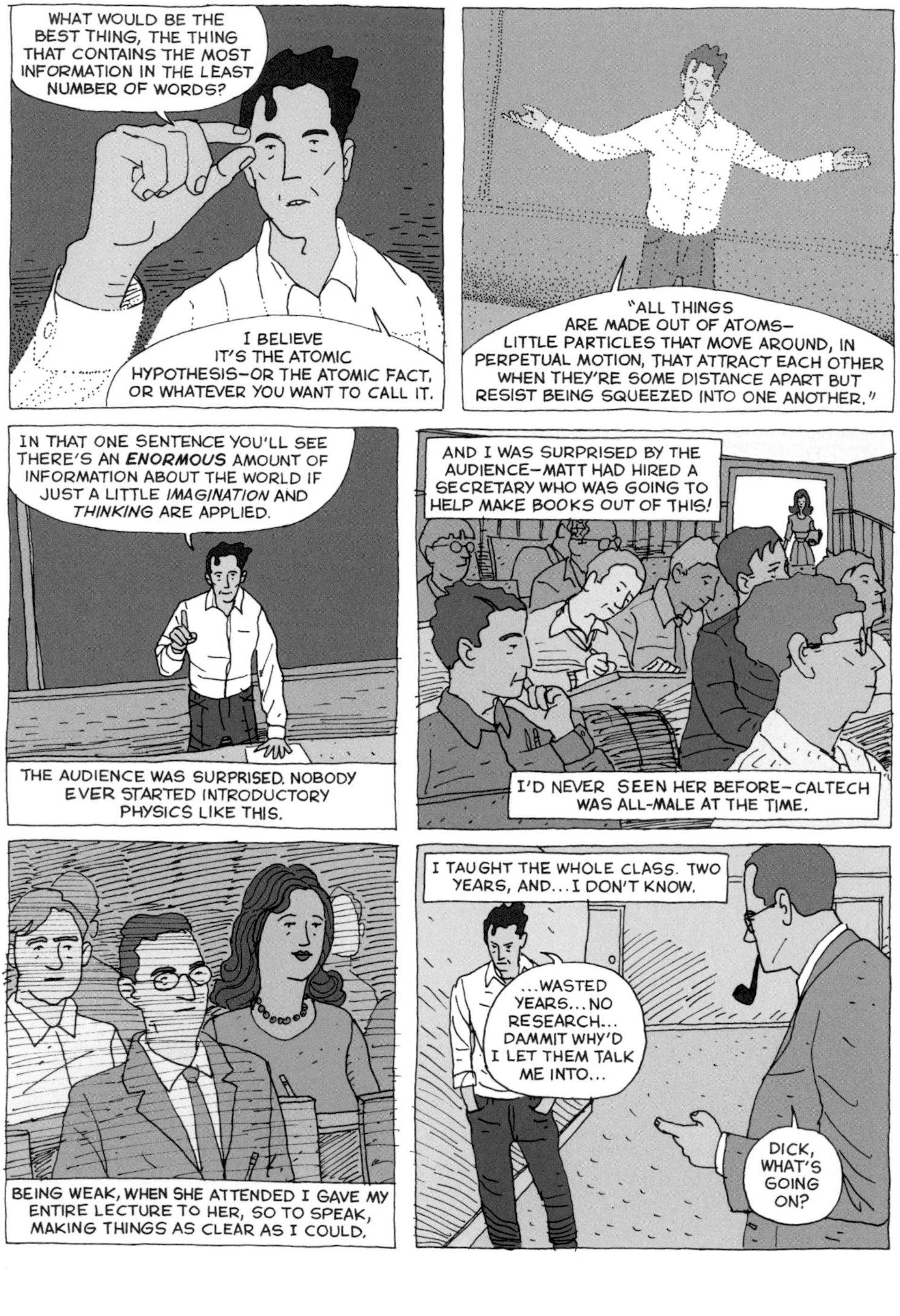
WHAT WOULD BE THE BEST THING, THE THING THAT CONTAINS THE MOST INFORMATION IN THE LEAST NUMBER OF WORDS?
I BELIEVE IT'S THE ATOMIC HYPOTHESIS—OR THE ATOMIC FACT, OR WHATEVER YOU WANT TO CALL IT.
"ALL THINGS ARE MADE OUT OF ATOMS—LITTLE PARTICLES THAT MOVE AROUND, IN PERPETUAL MOTION, THAT ATTRACT EACH OTHER WHEN THEY'RE SOME DISTANCE APART BUT RESIST BEING SQUEEZED INTO ONE ANOTHER."
IN THAT ONE SENTENCE YOU'LL SEE THERE'S AN ***ENORMOUS*** AMOUNT OF INFORMATION ABOUT THE WORLD IF JUST A LITTLE *IMAGINATION* AND *THINKING* ARE APPLIED.
THE AUDIENCE WAS SURPRISED. NOBODY EVER STARTED INTRODUCTORY PHYSICS LIKE THIS.
AND I WAS SURPRISED BY THE AUDIENCE—MATT HAD HIRED A SECRETARY WHO WAS GOING TO HELP MAKE BOOKS OUT OF THIS!
I'D NEVER SEEN HER BEFORE—CALTECH WAS ALL-MALE AT THE TIME.
BEING WEAK, WHEN SHE ATTENDED I GAVE MY ENTIRE LECTURE TO HER, SO TO SPEAK, MAKING THINGS AS CLEAR AS I COULD.
I TAUGHT THE WHOLE CLASS. TWO YEARS, AND... I DON'T KNOW.
...WASTED YEARS... NO RESEARCH... DAMMIT WHY'D I LET THEM TALK ME INTO...
DICK, WHAT'S GOING ON?

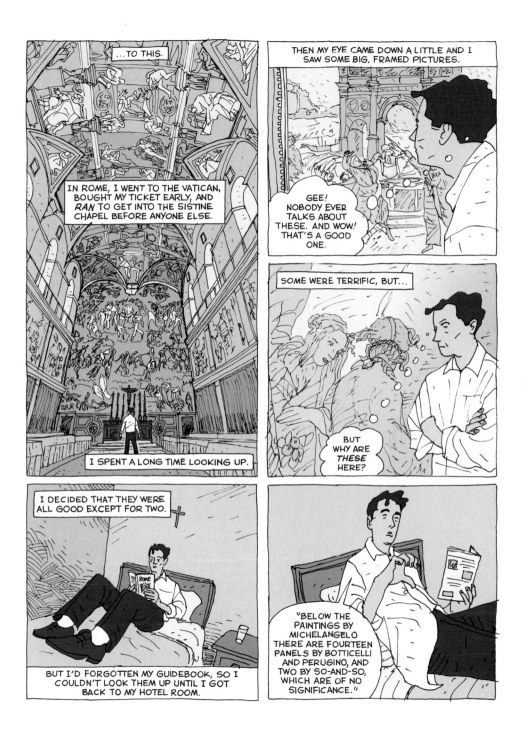

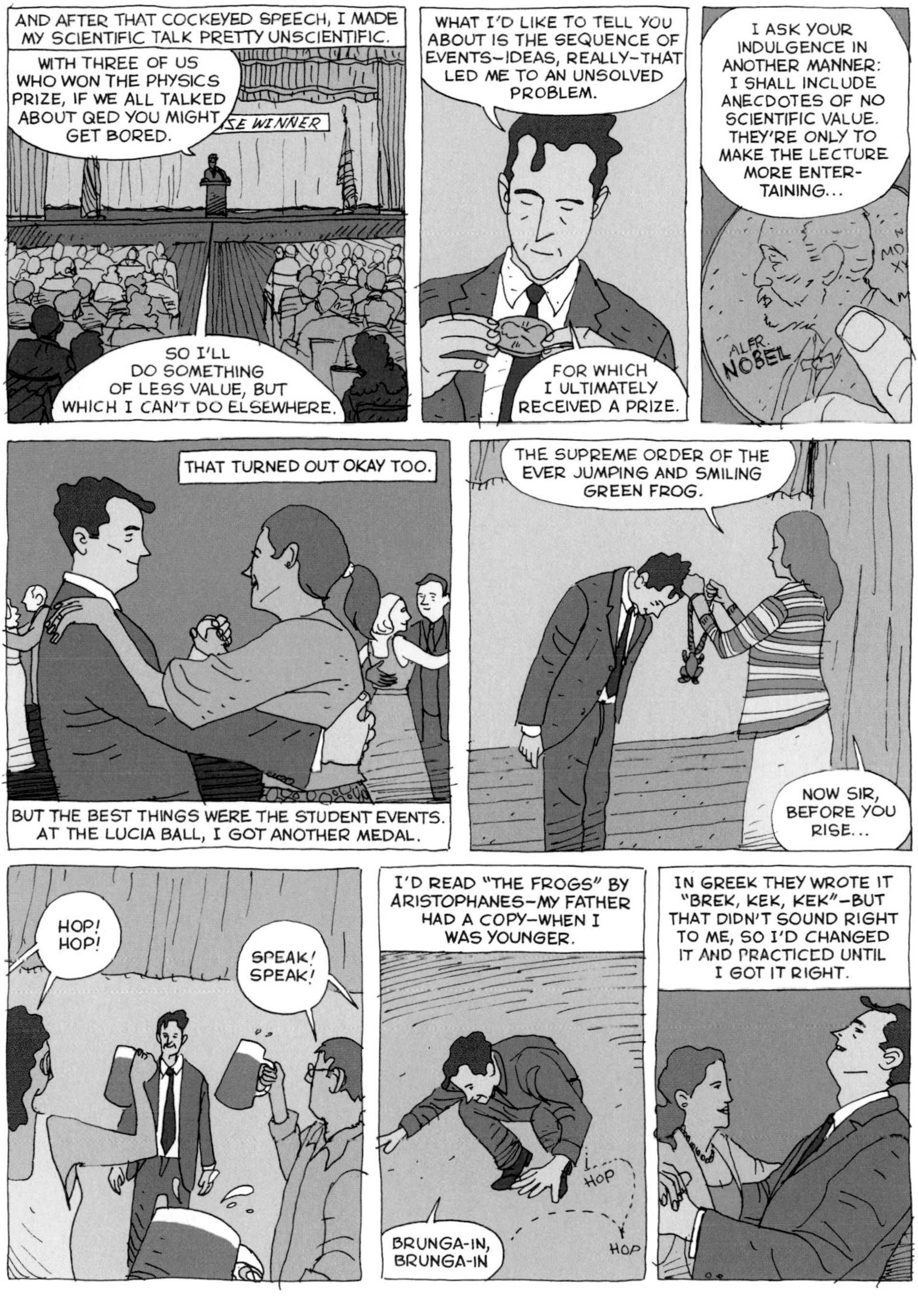
AND AFTER THAT COCKEYED SPEECH, I MADE MY SCIENTIFIC TALK PRETTY UNSCIENTIFIC.
WITH THREE OF US WHO WON THE PHYSICS PRIZE, IF WE ALL TALKED ABOUT QED YOU MIGHT GET BORED.
SE WINNER
SO I'LL DO SOMETHING OF LESS VALUE, BUT WHICH I CAN'T DO ELSEWHERE.
WHAT I'D LIKE TO TELL YOU ABOUT IS THE SEQUENCE OF EVENTS–IDEAS, REALLY–THAT LED ME TO AN UNSOLVED PROBLEM.
FOR WHICH I ULTIMATELY RECEIVED A PRIZE.
I ASK YOUR INDULGENCE IN ANOTHER MANNER: I SHALL INCLUDE ANECDOTES OF NO SCIENTIFIC VALUE. THEY'RE ONLY TO MAKE THE LECTURE MORE ENTER-TAINING...
ALFR. NOBEL
THAT TURNED OUT OKAY TOO.
BUT THE BEST THINGS WERE THE STUDENT EVENTS. AT THE LUCIA BALL, I GOT ANOTHER MEDAL.
THE SUPREME ORDER OF THE EVER JUMPING AND SMILING GREEN FROG.
NOW SIR, BEFORE YOU RISE...
HOP! HOP!
SPEAK! SPEAK!
I'D READ "THE FROGS" BY ARISTOPHANES–MY FATHER HAD A COPY–WHEN I WAS YOUNGER.
HOP
HOP
BRUNGA-IN, BRUNGA-IN
IN GREEK THEY WROTE IT "BREK, KEK, KEK"–BUT THAT DIDN'T SOUND RIGHT TO ME, SO I'D CHANGED IT AND PRACTICED UNTIL I GOT IT RIGHT.

*SEE THE NOTES AT THE END OF THE BOOK TO FIND OUT WHY TOMONAGA DIDN'T MAKE IT TO THE CEREMONY.

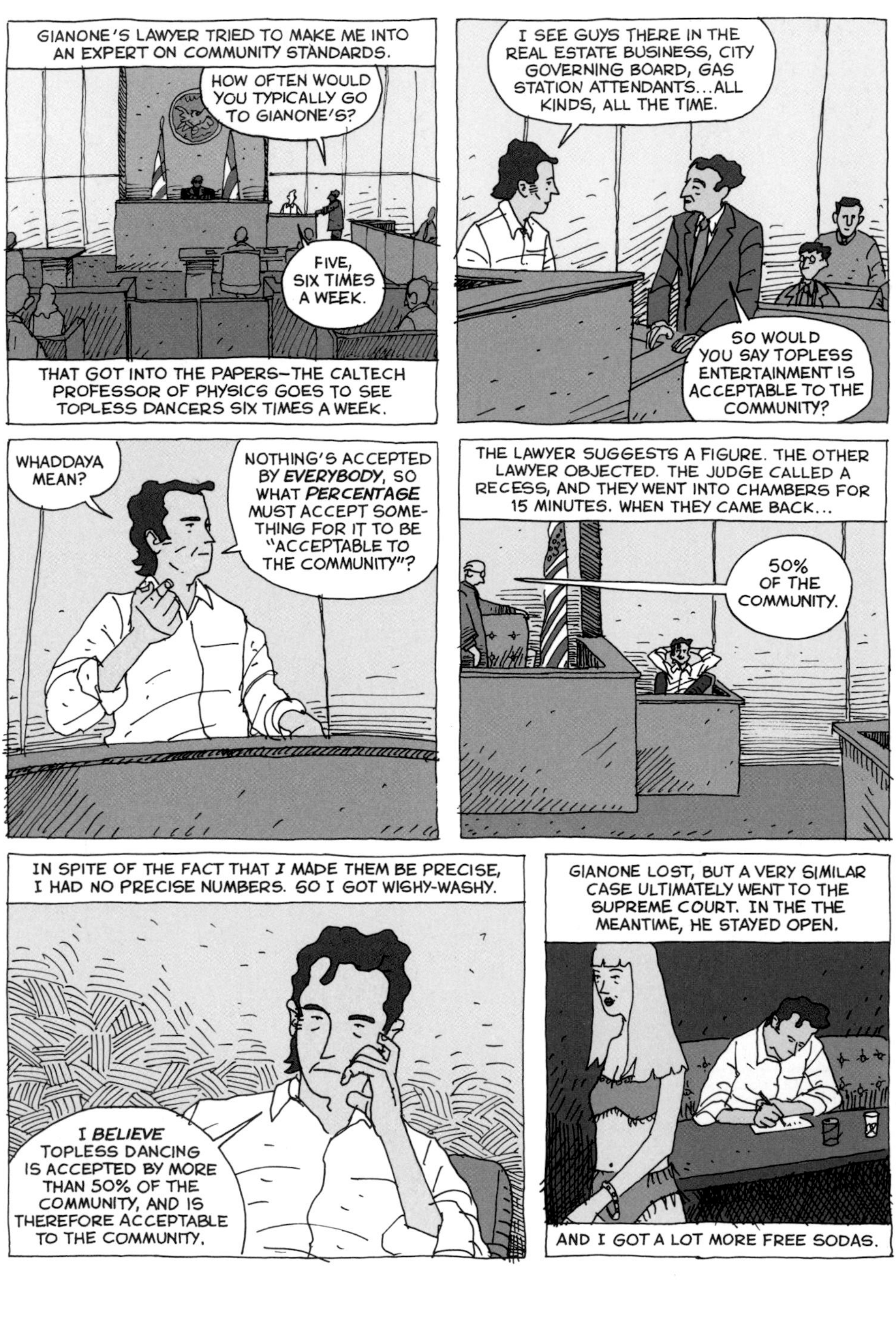
GIANONE'S LAWYER TRIED TO MAKE ME INTO AN EXPERT ON COMMUNITY STANDARDS.
HOW OFTEN WOULD YOU TYPICALLY GO TO GIANONE'S?
FIVE, SIX TIMES A WEEK.
THAT GOT INTO THE PAPERS—THE CALTECH PROFESSOR OF PHYSICS GOES TO SEE TOPLESS DANCERS SIX TIMES A WEEK.
I SEE GUYS THERE IN THE REAL ESTATE BUSINESS, CITY GOVERNING BOARD, GAS STATION ATTENDANTS...ALL KINDS, ALL THE TIME.
SO WOULD YOU SAY TOPLESS ENTERTAINMENT IS ACCEPTABLE TO THE COMMUNITY?
WHADDAYA MEAN?
NOTHING'S ACCEPTED BY *EVERYBODY*, SO WHAT *PERCENTAGE* MUST ACCEPT SOMETHING FOR IT TO BE "ACCEPTABLE TO THE COMMUNITY"?
THE LAWYER SUGGESTS A FIGURE. THE OTHER LAWYER OBJECTED. THE JUDGE CALLED A RECESS, AND THEY WENT INTO CHAMBERS FOR 15 MINUTES. WHEN THEY CAME BACK...
50% OF THE COMMUNITY.
IN SPITE OF THE FACT THAT *I* MADE THEM BE PRECISE, I HAD NO PRECISE NUMBERS. SO I GOT WISHY-WASHY.
I *BELIEVE* TOPLESS DANCING IS ACCEPTED BY MORE THAN 50% OF THE COMMUNITY, AND IS THEREFORE ACCEPTABLE TO THE COMMUNITY.
GIANONE LOST, BUT A VERY SIMILAR CASE ULTIMATELY WENT TO THE SUPREME COURT. IN THE THE MEANTIME, HE STAYED OPEN.
AND I GOT A LOT MORE FREE SODAS.

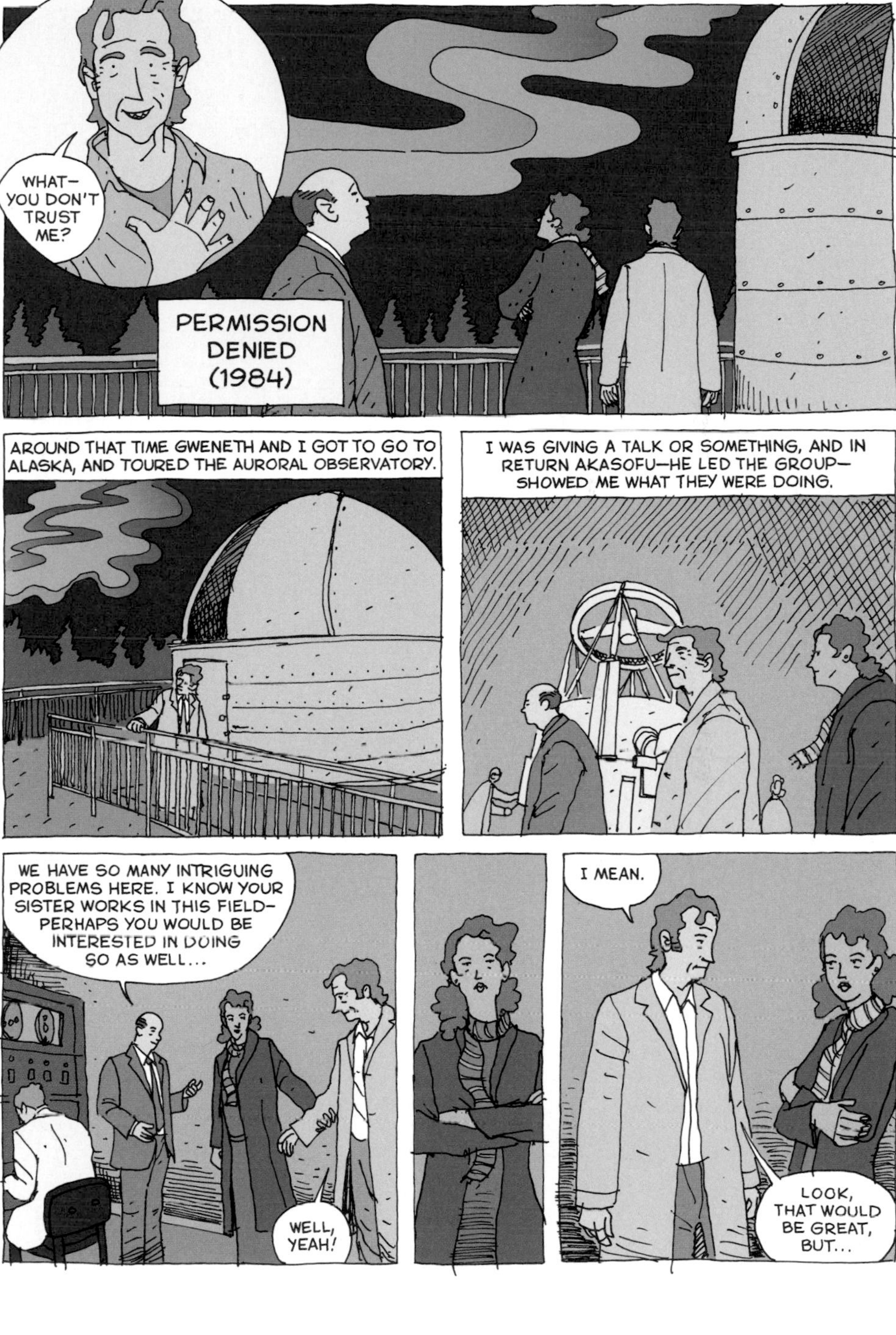
WHAT—
YOU DON'T
TRUST
ME?
PERMISSION
DENIED
(1984)
AROUND THAT TIME GWENETH AND I GOT TO GO TO ALASKA, AND TOURED THE AURORAL OBSERVATORY.
I WAS GIVING A TALK OR SOMETHING, AND IN RETURN AKASOFU—HE LED THE GROUP—SHOWED ME WHAT THEY WERE DOING.
WE HAVE SO MANY INTRIGUING PROBLEMS HERE. I KNOW YOUR SISTER WORKS IN THIS FIELD—PERHAPS YOU WOULD BE INTERESTED IN DOING SO AS WELL...
WELL, YEAH!
I MEAN.
LOOK, THAT WOULD BE GREAT, BUT...

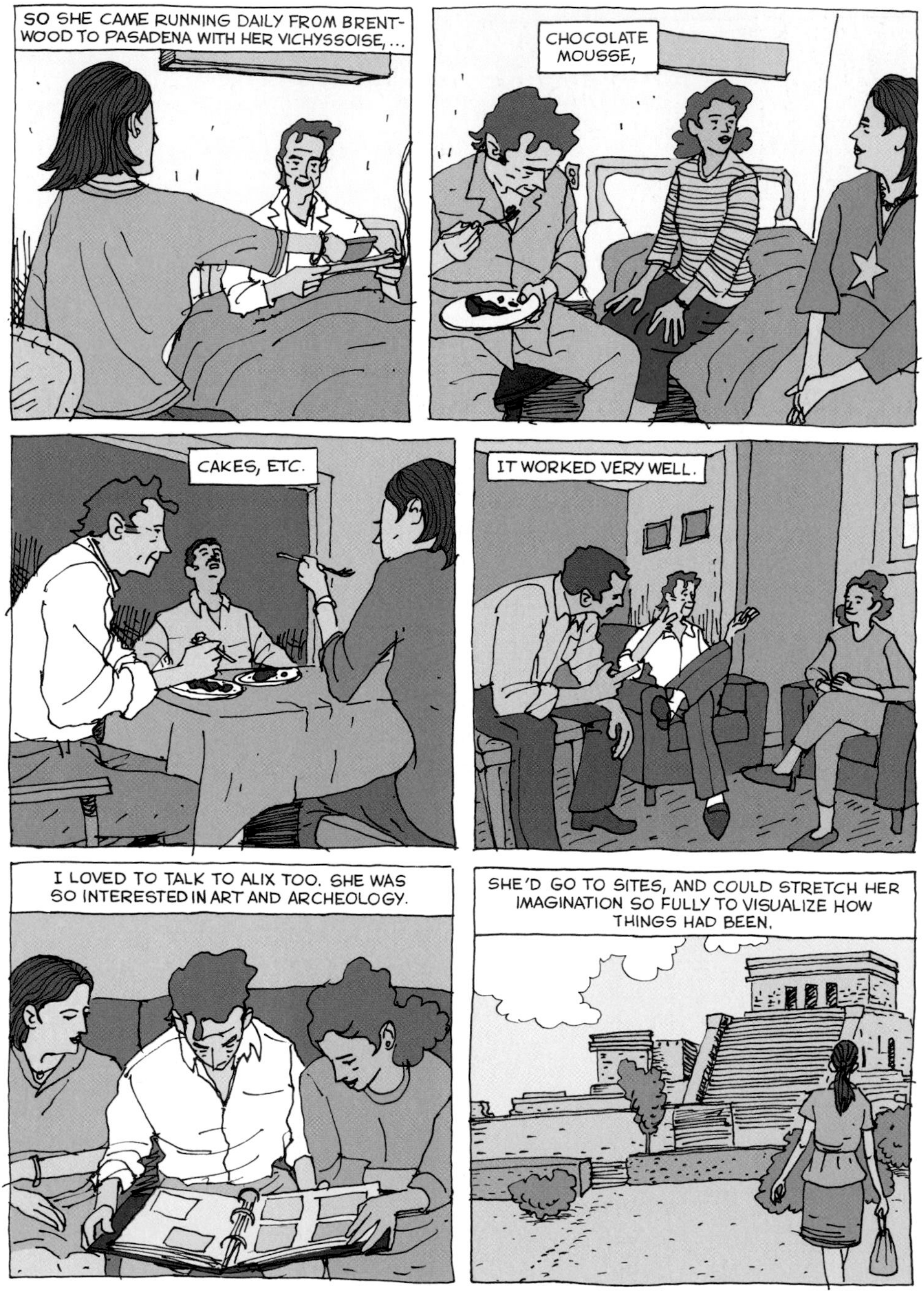
SO SHE CAME RUNNING DAILY FROM BRENTWOOD TO PASADENA WITH HER VICHYSSOISE, ...
CHOCOLATE MOUSSE,
CAKES, ETC.
IT WORKED VERY WELL.
I LOVED TO TALK TO ALIX TOO. SHE WAS SO INTERESTED IN ART AND ARCHEOLOGY.
SHE'D GO TO SITES, AND COULD STRETCH HER IMAGINATION SO FULLY TO VISUALIZE HOW THINGS HAD BEEN.

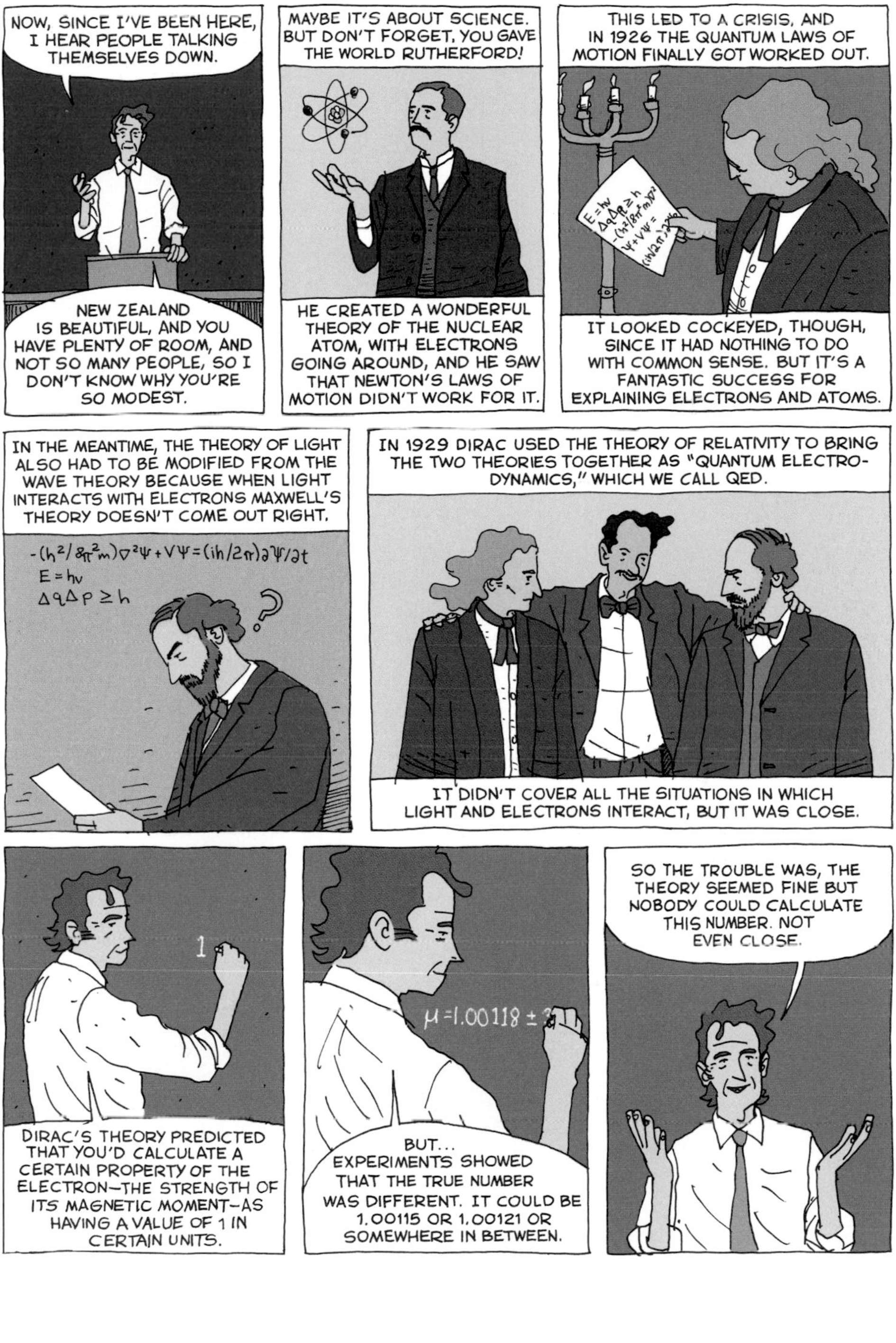

NOW, SINCE I'VE BEEN HERE, I HEAR PEOPLE TALKING THEMSELVES DOWN.
NEW ZEALAND IS BEAUTIFUL, AND YOU HAVE PLENTY OF ROOM, AND NOT SO MANY PEOPLE, SO I DON'T KNOW WHY YOU'RE SO MODEST.
MAYBE IT'S ABOUT SCIENCE. BUT DON'T FORGET, YOU GAVE THE WORLD RUTHERFORD!
HE CREATED A WONDERFUL THEORY OF THE NUCLEAR ATOM, WITH ELECTRONS GOING AROUND, AND HE SAW THAT NEWTON'S LAWS OF MOTION DIDN'T WORK FOR IT.
THIS LED TO A CRISIS, AND IN 1926 THE QUANTUM LAWS OF MOTION FINALLY GOT WORKED OUT.
IT LOOKED COCKEYED, THOUGH, SINCE IT HAD NOTHING TO DO WITH COMMON SENSE. BUT IT'S A FANTASTIC SUCCESS FOR EXPLAINING ELECTRONS AND ATOMS.
IN THE MEANTIME, THE THEORY OF LIGHT ALSO HAD TO BE MODIFIED FROM THE WAVE THEORY BECAUSE WHEN LIGHT INTERACTS WITH ELECTRONS MAXWELL'S THEORY DOESN'T COME OUT RIGHT.
$-(h^2/8\pi^2 m)\nabla^2\psi + V\psi = (ih/2\pi)\partial\psi/\partial t$
$E = h\nu$
$\Delta q \Delta p \geq h$
?
IN 1929 DIRAC USED THE THEORY OF RELATIVITY TO BRING THE TWO THEORIES TOGETHER AS "QUANTUM ELECTRO-DYNAMICS," WHICH WE CALL QED.
IT DIDN'T COVER ALL THE SITUATIONS IN WHICH LIGHT AND ELECTRONS INTERACT, BUT IT WAS CLOSE.
1
DIRAC'S THEORY PREDICTED THAT YOU'D CALCULATE A CERTAIN PROPERTY OF THE ELECTRON—THE STRENGTH OF ITS MAGNETIC MOMENT—AS HAVING A VALUE OF 1 IN CERTAIN UNITS.
$\mu = 1.00118 \pm$
BUT... EXPERIMENTS SHOWED THAT THE TRUE NUMBER WAS DIFFERENT. IT COULD BE 1.00115 OR 1.00121 OR SOMEWHERE IN BETWEEN.
SO THE TROUBLE WAS, THE THEORY SEEMED FINE BUT NOBODY COULD CALCULATE THIS NUMBER. NOT EVEN CLOSE.

IT WAS ABSURD, AND IT LASTED FOR A LONG TIME. IN THE 1940S THERE BEGAN A LOT OF EFFORT TO GET THE THEORY STRAIGHTENED OUT.

IT TURNS OUT SURPRISINGLY THAT THREE GUYS —ONE OF WHICH YOU SEE HERE—WORKED IT OUT INDEPENDENTLY, AND THEY GOT NOBEL PRIZES...

SCHWINGER—ONE OF THE OTHER GUYS WHO'S NOT ME—FIGURED OUT THAT THE ORIGINAL THEORY WAS VERY NEARLY RIGHT. MAYBE 97% CORRECT.

AND HE FIGURED OUT THAT THE NUMBER WAS CLOSER TO 1.00116, THEORETICALLY.

NOW, 30 YEARS LATER, THE EXPERIMENTERS HAVE GOTTEN BETTER AT MEASURING THIS AND NOW HAVE IT PEGGED AT 1.0011596524 ± 2.

$1.0011596524 \pm 2.$

IN THE MEANTIME, THE POOR GUYS USING CALCULATORS AND WRITING MARKS ON PIECES OF PAPER HAVE PREDICTED THAT THE SAME VALUE SHOULD BE 1.0011596523 ± 3

WHY DOES THE THEORY HAVE A ±? WELL, EVERYBODY GETS EXHAUSTED COMPUTING THIS, SO WE STOP BEFORE IT'S FINISHED!

THIS UNCERTAINTY IS PRETTY SMALL, THOUGH. IT'S LIKE IF YOU MEASURED THE DISTANCE FROM LOS ANGELES TO NEW YORK AND YOU COULD DO IT TO AN ACCURACY OF THE THICKNESS OF ONE OF THE HAIRS ON MY HEAD.

LA   NY

I SAY ALL THIS TO *INTIMIDATE* YOU INTO BELIEVING THE THEORY AND EXPERIMENT AGREE TO A HIGH DEGREE OF ACCURACY.

AND THIS THEORY— OF HOW ELECTRONS AND LIGHT INTERACT—BASICALLY DESCRIBES ALMOST EVERY-THING WE ORDINARILY EXPERIENCE.

IN FACT, IT'S EASIER TO TALK ABOUT WHAT IT DOESN'T EXPLAIN. GRAVITY? NOT EXPLAINED BY QED. RADIOACTIVITY? NOPE.

BUT IF IT INVOLVES ELECTRONS, YEAH. THAT MEANS ALL OF CHEMISTRY AND OBSERVABLE PHENOMENA.

THE *COLORS* OF THINGS, THE SOFTNESS OF MATERIALS, HOW QUICKLY THINGS GET HOT WHEN THEY'RE IN THE SUN, SOUND...

ALL THESE PHENOMENA, EVERYTHING TO DO WITH THE OUTSIDE OF THE ATOM? WE *GOT* IT.

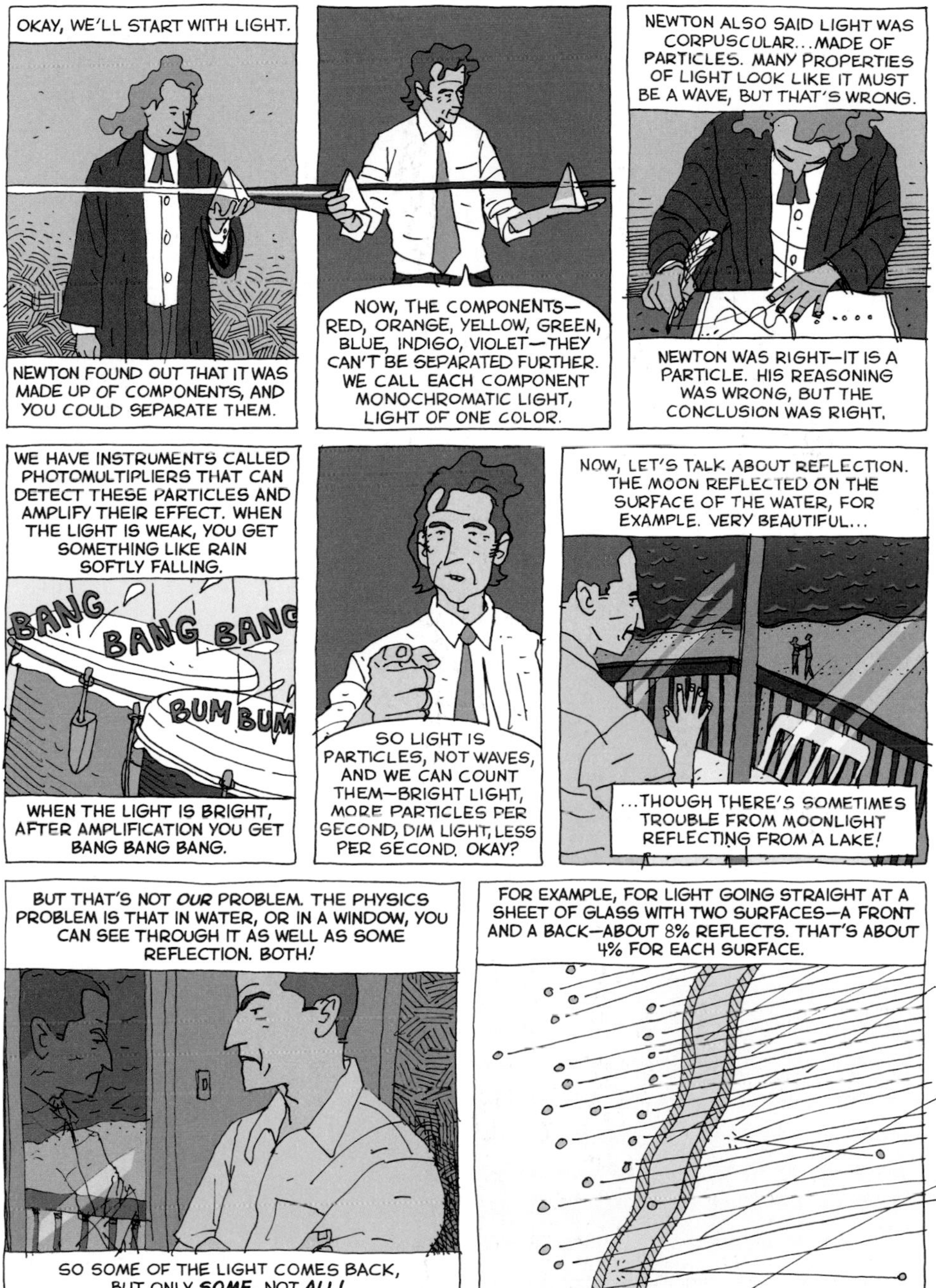
OKAY, WE'LL START WITH LIGHT.
NEWTON FOUND OUT THAT IT WAS MADE UP OF COMPONENTS, AND YOU COULD SEPARATE THEM.
NOW, THE COMPONENTS—RED, ORANGE, YELLOW, GREEN, BLUE, INDIGO, VIOLET—THEY CAN'T BE SEPARATED FURTHER. WE CALL EACH COMPONENT MONOCHROMATIC LIGHT, LIGHT OF ONE COLOR.
NEWTON ALSO SAID LIGHT WAS CORPUSCULAR...MADE OF PARTICLES. MANY PROPERTIES OF LIGHT LOOK LIKE IT MUST BE A WAVE, BUT THAT'S WRONG.
NEWTON WAS RIGHT—IT IS A PARTICLE. HIS REASONING WAS WRONG, BUT THE CONCLUSION WAS RIGHT.
WE HAVE INSTRUMENTS CALLED PHOTOMULTIPLIERS THAT CAN DETECT THESE PARTICLES AND AMPLIFY THEIR EFFECT. WHEN THE LIGHT IS WEAK, YOU GET SOMETHING LIKE RAIN SOFTLY FALLING.
BANG
BANG BANG
BUM BUM
WHEN THE LIGHT IS BRIGHT, AFTER AMPLIFICATION YOU GET BANG BANG BANG.
SO LIGHT IS PARTICLES, NOT WAVES, AND WE CAN COUNT THEM—BRIGHT LIGHT, MORE PARTICLES PER SECOND, DIM LIGHT, LESS PER SECOND. OKAY?
NOW, LET'S TALK ABOUT REFLECTION. THE MOON REFLECTED ON THE SURFACE OF THE WATER, FOR EXAMPLE. VERY BEAUTIFUL...
...THOUGH THERE'S SOMETIMES TROUBLE FROM MOONLIGHT REFLECTING FROM A LAKE!
BUT THAT'S NOT *OUR* PROBLEM. THE PHYSICS PROBLEM IS THAT IN WATER, OR IN A WINDOW, YOU CAN SEE THROUGH IT AS WELL AS SOME REFLECTION. BOTH!
SO SOME OF THE LIGHT COMES BACK, BUT ONLY **SOME**. NOT ***ALL!***
FOR EXAMPLE, FOR LIGHT GOING STRAIGHT AT A SHEET OF GLASS WITH TWO SURFACES—A FRONT AND A BACK—ABOUT 8% REFLECTS. THAT'S ABOUT 4% FOR EACH SURFACE.

NOW, HOW CAN LIGHT BE PARTIALLY REFLECTED? FOR A SINGLE COLOR OF LIGHT, EACH PARTICLE HAS THE *EXACT SAME* STRENGTH, THE *EXACT SAME* ENERGY. THERE ARE NO HALF-PARTICLES.

SO WE LOOK AT THE LIGHT AND WE HAVE TO ASK "HOW DOES A PARTICULAR PHOTON MAKE UP ITS MIND WHETHER TO REFLECT OR GO THROUGH?"

HA HA HA

HEY, WE CAN'T JUST *LAUGH!* WE NEED A THEORY.

PEOPLE CAME UP WITH A LOT OF THEM, BUT IN THE END IT'S THIS: WE CAN'T PREDICT WHAT A PARTICULAR PHOTON WILL DO. NATURE ONLY ALLOWS US TO CALCULATE PROBABILITIES.

I DON'T LIKE IT?

HOW CAN IT BE?

I DON'T UNDERSTAND.

I CAN SEE YOU SAYING "I DON'T UNDERSTAND." I CAN SEE YOU THINKING "I DON'T LIKE IT."

I CAN SEE YOU TURNING OFF.

TOUGH.

I DON'T UNDERSTAND IT EITHER. I DON'T LIKE IT EITHER.

BUT THAT'S THE WAY IT IS.

BACK TO WATER. IF YOU HAVE A SOAP BUBBLE INSTEAD OF A MOONLIT LAKE, YOU HAVE TWO SURFACES — INSIDE AND OUTSIDE OF THE BUBBLE. AND WHEN REGULAR SUNLIGHT HITS IT, YOU SEE COLORS!

IF IT'S MONOCHROMATIC RED LIGHT THAT HITS, YOU SEE BANDS — BLACK AND RED.

SOME AREAS REFLECT THE RED LIGHT, OTHERS DON'T REFLECT IT AT ALL. IT HAS TO DO WITH THE *THICKNESS* — NEWTON FIGURED THIS OUT AND DID EXPERIMENTS WITH GLASS.

POP

IF YOU CHANGED THE THICKNESS YOU GOT DIFFERENT PERCENTAGES OF PROBABILITY OF REFLECTION.

204

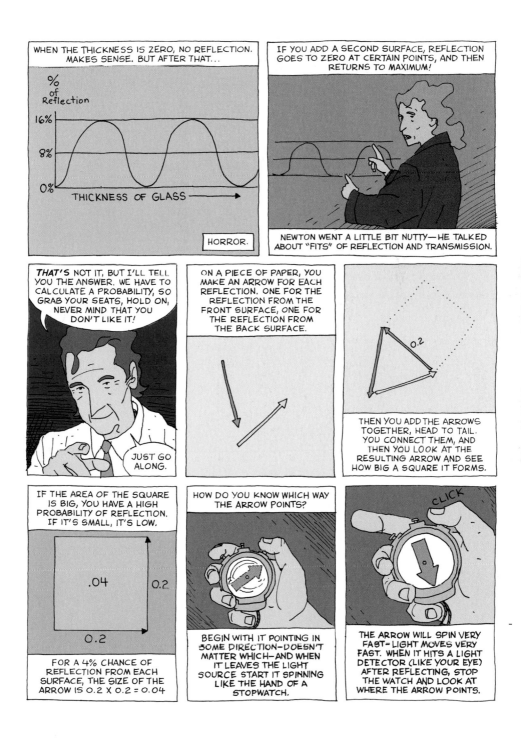

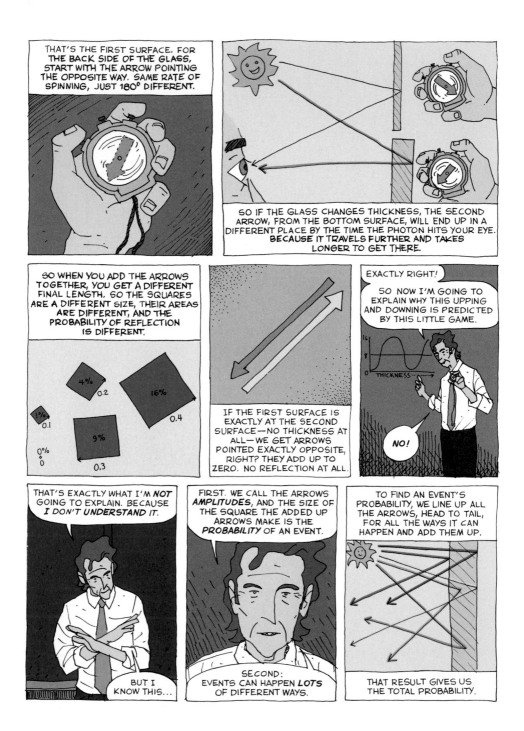

THAT'S THE FIRST SURFACE. FOR THE BACK SIDE OF THE GLASS, START WITH THE ARROW POINTING THE OPPOSITE WAY. SAME RATE OF SPINNING, JUST 180° DIFFERENT.

SO IF THE GLASS CHANGES THICKNESS, THE SECOND ARROW, FROM THE BOTTOM SURFACE, WILL END UP IN A DIFFERENT PLACE BY THE TIME THE PHOTON HITS YOUR EYE. BECAUSE IT TRAVELS FURTHER AND TAKES LONGER TO GET THERE.

SO WHEN YOU ADD THE ARROWS TOGETHER, YOU GET A DIFFERENT FINAL LENGTH, SO THE SQUARES ARE A DIFFERENT SIZE, THEIR AREAS ARE DIFFERENT, AND THE PROBABILITY OF REFLECTION IS DIFFERENT.

4% 0.2
16% 0.4
1% 0.1
9% 0.3
0% 0

IF THE FIRST SURFACE IS EXACTLY AT THE SECOND SURFACE—NO THICKNESS AT ALL—WE GET ARROWS POINTED EXACTLY OPPOSITE, RIGHT? THEY ADD UP TO ZERO. NO REFLECTION AT ALL.

EXACTLY RIGHT!

SO NOW I'M GOING TO EXPLAIN WHY THIS UPPING AND DOWNING IS PREDICTED BY THIS LITTLE GAME.

16
8
0
THICKNESS

NO!

THAT'S EXACTLY WHAT I'M *NOT* GOING TO EXPLAIN. BECAUSE *I DON'T UNDERSTAND IT.*

BUT I KNOW THIS...

FIRST, WE CALL THE ARROWS *AMPLITUDES*, AND THE SIZE OF THE SQUARE THE ADDED UP ARROWS MAKE IS THE *PROBABILITY* OF AN EVENT.

SECOND: EVENTS CAN HAPPEN *LOTS* OF DIFFERENT WAYS.

TO FIND AN EVENT'S PROBABILITY, WE LINE UP ALL THE ARROWS, HEAD TO TAIL, FOR ALL THE WAYS IT CAN HAPPEN AND ADD THEM UP.

THAT RESULT GIVES US THE TOTAL PROBABILITY.

THIRD: IT WORKS FOR MORE THAN LIGHT! IT WORKS FOR ELECTRONS TOO, AND ELECTRONS INTERACTING WITH PHOTONS OR OTHER ELECTRONS.

AND THAT'S QED.

IT EXPLAINS LIGHT TRAVELING IN A STRAIGHT LINE, LIGHT FOCUSED BY LENSES, LIGHT REFLECTING OFF MIRRORS AT THE SAME ANGLE IT CAME IN, MIRAGES...

EVERYTHING. IT'S ALL IN THERE.

REALLY, THE CHALLENGE IS TO CONTROL MYSELF AND NOT SHOW ALL THE EXAMPLES!

BUT, I GOTTA SHOW AT LEAST ONE, SO LET'S START WITH A MIRROR.

SCREEN

EXPECTED PATH

ANGLE OF INCIDENCE

ANGLE OF REFLECTION

OF REFLECTION

MIRROR

YOU KNOW... OR YOU THINK YOU KNOW, THAT WHEN LIGHT STARTS AT ONE POINT, REFLECTS OFF A MIRROR, AND IS DETECTED AT ANOTHER POINT, THE PATH IS LIKE THIS.

BUT SUPPOSE THE SURFACE IS DIVIDED INTO LITTLE SECTIONS. NOW THERE ARE SEVERAL WAYS A PHOTON CAN GO FROM THE SOURCE TO YOUR EYE.

A B C D E F G H I J K L M N O P

IT CAN GO TOWARD THIS SECTION, AND THEN BOUNCE OVER TO HERE.

I CAN HEAR YOU SAYING IT AGAIN, BUT I'M NOT CRAZY.

THAT'S WHAT REALLY HAPPENS.

YOU'RE CRAZY!

THE ANGLE AIN'T EQUAL.

I DON'T LIKE IT!

ANOTHER POSSIBILITY IS IT COULD COME HERE OR HERE OR HERE AND GO— OR IT COULD COME WHEREVER YOU'D LIKE IT TO COME, AND GO WHEREVER.

AND IT CAN GO OVER HERE AND GO, AND ON AND ON AND ON TO ALL POSSIBILITIES.

A B C D E F G H I J K L M N O P Q R S

THE IDEA IS THERE'S ARROWS—AMPLITUDES —FOR EACH OF THESE PATHS, AND WE USE THEM ALL TO FIGURE OUT THE TOTAL PROBABILITY IT GETS THERE.

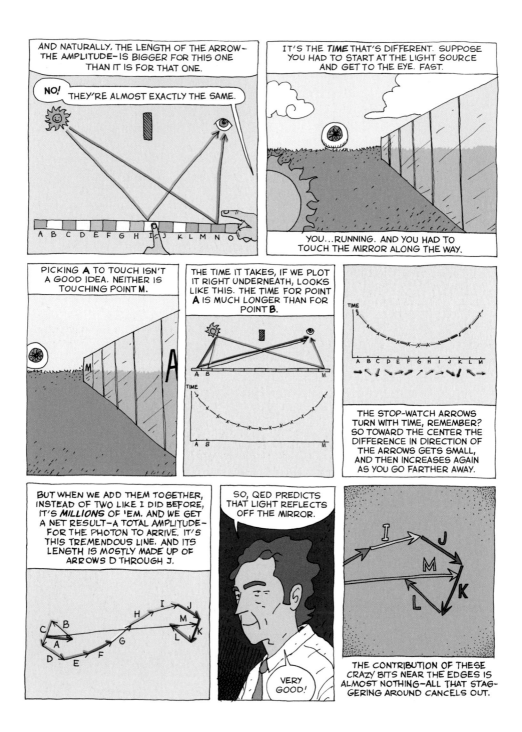

AND NATURALLY, THE LENGTH OF THE ARROW—THE AMPLITUDE—IS BIGGER FOR THIS ONE THAN IT IS FOR THAT ONE.

NO! THEY'RE ALMOST EXACTLY THE SAME.

A B C D E F G H I J K L M N O

IT'S THE *TIME* THAT'S DIFFERENT. SUPPOSE YOU HAD TO START AT THE LIGHT SOURCE AND GET TO THE EYE. FAST.

YOU...RUNNING. AND YOU HAD TO TOUCH THE MIRROR ALONG THE WAY.

PICKING **A** TO TOUCH ISN'T A GOOD IDEA. NEITHER IS TOUCHING POINT **M**.

M

A

THE TIME IT TAKES, IF WE PLOT IT RIGHT UNDERNEATH, LOOKS LIKE THIS. THE TIME FOR POINT **A** IS MUCH LONGER THAN FOR POINT **B**.

A B M

TIME

A B M

TIME

A B C D E F G H I J K L M

THE STOP-WATCH ARROWS TURN WITH TIME, REMEMBER? SO TOWARD THE CENTER THE DIFFERENCE IN DIRECTION OF THE ARROWS GETS SMALL, AND THEN INCREASES AGAIN AS YOU GO FARTHER AWAY.

BUT WHEN WE ADD THEM TOGETHER, INSTEAD OF TWO LIKE I DID BEFORE, IT'S *MILLIONS* OF 'EM. AND WE GET A NET RESULT—A TOTAL AMPLITUDE—FOR THE PHOTON TO ARRIVE. IT'S THIS TREMENDOUS LINE. AND ITS LENGTH IS MOSTLY MADE UP OF ARROWS D THROUGH J.

C B
A
D E F G H I J
M
L K

SO, QED PREDICTS THAT LIGHT REFLECTS OFF THE MIRROR.

VERY GOOD!

I
J
M
L K

THE CONTRIBUTION OF THESE CRAZY BITS NEAR THE EDGES IS ALMOST NOTHING—ALL THAT STAGGERING AROUND CANCELS OUT.

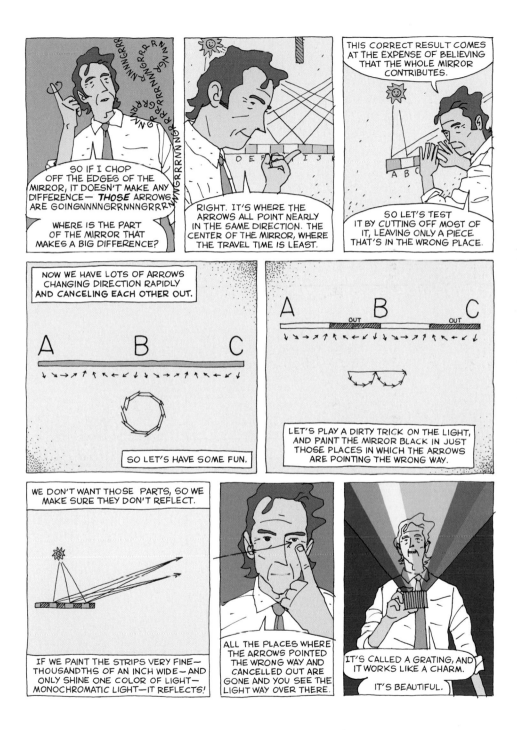

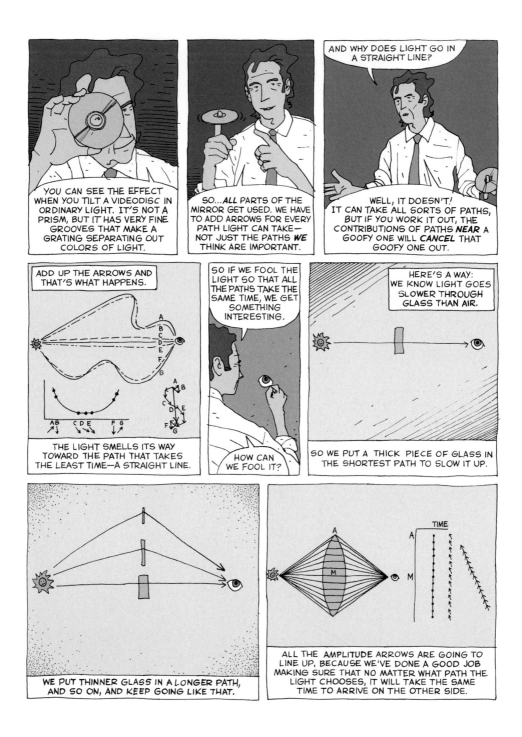

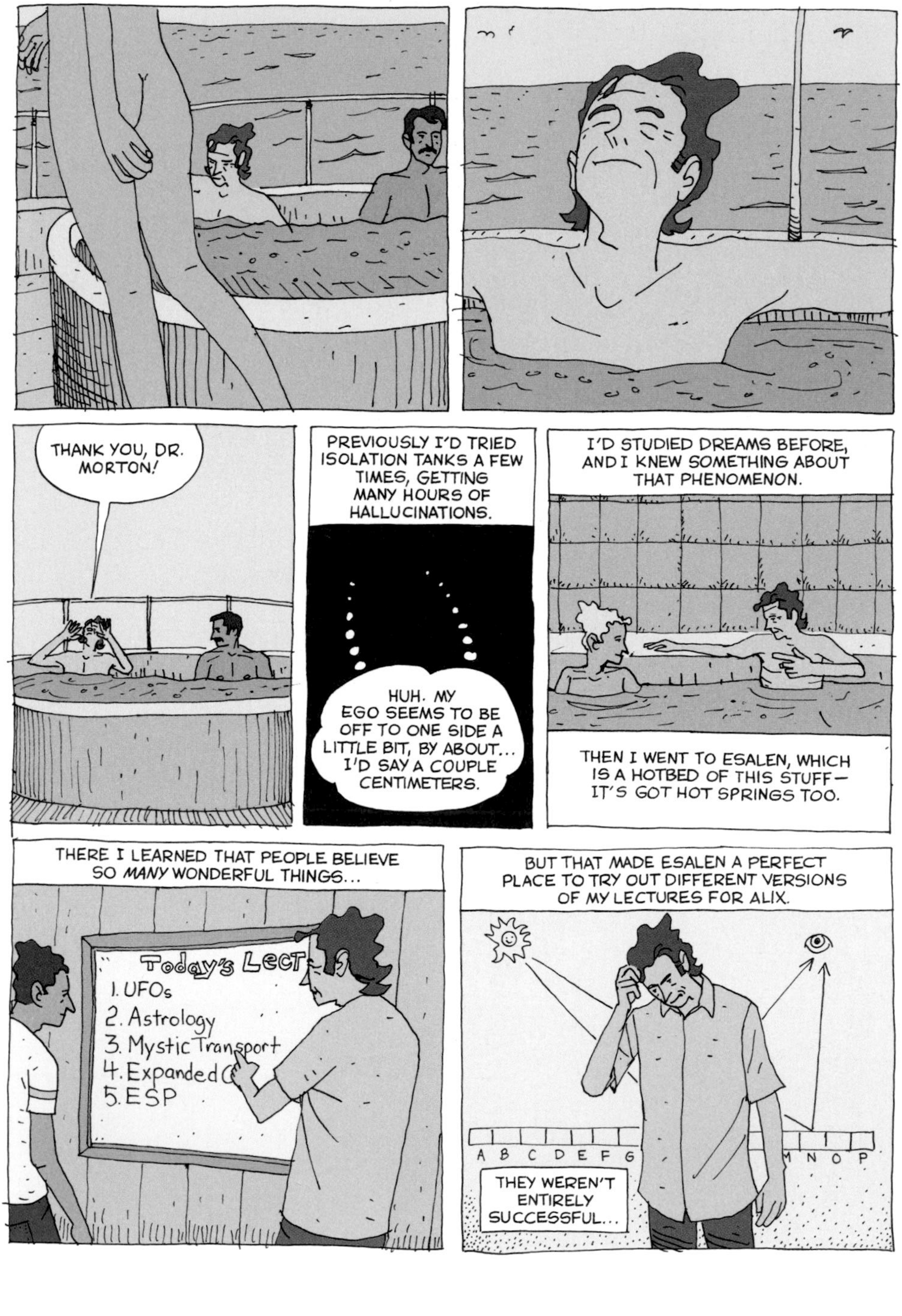
THANK YOU, DR. MORTON!
PREVIOUSLY I'D TRIED ISOLATION TANKS A FEW TIMES, GETTING MANY HOURS OF HALLUCINATIONS.
HUH. MY EGO SEEMS TO BE OFF TO ONE SIDE A LITTLE BIT, BY ABOUT... I'D SAY A COUPLE CENTIMETERS.
I'D STUDIED DREAMS BEFORE, AND I KNEW SOMETHING ABOUT THAT PHENOMENON.
THEN I WENT TO ESALEN, WHICH IS A HOTBED OF THIS STUFF— IT'S GOT HOT SPRINGS TOO.
THERE I LEARNED THAT PEOPLE BELIEVE SO *MANY* WONDERFUL THINGS...
Today's Lect
1. UFOs
2. Astrology
3. Mystic Transport
4. Expanded C
5. ESP
BUT THAT MADE ESALEN A PERFECT PLACE TO TRY OUT DIFFERENT VERSIONS OF MY LECTURES FOR ALIX.
A B C D E F G
M N O P
THEY WEREN'T ENTIRELY SUCCESSFUL...

215

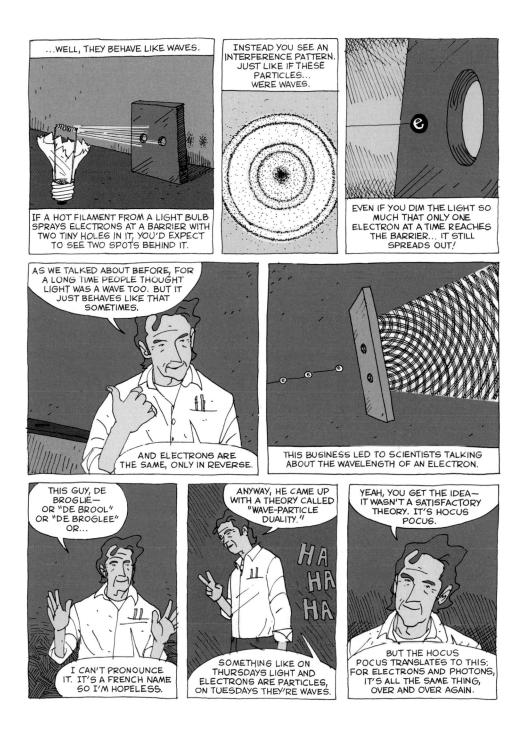

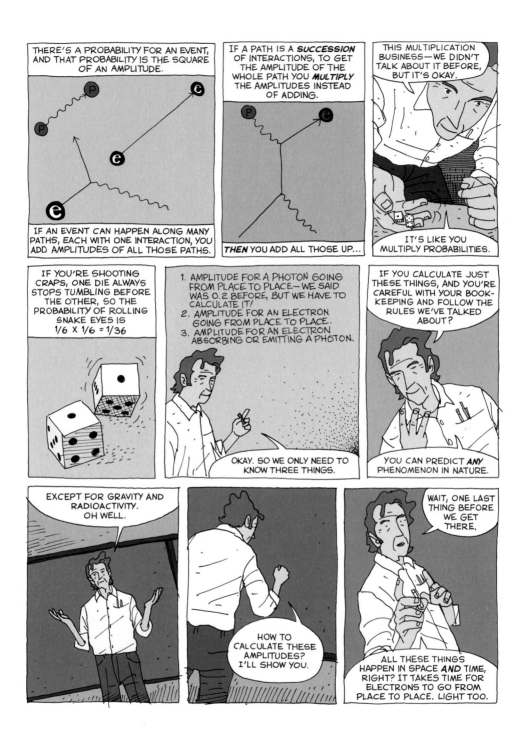

THERE'S A PROBABILITY FOR AN EVENT, AND THAT PROBABILITY IS THE SQUARE OF AN AMPLITUDE.

IF AN EVENT CAN HAPPEN ALONG MANY PATHS, EACH WITH ONE INTERACTION, YOU ADD AMPLITUDES OF ALL THOSE PATHS.

IF A PATH IS A *SUCCESSION* OF INTERACTIONS, TO GET THE AMPLITUDE OF THE WHOLE PATH YOU *MULTIPLY* THE AMPLITUDES INSTEAD OF ADDING.

THEN YOU ADD ALL THOSE UP...

THIS MULTIPLICATION BUSINESS—WE DIDN'T TALK ABOUT IT BEFORE, BUT IT'S OKAY.

IT'S LIKE YOU MULTIPLY PROBABILITIES.

IF YOU'RE SHOOTING CRAPS, ONE DIE ALWAYS STOPS TUMBLING BEFORE THE OTHER, SO THE PROBABILITY OF ROLLING SNAKE EYES IS 1/6 X 1/6 = 1/36

1. AMPLITUDE FOR A PHOTON GOING FROM PLACE TO PLACE.— WE SAID WAS 0.2 BEFORE, BUT WE HAVE TO CALCULATE IT!
2. AMPLITUDE FOR AN ELECTRON GOING FROM PLACE TO PLACE.
3. AMPLITUDE FOR AN ELECTRON ABSORBING OR EMITTING A PHOTON.

OKAY. SO WE ONLY NEED TO KNOW THREE THINGS.

IF YOU CALCULATE JUST THESE THINGS, AND YOU'RE CAREFUL WITH YOUR BOOK-KEEPING AND FOLLOW THE RULES WE'VE TALKED ABOUT?

YOU CAN PREDICT *ANY* PHENOMENON IN NATURE.

EXCEPT FOR GRAVITY AND RADIOACTIVITY. OH WELL.

HOW TO CALCULATE THESE AMPLITUDES? I'LL SHOW YOU.

WAIT, ONE LAST THING BEFORE WE GET THERE.

ALL THESE THINGS HAPPEN IN SPACE *AND* TIME, RIGHT? IT TAKES TIME FOR ELECTRONS TO GO FROM PLACE TO PLACE, LIGHT TOO.

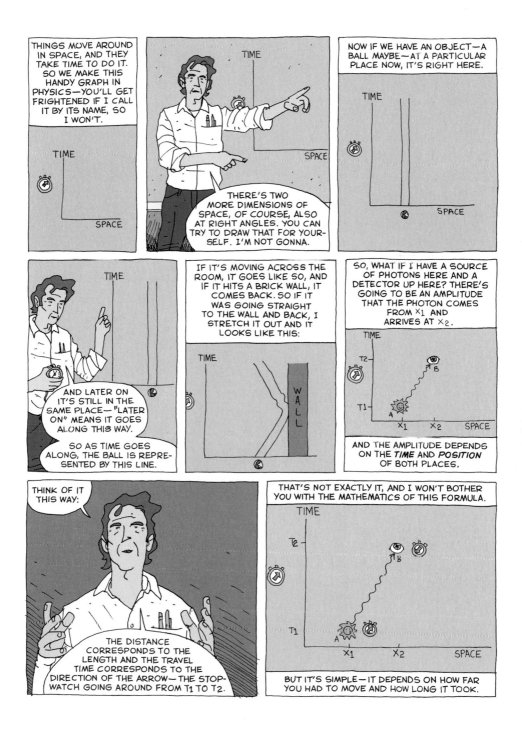

THINGS MOVE AROUND IN SPACE, AND THEY TAKE TIME TO DO IT. SO WE MAKE THIS HANDY GRAPH IN PHYSICS—YOU'LL GET FRIGHTENED IF I CALL IT BY ITS NAME, SO I WON'T.

TIME

SPACE

TIME

SPACE

THERE'S TWO MORE DIMENSIONS OF SPACE, OF COURSE, ALSO AT RIGHT ANGLES. YOU CAN TRY TO DRAW THAT FOR YOUR- SELF. I'M NOT GONNA.

NOW IF WE HAVE AN OBJECT—A BALL MAYBE—AT A PARTICULAR PLACE NOW, IT'S RIGHT HERE.

TIME

SPACE

TIME

AND LATER ON IT'S STILL IN THE SAME PLACE—"LATER ON" MEANS IT GOES ALONG THIS WAY.

SO AS TIME GOES ALONG, THE BALL IS REPRE- SENTED BY THIS LINE.

IF IT'S MOVING ACROSS THE ROOM, IT GOES LIKE SO, AND IF IT HITS A BRICK WALL, IT COMES BACK. SO IF IT WAS GOING STRAIGHT TO THE WALL AND BACK, I STRETCH IT OUT AND IT LOOKS LIKE THIS:

TIME

WALL

SO, WHAT IF I HAVE A SOURCE OF PHOTONS HERE AND A DETECTOR UP HERE? THERE'S GOING TO BE AN AMPLITUDE THAT THE PHOTON COMES FROM x_1 AND ARRIVES AT x_2.

TIME

T_2

T_1

B

A

x_1 x_2 SPACE

AND THE AMPLITUDE DEPENDS ON THE *TIME* AND *POSITION* OF BOTH PLACES.

THINK OF IT THIS WAY:

THE DISTANCE CORRESPONDS TO THE LENGTH AND THE TRAVEL TIME CORRESPONDS TO THE DIRECTION OF THE ARROW—THE STOP- WATCH GOING AROUND FROM T_1 TO T_2.

THAT'S NOT EXACTLY IT, AND I WON'T BOTHER YOU WITH THE MATHEMATICS OF THIS FORMULA.

TIME

T_2

B

T_1

A

x_1 x_2 SPACE

BUT IT'S SIMPLE—IT DEPENDS ON HOW FAR YOU HAD TO MOVE AND HOW LONG IT TOOK.

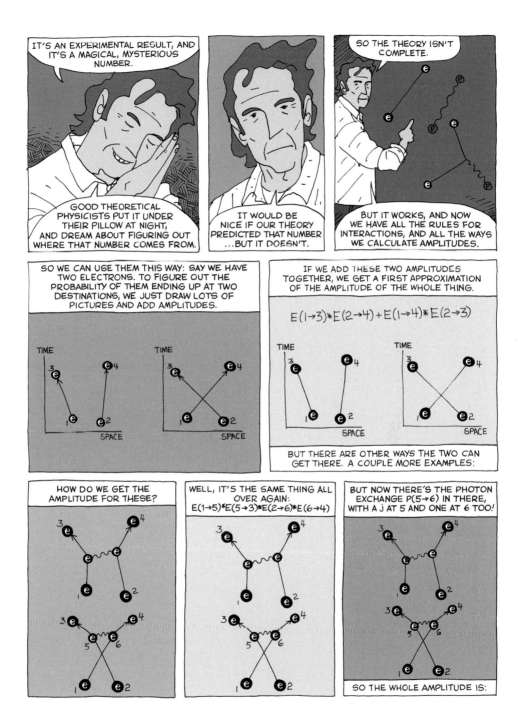

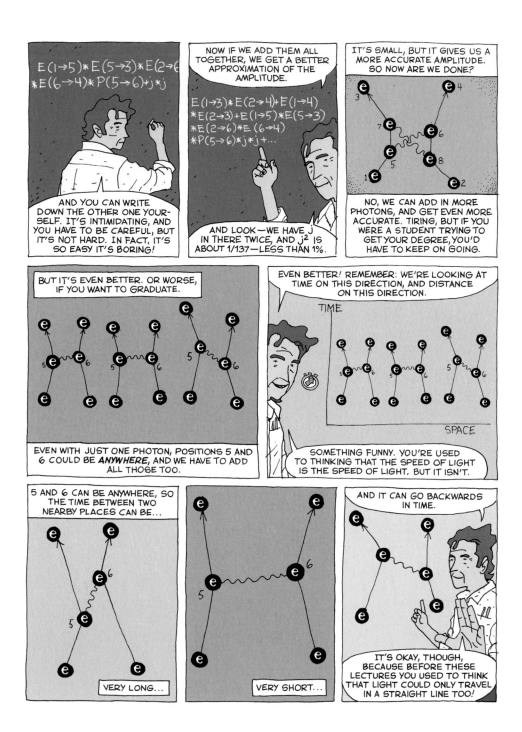

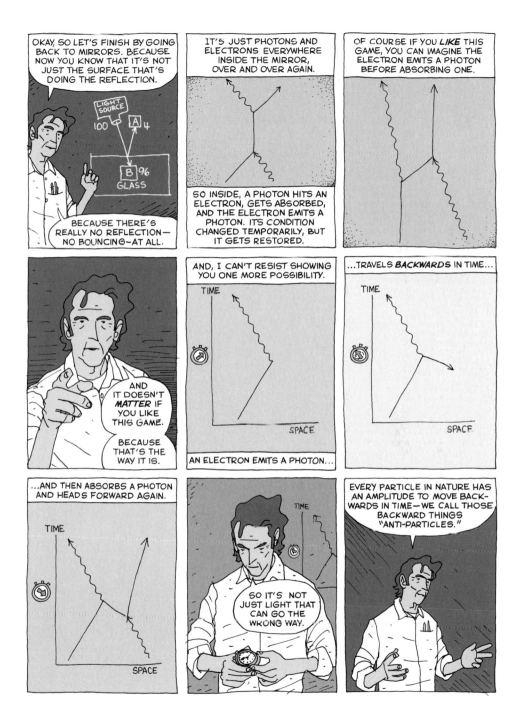

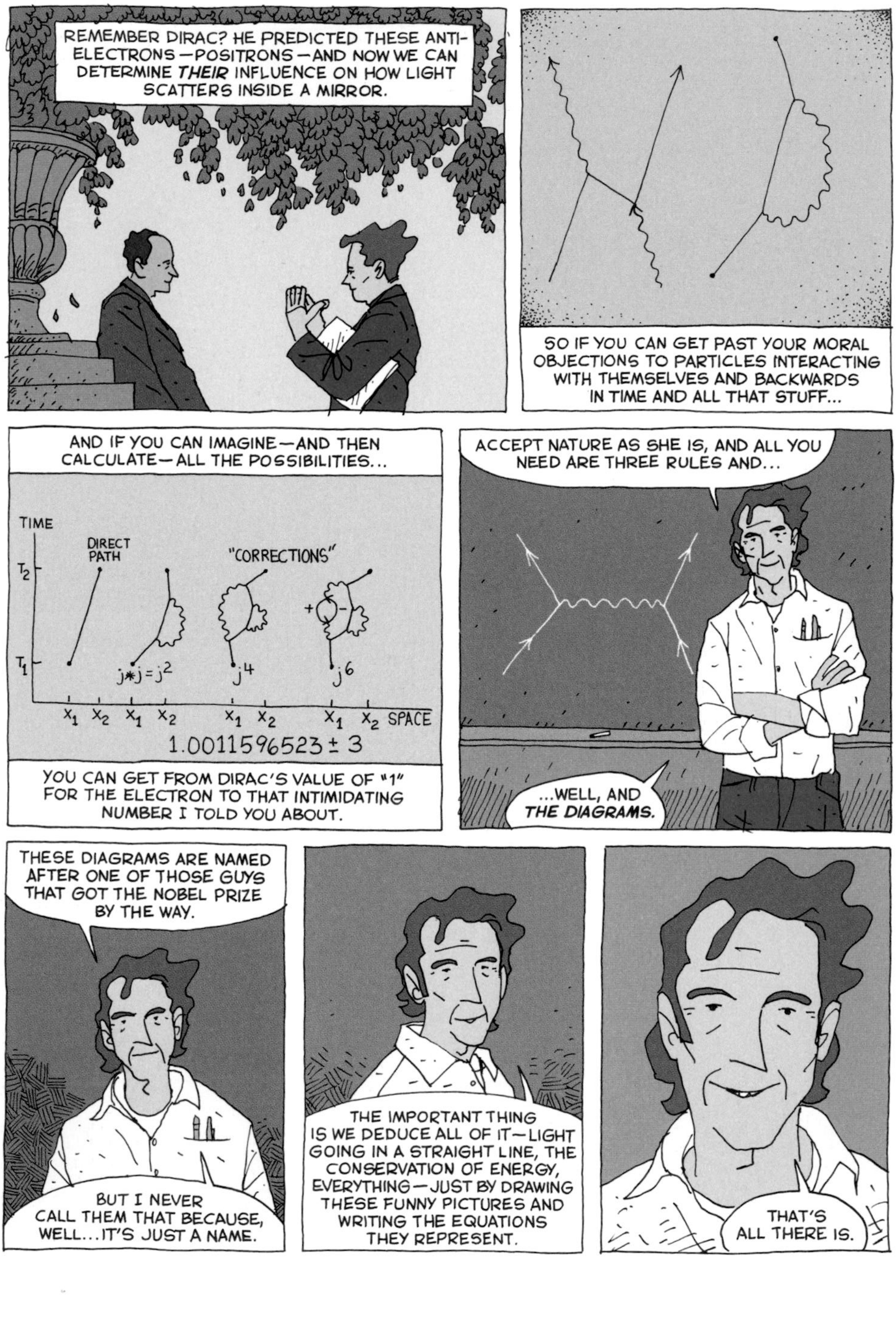
REMEMBER DIRAC? HE PREDICTED THESE ANTI-ELECTRONS—POSITRONS—AND NOW WE CAN DETERMINE *THEIR* INFLUENCE ON HOW LIGHT SCATTERS INSIDE A MIRROR.
SO IF YOU CAN GET PAST YOUR MORAL OBJECTIONS TO PARTICLES INTERACTING WITH THEMSELVES AND BACKWARDS IN TIME AND ALL THAT STUFF...
AND IF YOU CAN IMAGINE—AND THEN CALCULATE—ALL THE POSSIBILITIES...
TIME
DIRECT PATH
"CORRECTIONS"
T_2
T_1
$j*j=j^2$
j^4
j^6
x_1 x_2 x_1 x_2 x_1 x_2 x_1 x_2 SPACE
1.0011596523 ± 3
YOU CAN GET FROM DIRAC'S VALUE OF "1" FOR THE ELECTRON TO THAT INTIMIDATING NUMBER I TOLD YOU ABOUT.
ACCEPT NATURE AS SHE IS, AND ALL YOU NEED ARE THREE RULES AND...
...WELL, AND *THE DIAGRAMS.*
THESE DIAGRAMS ARE NAMED AFTER ONE OF THOSE GUYS THAT GOT THE NOBEL PRIZE BY THE WAY.
BUT I NEVER CALL THEM THAT BECAUSE, WELL... IT'S JUST A NAME.
THE IMPORTANT THING IS WE DEDUCE ALL OF IT—LIGHT GOING IN A STRAIGHT LINE, THE CONSERVATION OF ENERGY, EVERYTHING—JUST BY DRAWING THESE FUNNY PICTURES AND WRITING THE EQUATIONS THEY REPRESENT.
THAT'S ALL THERE IS.

MEEEEEEEEEE!

YES, OF COURSE, MR. FEYNMAN. I WAS WONDERING IF ANYONE *ELSE* WOULD VOLUNTEER TO BE HYPNOTIZED.

MARILYN TELLS ME THAT YOU'RE A PROFESSIONAL GAMBLER, NICK.

THAT'S RIGHT—THEY CALL ME "THE GREEK."

SURE. BUT WHAT I WANT TO KNOW IS HOW DO YOU DO THAT? I'VE FIGURED THE ODDS FOR CRAPS, SEE...

IT'S A COMMISSION FOR A MASSAGE PARLOR. SEE, THEY WANT THIS TOREADOR...

THIS BOOK ALSO DID VERY WELL.

I GOT A LOT OF MAIL, AND IT WAS TRANSLATED INTO A BUNCH OF LANGUAGES.

BETTE, I'LL HAND SIGN FOR THIS KID.

THAT GAVE ME A KICK, BUT NOT EVERYBODY UNDERSTOOD MY PURPOSE IN WRITING THE BOOK.

"...SOME PARTS ARE NOT SO IMPORTANT FOR THE GERMAN READER."??

NOTHING AT ALL IS *IMPORTANT*—TO ANY READER!

TELL 'EM TO GIVE IT TO A TRANSLATOR WITH A SENSE OF HUMOR AND A HEALTHY DISRESPECT FOR POMPOUSNESS.

SCIENCE IT IS NOT!

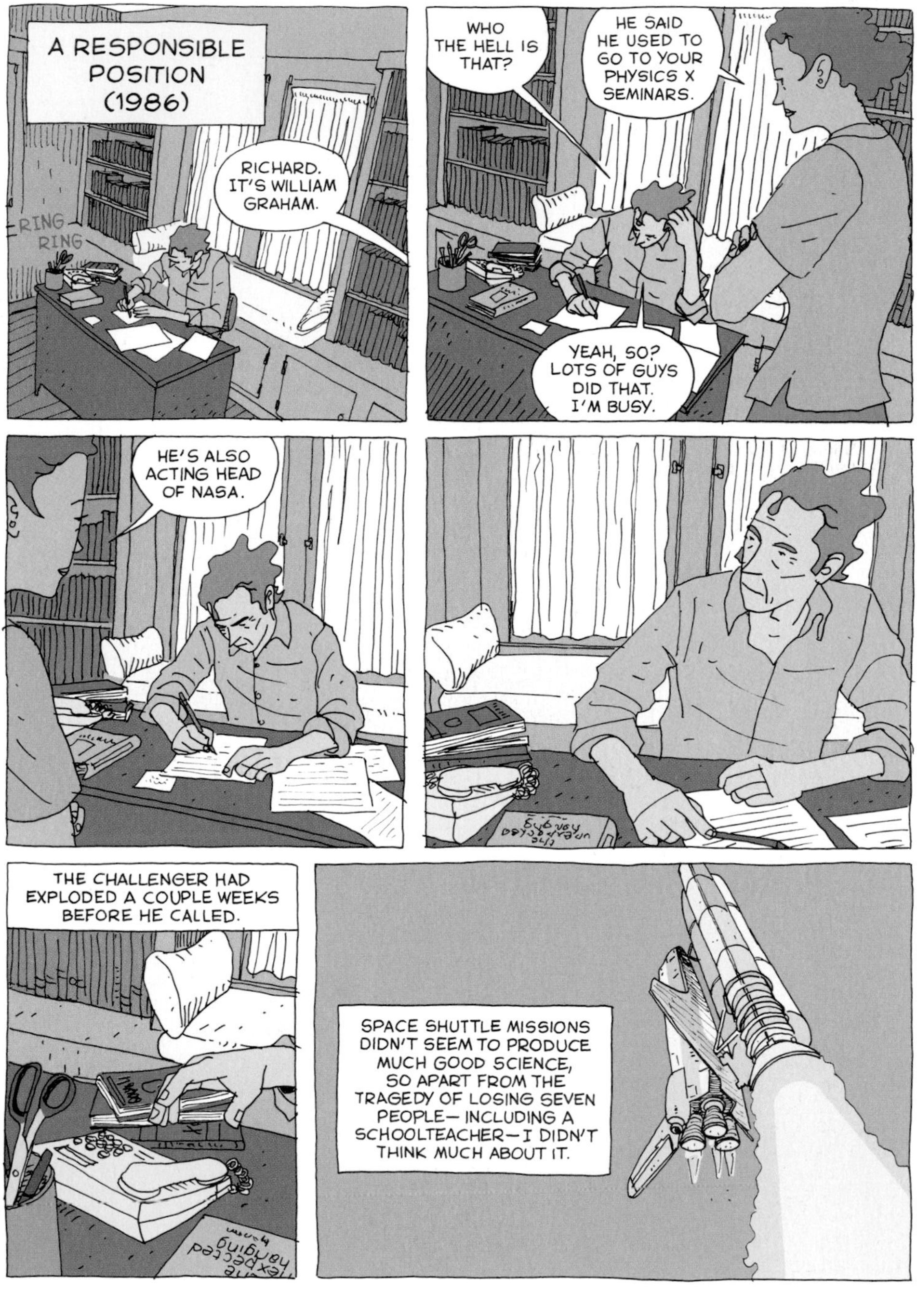
A RESPONSIBLE POSITION (1986)
RING RING
RICHARD. IT'S WILLIAM GRAHAM.
WHO THE HELL IS THAT?
HE SAID HE USED TO GO TO YOUR PHYSICS X SEMINARS.
YEAH, SO? LOTS OF GUYS DID THAT. I'M BUSY.
HE'S ALSO ACTING HEAD OF NASA.
THE CHALLENGER HAD EXPLODED A COUPLE WEEKS BEFORE HE CALLED.
SPACE SHUTTLE MISSIONS DIDN'T SEEM TO PRODUCE MUCH GOOD SCIENCE, SO APART FROM THE TRAGEDY OF LOSING SEVEN PEOPLE— INCLUDING A SCHOOLTEACHER—I DIDN'T THINK MUCH ABOUT IT.

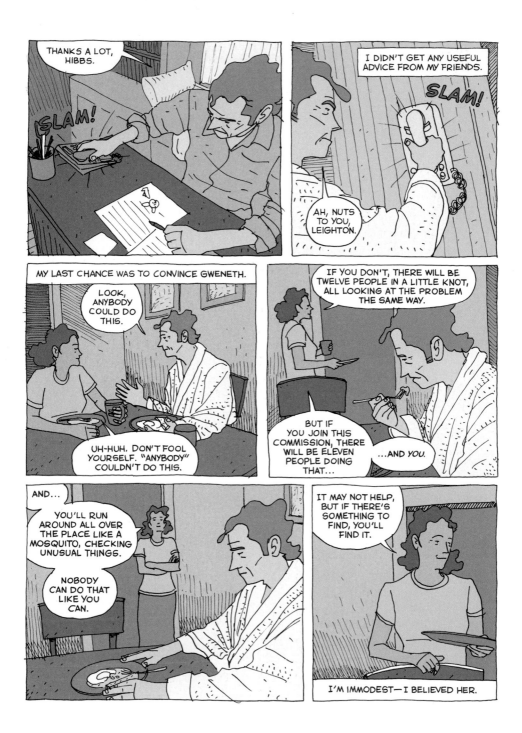

SO ON MONDAY I GOT APPOINTED TO THE "ROGERS COMMISSION" AND ON TUESDAY AL HIBBS ASSEMBLED SOME GUYS AT NASA'S JET PROPULSION LAB TO BRIEF ME.

IT WAS REALLY QUITE EXCITING.

AND THEY REALLY KNEW WHAT THEY WERE DOING: MY SECOND LINE OF NOTES SAID "O-RINGS SHOW SOME SCORCHING."

MY WAY OF LEARNING THINGS IS YOU DON'T JUST SIT THERE.

NO, NO. IT'S LIKE THIS...

YOU ASK LOTS OF DUMB-SOUNDING QUESTIONS, GET QUICK ANSWERS, AND LEARN WHAT TO ASK TO GET THE NEXT PIECE OF INFORMATION YOU NEED.

I TOOK THE RED-EYE TO WASHINGTON THE NEXT DAY, AND GOT LOST ON MY WAY TO THE FIRST FORMAL MEETING.

FINALLY I MADE IT TO BILL GRAHAM'S OFFICE, AND THEY HELPED ME FIND WHERE THE COMMISSION WAS.

I DON'T KNOW... HE SIMPLY WANDERED IN HERE!

WHEN I GOT THERE THE ONLY ONE I'D EVER HEARD OF BEFORE WAS NEIL ARMSTRONG, THE MOON MAN.

I DIDN'T RECOGNIZE WHO SALLY RIDE WAS UNTIL LATER.

235

BUT IT TURNS OUT THAT BESIDES MR. ROGERS, THE GUY HEADING THE COMMISSION, MOST EVERYBODY HAD TECHNICAL BACKGROUNDS.

ARMSTRONG WAS AN AERONAUTICAL ENGINEER, FOR INSTANCE. RIDE WAS A PHYSICIST.

EVEN THE GENERAL, KUTYNA, HAD AN AERO-NAUTICS DEGREE FROM MIT. SO IT WAS GOOD.

CAN SOME-ONE TELL ME WHERE THE NEAREST METRO STATION IS?

ANY GENERAL THAT RIDES THE SUBWAY CAN'T BE ALL BAD!

I DON'T LIKE UNIFORMS MUCH, BUT I LIKED HIM FOR THAT, AND FOR OTHER STUFF HE DID.

THE NEXT MORNING, THEY SENT A LIMO FOR ME—THE FIRST "OFFICIAL" MEETING WAS GOING TO BE ON TV, AFTER ALL.

I UNDERSTAND A LOT OF IMPORTANT PEOPLE ARE ON YOUR COMMISSION.

YEAH, I S'POSE...

WELL, COULD YOU DO ME A FAVOR? I COLLECT AUTOGRAPHS.

SURE. I'D BE HAPPY TO...

COULD YOU POINT OUT NEIL ARMSTRONG FOR ME?

HAH!

236

WHEN WE GOT THERE, I SAT NEXT TO GENERAL KUTYNA.

SALLY RIDE

AL KEEL

RICHARD FEYNMAN

COPILOT TO PILOT.

THE TV CAMERAS WERE POINTING AT US EVERY TIME WE SCRATCHED OUR NOSES.

COMB YOUR HAIR.

WHAT TH—?

RICHARD FEYNMAN

KUTYNA THOUGHT I'D BE ANGRY, BUT WHAT THE HELL.

HE HAD A PRETTY GOOD IDEA OF HOW WASHINGTON WORKS.

YOU GOTTA COMB?

I DON'T, SO HE BRIEFED ME ON THE BIG PICTURE.

...AND SINCE YOU'VE WORKED ON SECRET PROJECTS, I CAN GET YOU CLEARED.

ABSOLUTELY NOT.

I DON'T DO THAT ANYMORE, AND I DON'T WANT MY BRAIN CLOGGED WITH STUFF I CAN'T TALK ABOUT.

HE TAUGHT ME A LOT ABOUT THE SPACE PROGRAM, AND MILITARY APPLICATIONS...

...AND POLITICS.

HEY, I DON'T WANT TO KNOW THAT STUFF EITHER.

YOU SHOULD. POLITICS MATTERS IF YOU WORK HERE.

LOOK, I'M VULNERABLE BECAUSE OF MY CONNECTIONS TO THE SHUTTLE PROGRAM.

SALLY RIDE STILL HAS A JOB AT NASA, CHUCK YEAGER HAS CONNECTIONS IN THE AIR FORCE, AND SO ON...

SO THAT WAS IT. I CALLED BILL GRAHAM.

THE NEXT MORNING, BEFORE ANOTHER TELEVISED MEETING, I PUT ON MY *COSTUME* —THE ONE THAT MADE ME LESS CONSPICUOUS AMONG THE NATIVES...

HEY, I NEED TO GET TO A HARDWARE STORE.

SIR, WE'RE RIGHT BETWEEN THE WHITE HOUSE AND THE CAPITOL. DO YOU REALLY THINK...?

BUT HE FOUND ONE, AND I BOUGHT STUFF NASA ADMINISTRATORS DON'T USUALLY KEEP IN THEIR OFFICES.

ARDWARE
SALE

WHAT I KNEW BILL *DID* HAVE WAS AN EXAMPLE OF THE JOINT USED ON THE CHALLENGER TANK THAT EXPLODED.

SO...I'M ASHAMED TO ADMIT THAT I CHEATED, BUT I COULDN'T RESIST:

GRAHAM

I TRIED THE EXPERIMENT *BEFORE* GETTING IN FRONT OF THE CAMERAS.

IT WOULD HAVE BEEN MORE IN-TER-ES-TING TO WAIT FOR THE MEETING.

WILLIAM ROGERS   SALLY RIDE   AL KEEL   RICHARD FEYNMAN

BUT IT WAS OKAY, SINCE NOBODY KNEW WHAT I WAS UP TO ANYWAY.

I BELIEVE THAT HAS SOME SIGNIFICANCE FOR OUR PROBLEM.

DURING THE LUNCH BREAK, THE QUESTIONS I GOT WERE DOPEY. BECAUSE OF WHEN I DID THE DEMONSTRATION, I DIDN'T THINK ANYBODY UNDERSTOOD THE SIGNIFICANCE.

THAT MADE ME MAD.

YOU SHOULD HAVE LET ME TALK WHEN I WANTED TO.

CONFERE

YOU RUINED MY EXPERIMENT.

BUT THAT NIGHT IT WAS ON ALL THE NEWS SHOWS, AND THE NEWSPAPER ARTICLES THE NEXT DAY EXPLAINED IT EXACTLY RIGHT.

WHAT ARE THE ODDS? (MARCH-APRIL 1986)

HEY, KUTYNA.

The New York Times

YOU'RE NOT ALL BAD!

SOME OF THE OTHER PEOPLE ON THE COMMISSION DIDN'T LIKE IT AS MUCH, THOUGH.

FEYNMAN'S BECOMING A REAL PAIN IN THE ASS.

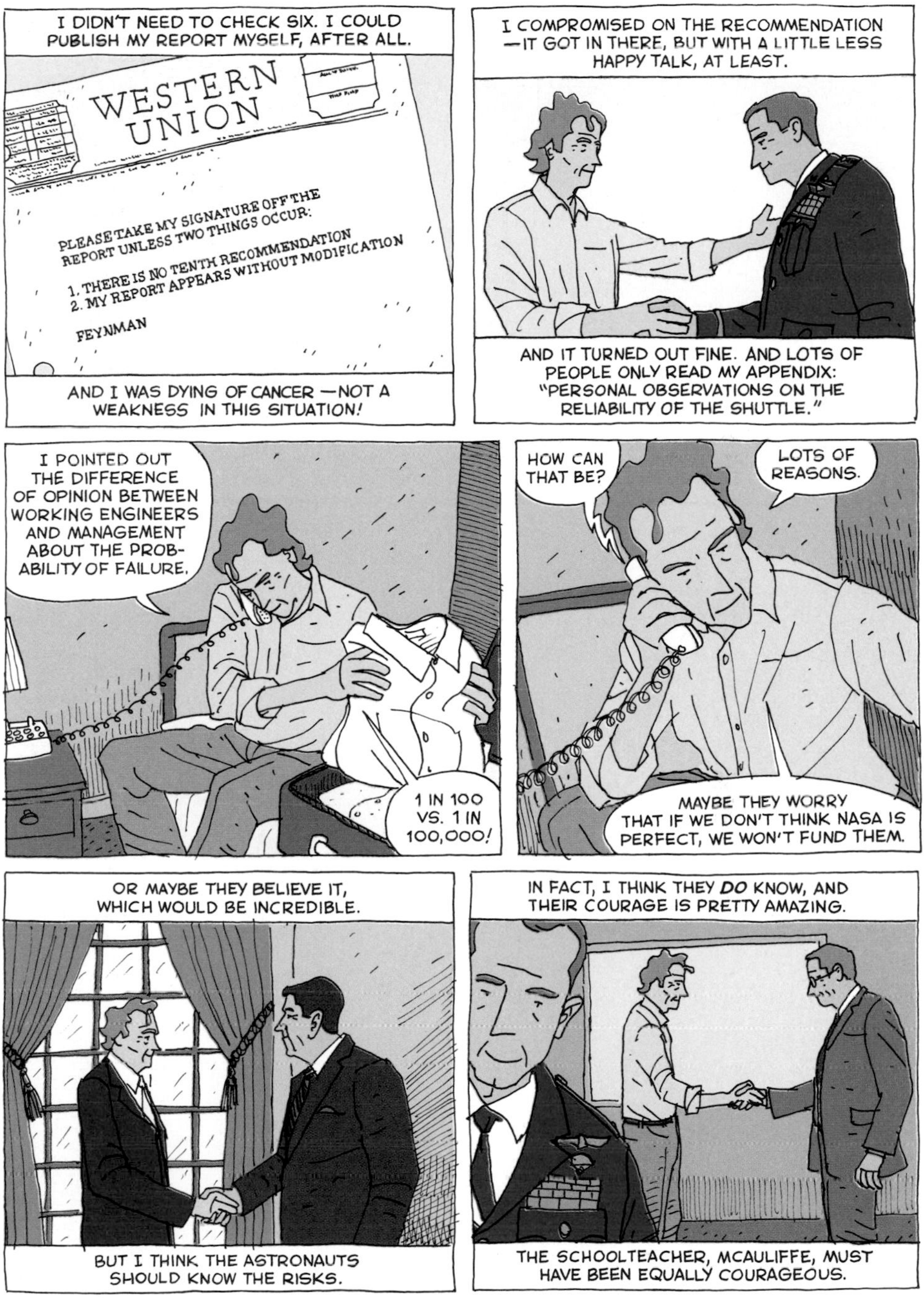

I DIDN'T NEED TO CHECK SIX. I COULD PUBLISH MY REPORT MYSELF, AFTER ALL.
WESTERN UNION
PLEASE TAKE MY SIGNATURE OFF THE REPORT UNLESS TWO THINGS OCCUR:
1. THERE IS NO TENTH RECOMMENDATION
2. MY REPORT APPEARS WITHOUT MODIFICATION
FEYNMAN
AND I WAS DYING OF CANCER —NOT A WEAKNESS IN THIS SITUATION!
I COMPROMISED ON THE RECOMMENDATION —IT GOT IN THERE, BUT WITH A LITTLE LESS HAPPY TALK, AT LEAST.
AND IT TURNED OUT FINE. AND LOTS OF PEOPLE ONLY READ MY APPENDIX: "PERSONAL OBSERVATIONS ON THE RELIABILITY OF THE SHUTTLE."
I POINTED OUT THE DIFFERENCE OF OPINION BETWEEN WORKING ENGINEERS AND MANAGEMENT ABOUT THE PROBABILITY OF FAILURE.
1 IN 100 VS. 1 IN 100,000!
HOW CAN THAT BE?
LOTS OF REASONS.
MAYBE THEY WORRY THAT IF WE DON'T THINK NASA IS PERFECT, WE WON'T FUND THEM.
OR MAYBE THEY BELIEVE IT, WHICH WOULD BE INCREDIBLE.
BUT I THINK THE ASTRONAUTS SHOULD KNOW THE RISKS.
IN FACT, I THINK THEY DO KNOW, AND THEIR COURAGE IS PRETTY AMAZING.
THE SCHOOLTEACHER, MCAULIFFE, MUST HAVE BEEN EQUALLY COURAGEOUS.

SHE TRAINED WITH ASTRONAUTS. SHE HAD TO KNOW THE TRUE SITUATION BETTER THAN NASA OFFICIALS.

NASA HAS TO DEAL IN A WORLD OF REALITY TO UNDERSTAND TECHNOLOGICAL WEAKNESSES WELL ENOUGH TO ACTIVELY TRY TO ELIMINATE THEM.

THEY SHOULD PROPOSE ONLY REALISTIC FLIGHT SCHEDULES THEY HAVE A REASONABLE CHANCE OF MEETING.

IF THAT MEANS WE WOULDN'T SUPPORT THEM, WELL... SO BE IT.

FOR A SUCCESSFUL TECHNOLOGY, REALITY MUST TAKE PRECEDENCE OVER PUBLIC RELATIONS, FOR NATURE CANNOT BE FOOLED.

THAT WAS IT. I WAS DONE. I ONLY GAVE TWO INTERVIEWS— ONE TO A LOCAL PAPER, ONE TO THE *NATIONAL ENQUIRER*.

...HEY, IF I SAID SOMETHING DOPEY AND THEY QUOTE IT, NOBODY WILL BLAME *ME!*

IT'S GOOD TO BE HOME, BUT I'M GOING TO LEAVE THIS BAG PACKED...

WE'RE GOING TO KYZYL!

RICHARD FEYNMAN DIDN'T MAKE IT TO TUVA.
THE OFFICIAL, FORMAL INVITATION FROM MOSCOW PERMITTING THE VISIT
WAS DATED FEBRUARY 19, 1988—FOUR DAYS AFTER HE DIED.

HIS LAST WORDS, UPON FORCING HIMSELF AWAKE FROM A COMA:

"I'D HATE TO DIE TWICE. IT'S SO BORING."

(ALMOST COMPLETE*) BIBLIOGRAPHY & EARLY SKETCHES

OUR STACK OF FEYNMAN MATERIAL IS OVER A METER HIGH AND RISING.
YOURS MAY NOT GROW THAT TALL, BUT IF YOU LIKED THIS STORY, YOU'LL
ENJOY THE FOLLOWING...AND BE SURPRISED AT HOW MUCH WE HAD TO
LEAVE OUT. SO PLEASE READ MORE, STARTING WITH THE BOOKS BY
FEYNMAN HIMSELF:

THE CHARACTER OF PHYSICAL LAW (CAMBRIDGE, MA: MIT PRESS, 1965).
    THE PERFECT BOOK TO READ TO GET A FEEL FOR QUANTUM
    PHYSICS. OUR OPENING SCENE CAME FROM AN ANECDOTE
    RECOUNTED IN JAMES GLEICK'S INTRODUCTION TO THE 1994
    MODERN LIBRARY EDITION, SO SEEK THAT ONE OUT AS WELL.

CLASSIC FEYNMAN: ALL THE ADVENTURES OF A CURIOUS CHARACTER
(NY: W.W. NORTON, 2006).
    I STILL LIKE THE ORIGINAL VOLUMES—*SURELY YOU'RE JOKING,
    MR. FEYNMAN!* (1985) AND *WHAT DO YOU CARE WHAT OTHER
    PEOPLE THINK?* (1988)—SINCE READING FEYNMAN STORIES OUT
    OF ORDER IS A GREAT WAY TO EXPERIENCE A LIFE THE WAY
    IT IS: MESSY, AND WITHOUT A DISCERNABLE PLOT! BUT THIS
    MAY JUST BE BIAS RESULTING FROM THOSE BEING MY FIRST
    EXPOSURE TO THEM, SO IF YOU ONLY GET ONE BOOK, THE
    SPLENDID *CLASSIC FEYNMAN* IS YOUR BEST BET. IT NOT ONLY
    HAS ALL THE STORIES FROM ITS PREDECESSORS, BUT ALSO

INCLUDES A CD OF FEYNMAN TALKING ABOUT "LOS ALAMOS FROM BELOW." CARL AND MICHELLE FEYNMAN CONTRIBUTE TO THIS OMNIBUS EDITION AS WELL, AS DO FREEMAN DYSON AND ALAN ALDA. IT'S GREAT.

THE FEYNMAN LECTURES ON PHYSICS, VOLUMES I–III, BY RICHARD FEYNMAN, ROBERT LEIGHTON, AND MATTHEW SANDS (READING, MA: ADDISON-WESLEY, 1964).

ALONG WITH *QED* (PAGE 255), WITH THIS YOU HAVE ALL OF PHYSICS, RIGHT THERE WAITING FOR YOU. OKAY, NOT REALLY ALL, BUT CLOSE ENOUGH! THE *LECTURES* ARE TOUGHER SLEDDING, AND I'VE ONLY DIPPED INTO THEM HERE AND THERE MYSELF. BUT THEY'RE WELL WORTH THE EFFORT. (I RECOMMEND VOLUME II'S CHAPTER 19, "THE PRINCIPLE OF LEAST ACTION", AS YOUR FIRST SAMPLE.)

FEYNMAN'S TIPS ON PHYSICS, BY RICHARD FEYNMAN, MICHAEL A. GOTTLIEB, AND RALPH LEIGHTON (SAN FRANCISCO: PEARSON ADDISON-WESLEY, 2006).

NOT ONLY DOES FEYNMAN PROVIDE TIPS ON SOLVING PHYSICS PROBLEMS, HE ALSO PROVIDES TIPS ON HOW TO DEAL WITH BEING BELOW AVERAGE. THE LATTER ARE SURPRISINGLY GOOD, GIVEN HE HAD NO PRACTICAL EXPERIENCE WITH THAT POSITION. MATT SANDS' INTRODUCTION, DESCRIBING THE ORIGINS OF THE FEYNMAN LECTURES, IS ALSO ENTERTAINING.

THE MEANING OF IT ALL: THOUGHTS OF A CITIZEN SCIENTIST (READING, MA: PERSEUS BOOKS, 1998).

>THESE LECTURES ARE SOME OF THE RESULTS OF THE MIDDLE-AGED DISEASE FEYNMAN TALKED ABOUT ON PAGE 156. THEY'RE REALLY NOT BAD! THESE CLEANED UP VERSIONS MAKE AN INTERESTING COUNTERPOINT TO THE RAW TRANSCRIPTIONS AVAILABLE IN THE CALTECH ARCHIVES—WHICH I ENJOYED READING AND CONSULTING EVEN MORE, AND SOME OF WHICH MADE THEIR WAY INTO THIS BOOK.

NOBEL ACCEPTANCE AND "THE DEVELOPMENT OF THE SPACE-TIME VIEW OF QUANTUM ELECTRODYNAMICS," FROM *LES PRIX NOBEL EN 1965* (STOCKHOLM: IMPRIMERIE ROYALE P.A. NORSTEDT & SÖNER, 1966).

>EVEN CONSTRAINED BY A TUXEDO AND ROYALTY, FEYNMAN REMAINED QUOTABLE.

THE PLEASURE OF FINDING THINGS OUT, EDITED BY JEFFREY ROBBINS (CAMBRIDGE, MA: HELIX BOOKS, 1999).

>THESE ESSAYS ARE ALL TERRIFIC, AS IS FREEMAN DYSON'S FOREWORD. READ THEM ALL, BUT IF YOU'RE SHORT ON TIME THE BEST ONES ARE "THE PLEASURE OF FINDING THINGS OUT," "THERE'S PLENTY OF ROOM AT THE BOTTOM," "THE SMARTEST MAN IN THE WORLD," "CARGO CULT SCIENCE," AND...AW, WHO AM I KIDDING? YOU SHOULD READ THEM ALL!

PERFECTLY REASONABLE DEVIATIONS FROM THE BEATEN TRACK (NY: BASIC BOOKS, 2005).

>BEFORE E-MAIL, PEOPLE WROTE LETTERS. AND IN 1968 RICHARD FEYNMAN STARTED DONATING HIS PERSONAL PAPERS TO THE CALTECH ARCHIVES. THANK GOODNESS. MICHELLE FEYNMAN EDITED THE COLLECTION AND ADDED COMMENTARY AS WELL AS MANY LOVELY PHOTOGRAPHS.

QED: THE STRANGE THEORY OF LIGHT AND MATTER (PRINCETON, NJ: PRINCETON UNIVERSITY PRESS, 1985).

>FEYNMAN WROTE THIS SPECIFICALLY FOR PEOPLE—LIKE ALIX MAUTNER—WITH NO BACKGROUND IN MATH OR PHYSICS. YOU CAN SEE FEYNMAN DELIVER EARLY VERSIONS OF THE LECTURES IN NEW ZEALAND THANKS TO THE VEGA SCIENCE TRUST: *HTTP://WWW.VEGA.ORG.UK/VIDEO/SUBSERIES/8/*.

PAULI & EINSTEIN

THE REASON FOR ANTIPARTICLES, FROM "ELEMENTARY PARTICLES AND THE LAWS OF PHYSICS: THE 1986 DIRAC MEMORIAL LECTURES" (ALEXANDRIA, VA: SCIENTIFIC CONSULTING SERVICES, 1997) AND *ELEMENTARY PARTICLES AND THE LAWS OF PHYSICS: THE 1986 DIRAC MEMORIAL LECTURES*, BY RICHARD FEYNMAN AND STEVEN WEINBERG (CAMBRIDGE: CAMBRIDGE UNIVERSITY PRESS, 1987).

> IN THIS VIDEO/BOOK PAIRING FEYNMAN'S VISUAL, AND PHYSICAL, LECTURE STYLE IS IN FULL FORCE DURING HIS DEMONSTRATION OF THE IMPORTANCE OF SPIN AND ROTATION IN PHYSICAL THEORIES.

SIX EASY PIECES: ESSENTIALS OF PHYSICS EXPLAINED BY ITS MOST BRILLIANT TEACHER (READING, MA: HELIX BOOKS, 1994) AND *SIX NOT-SO-EASY PIECES: EINSTEIN'S RELATIVITY, SYMMETRY, AND SPACE-TIME* (READING, MA: HELIX BOOKS, 1997).

> THOUGH THE SECOND BOOK MAY CHALLENGE YOU WITH ITS COMPLEX IDEAS, BOTH ARE STILL A WHOLE LOT OF FUN! I RECOMMEND THE AUDIO VERSIONS TO GET THE FULL FLAVOR OF FEYNMAN'S STYLE.

I ALSO RECOMMEND THE FOLLOWING SECONDARY SOURCES, MANY BY PEOPLE WHO KNEW FEYNMAN WELL:

THE BEAT OF A DIFFERENT DRUM: THE LIFE AND SCIENCE OF RICHARD FEYNMAN, BY JAGDISH MEHRA (OXFORD: OXFORD UNIVERSITY PRESS, 1994).

PLENTY OF PHYSICS, AND MATHEMATICAL PHYSICS AT THAT, BUT THIS IS STILL MY FAVORITE BIOGRAPHY OF FEYNMAN BOTH BECAUSE OF ITS COMPLETENESS AND THE OBVIOUS CARE MEHRA TOOK IN INTERVIEWING FEYNMAN AND WEAVING TOGETHER THE WHOLE OF HIS LIFE.

THE BEST MIND SINCE EINSTEIN, PRODUCED BY CHRISTOPHER SYKES AND MELANIE WALLACE (BOSTON: WGBH/PBS/NOVA SERIES, ORIGINALLY BROADCAST DECEMBER 21, 1993).

A TERRIFIC OVERVIEW OF FEYNMAN'S LIFE AND CAREER IN SCIENCE. WATCH THIS IF YOU CAN'T GET HOLD OF *NO ORDINARY GENIUS* (SEE PAGE 259), SINCE THIS IS A CONDENSED VERSION OF THAT PROGRAM.

CLIMBING THE MOUNTAIN: THE SCIENTIFIC BIOGRAPHY OF JULIAN SCHWINGER, BY JAGDISH MEHRA AND KIMBALL A. MILTON (OXFORD: OXFORD UNIVERSITY PRESS, 2000).

AN EXCELLENT COMPANION TO MEHRA'S *THE BEAT OF A DIFFERENT DRUM*.

DISTURBING THE UNIVERSE, BY FREEMAN DYSON (NY: HARPER AND ROW, 1979).

DYSON'S COMPARISON OF FEYNMAN TO JOF THE JUGGLER WILL STRIKE A CHORD WITH YOU. READ THE WHOLE BOOK, THOUGH. IT'S TERRIFIC.

FEYNMAN'S RAINBOW: A SEARCH FOR BEAUTY IN PHYSICS AND IN LIFE, BY LEONARD MLODINOW (NY: WARNER BOOKS, 2003).

SLIM AND SLIGHT, BUT I ENJOYED READING ABOUT MLODINOW'S BRIEF, PERSONAL, AND ALMOST INCIDENTAL ENCOUNTERS WITH FEYNMAN. I MARKED A NUMBER OF QUOTES AS I READ IT, BUT DIDN'T END UP USING THEM FOR THIS STORY. IT'S THAT KIND OF BOOK.

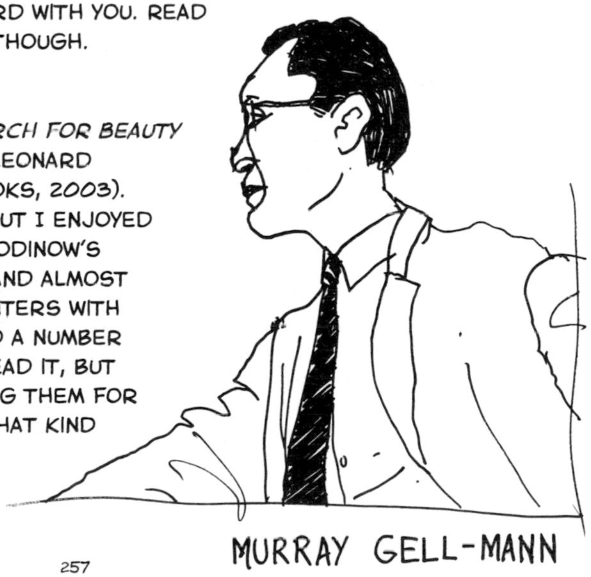
MURRAY GELL-MANN

FROM EROS TO GAIA, BY FREEMAN DYSON (NY: PENGUIN BOOKS, 1992).
GREAT THROUGHOUT, BUT DYSON'S FIRST-PERSON
RECOLLECTIONS OF FEYNMAN'S DISCOVERY OF QED
AND THE ROAD TRIP THAT RESULTED IN DYSON HIMSELF
BECOMING THE TRANSLATOR OF FEYNMAN'S IDIOSYNCRATIC
THEORY TO THE REST OF THE PHYSICS COMMUNITY MAKE IT
INDISPENSABLE.

FUN TO IMAGINE, PRODUCED BY CHRISTOPHER SYKES (BBC2,
ORIGINALLY BROADCAST IN 1983).
SNIPPETS OF PHYSICS AS VIEWED THROUGH THE FEYNMAN
LENS. THEY'RE QUICK AND A LOT OF FUN.

GENIUS: THE LIFE AND SCIENCE OF RICHARD FEYNMAN, BY JAMES
GLEICK (NY: PANTHEON, 1992).
THIS RIVALS MEHRA'S BOOK, BUT WITH LESS DEPTH IN THE
PHYSICS. IT'S STILL WORTH READING, BUT I DIDN'T FIND
MYSELF CONSULTING IT DURING THE PRODUCTION OF THIS
BOOK.

JULIAN SCHWINGER: THE PHYSICIST, THE TEACHER, AND THE MAN,
EDITED BY Y. JACK NG (NJ: WORLD SCIENTIFIC, 1996).
SCHWINGER, THOUGH FAR LESS FAMOUS THAN HIS
COUNTERPART, IS REMEMBERED JUST AS FONDLY BY THOSE
WHO KNEW HIM.

THE LAST JOURNEY OF A GENIUS/THE QUEST FOR TANNU TUVA,
PRODUCED BY CHRISTOPHER SYKES (BBC2 HORIZON SPECIAL/WGBH/
PBS/NOVA, ORIGINALLY BROADCAST JANUARY 24, 1989).
THE STORY OF FEYNMAN AND RALPH LEIGHTON'S EFFORTS
TO GET TO TUVA, WITH MANY ADVENTURES—INCLUDING THE
CHALLENGER INVESTIGATION—ALONG THE WAY. MOVING, SAD,
AND INSPIRING.

"MOST OF THE GOOD STUFF": MEMORIES OF RICHARD FEYNMAN,
EDITED BY LAURIE M. BROWN AND JOHN S. RIGDEN (NY: AMERICAN
INSTITUTE OF PHYSICS, 1993).
MISTITLED: THIS IS *GREAT* STUFF, INCLUDING DANNY HILLIS'
STORIES OF KNOWING, WORKING WITH, AND BEFRIENDING
FEYNMAN. HILLIS CONTINUES TO DO INTERESTING WORK, WITH
THE CLOCK OF THE LONG NOW (*WWW.LONGNOW.ORG*) BEING
MY FAVORITE OF HIS MOST RECENT PROJECTS.

ROBERT OPPENHEIMER

NANO: THE EMERGING SCIENCE OF NANOTECHNOLOGY, BY ED REGIS
(BOSTON: LITTLE BROWN, 1995).

> REGIS IS AN ENGAGING WRITER, AND HIS ACCOUNT OF
> THE LEAD-UP AND IMMEDIATE AFTERMATH OF FEYNMAN'S
> "PLENTY OF ROOM AT THE BOTTOM" SPEECH GIVES YOU THE
> FLAVOR OF THE TIMES.

NO ORDINARY GENIUS, PRODUCED BY CHRISTOPHER SYKES (BBC,
ORIGINALLY BROADCAST JANUARY 24, 1993).

> THE BEST FEYNMAN OVERVIEW ON VIDEO THAT I CAN THINK
> OF, BAR NONE. IT AIRED IN THE U.S. AS *THE BEST MIND
> SINCE EINSTEIN,* BUT THE NOVA/PBS VERSION IS ONLY HALF
> AS LONG, MEANING IT'S ONLY HALF AS GOOD.

NO ORDINARY GENIUS: THE ILLUSTRATED RICHARD FEYNMAN, BY
CHRISTOPHER SYKES (NY: W.W. NORTON, 1994).

> THIS BOOK HAS MEMORIES FROM FEYNMAN'S COLLEAGUES,
> FAMILY, AND FRIENDS ALONG WITH GREAT ILLUSTRATIONS
> AND PHOTOGRAPHS. BASED ON THE VIDEO OF THE SAME
> NAME, IT'S ALSO WONDERFUL.

ARLINE

THE PLEASURE OF FINDING THINGS OUT, PRODUCED BY
CHRISTOPHER SYKES (BBC2 HORIZON/NOVA, ORIGINALLY
BROADCAST 1981).
> MORE FEYNMAN, LIVE, AND ALMOST AS GOOD AS *NO
> ORDINARY GENIUS*.

PHYSICS TODAY, FEBRUARY 1989.
> A SPECIAL ISSUE DEVOTED TO FEYNMAN, WITH ARTICLES BY
> FREEMAN DYSON, MURRAY GELL-MANN, DAVID GOODSTEIN,
> JULIAN SCHWINGER, JOHN WHEELER, AND OTHERS. IT
> CONTAINS MANY PERSONAL AND PROFESSIONAL MEMORIES.

*QED AND THE MEN WHO MADE IT: DYSON, FEYNMAN, SCHWINGER,
AND TOMONAGA*, BY SILVAN S. SCHWEBER (PRINCETON, NJ:
PRINCETON UNIVERSITY PRESS, 1994).
> THIS DETAILED ACCOUNT OF HOW THE PROBLEMS IN
> QED GOT SWEPT UNDER THE RUG SUCCESSFULLY, AS
> FEYNMAN PUT IT, IS WRITTEN FOR A TECHNICAL AUDIENCE.
> IT HAS MANY GREAT ANECDOTES AS WELL, THOUGH, AND
> EXAMPLES OF HOW FEYNMAN'S SPEAKING AND WRITING
> STYLE LED TO A GREATER UNDERSTANDING OF THE
> FUNDAMENTAL PHYSICS BEHIND THE PROBLEM.

RICHARD FEYNMAN: A LIFE IN SCIENCE, BY JOHN GRIBBIN AND MARY GRIBBIN (NY: DUTTON, 1997).
> BESIDE MEHRA'S BOOK, MY FAVORITE BIOGRAPHY OF FEYNMAN, SINCE IT GIVES GENERAL READERS JUST ENOUGH OF A TASTE OF HIS PHYSICS TO MAKE THEM WANT TO LEARN MORE.

SIN-ITIRO TOMONAGA: LIFE OF A JAPANESE PHYSICIST, EDITED BY MAKINOSUKE MATSUI AND HIROSHI EZAWA, TRANSLATED FROM THE JAPANESE BY CHERYL FUJIMOTO AND TAKAKO SANO (TOKYO: MYU, 1995).
> THE ONLY ENGLISH-LANGUAGE BOOK ABOUT TOMONAGA THAT I FOUND READILY ACCESSIBLE. FORTUNATELY, IT'S VERY GOOD!

TAKE THE WORLD FROM ANOTHER POINT OF VIEW (YORKSHIRE TELEVISION, INTERVIEW SEGMENTS BY SIMON WELFARE 1973).
> FEYNMAN, INTERVIEWED IN MILIBACK, HIGH IN THE YORKSHIRE PENNINES, WHILE ON HOLIDAY NEAR GWENETH'S HOME. MANY OF THE STORIES HERE SHOW UP IN OTHER PLACES, BUT THE TAP-TAP-TAP ANECDOTE—AS TOLD TO THE FAMED ASTRONOMER SIR FRED HOYLE—MADE TRACKING THIS ONE DOWN WORTHWHILE. YOU CAN READ A TRANSCRIPT AT *HTTP://CALTECHES.LIBRARY.CALTECH.EDU/35/2/POINTOFVIEW.HTM*

TUVA OR BUST, BY RALPH LEIGHTON (NY: W.W. NORTON, 1991).
> HOW FEYNMAN ALMOST GOT TO TUVA. THIS IS AN ADVENTURE STORY WITH A SAD ENDING—GWENETH FEYNMAN ALSO DIED BEFORE SHE COULD MAKE IT TO KYZYL—BUT READING IT WILL STILL MAKE YOU HAPPY.

* AND...THERE'S EVEN MORE. WE CALLED THIS BIBLIOGRAPHY "ALMOST COMPLETE" BECAUSE DOZENS OF OTHER BOOKS AND ARTICLES AND EVEN A FEW WEBSITES ALSO HELPED US BUILD A PICTURE OF THE CENTURY FEYNMAN RACED ACROSS ON HIS WAY TO BECOMING A LEGEND. IF YOU'D LIKE TO START DOWN THAT PATH, I RECOMMEND THE EXCELLENT *A TALE OF TWO CONTINENTS* BY ABRAHAM PAIS AND *THE MAKING OF THE ATOMIC BOMB* BY RICHARD RHODES, BOTH OF WHICH CAN PROVIDE YOU WITH BACKGROUND ON FEYNMAN'S ERA IN PHYSICS AND THE WORLD. AND IF YOU WANT AN EVEN MORE TECHNICAL OVERVIEW THAN YOU GOT FROM MEHRA'S BOOK, YOU CAN CONSULT THE MASSIVE *SELECTED PAPERS OF RICHARD FEYNMAN* (RIVER EDGE, NJ: WORLD SCIENTIFIC, 2000).

AND IN ADDITION TO THINGS YOU CAN EASILY GET AT LIBRARIES OR
BOOKSTORES OR ON THE WEB, WE ALSO INCORPORATED INFORMATION,
STORIES, AND MANY FACTS FROM UNPUBLISHED MATERIALS HELD
IN THE CALIFORNIA INSTITUTE OF TECHNOLOGY'S ARCHIVES. WE
OWE JUDITH GOODSTEIN AND HER STAFF OUR THANKS FOR THE
ASSISTANCE AND HOSPITALITY THEY PROVIDED DURING MY VISIT
THERE. THEY EVEN RECOMMENDED A FINE MOTEL, RIGHT ON ROUTE
66. (I DIDN'T BARBEQUE, THOUGH.) OUR FAVORITE FIND WAS THE
TRANSCRIPT FOR HIS 1965 "ADDRESS TO FAR ROCKAWAY HIGH SCHOOL
AUDIENCE." MUCH OF THE SEQUENCE SHOWING FEYNMAN IN HIGH
SCHOOL COMES FROM THIS SPEECH. EVEN IF CALTECH WASN'T SUCH
A LOVELY PLACE, AND EVEN IF THEIR STUDENT UNION DIDN'T OFFER
TERRIFIC VEGETARIAN PIZZA BY THE SLICE, I'D RECOMMEND A TRIP
JUST TO READ IT.

FINALLY, ON PAGE 178 WE PROMISED YOU THE STORY OF WHY TOMONAGA
MISSED THE NOBEL CEREMONY. SO, IN HIS OWN WORDS AS QUOTED
ON PAGE 271 OF *SIN-ITIRO TOMONAGA: LIFE OF A JAPANESE PHYSICIST*
(MATSUI, ED.):

> ALTHOUGH I SENT A LETTER SAYING THAT I WOULD
> BE "PLEASED TO ATTEND," I LOATHED THE THOUGHT
> OF GOING, THINKING THAT THE COLD WOULD BE
> SEVERE, AS THE CEREMONY WAS TO BE HELD IN
> DECEMBER, AND THAT THE INEVITABLE FORMALITIES
> WOULD BE TIRESOME.

AFTER AFTER I WAS NAMED A NOBEL PRIZE AWARDEE, MANY PEOPLE CAME TO VISIT, BRINGING LIQUOR. I HAD BARRELS OF IT. ONE DAY, MY FATHER'S YOUNGER BROTHER, WHO LOVED WHISKEY, HAPPENED TO STOP BY AND WE BOTH BEGAN DRINKING GLEEFULLY. WE DRANK A LITTLE TOO MUCH, AND THEN, SEIZING THE OPPORTUNITY THAT MY WIFE HAD GONE OUT SHOPPING, I ENTERED THE BATHROOM TO TAKE A BATH. THERE I SLIPPED AND FELL DOWN, BREAKING SIX OF MY RIBS...IT WAS A PIECE OF GOOD LUCK IN THAT UNHAPPY INCIDENT.

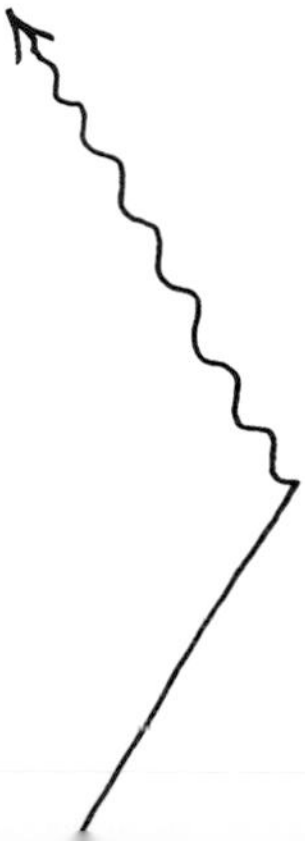

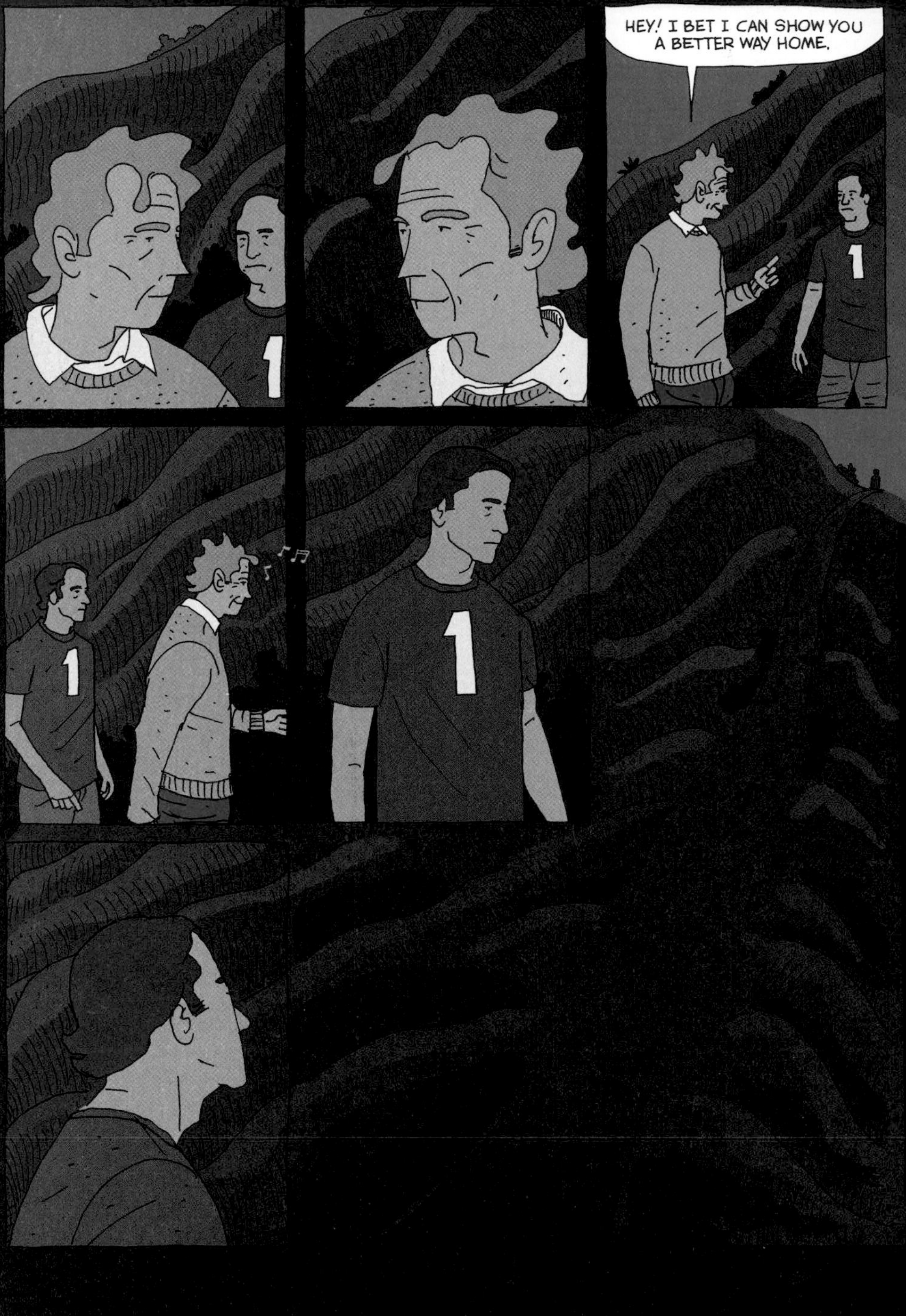
HEY! I BET I CAN SHOW YOU A BETTER WAY HOME.

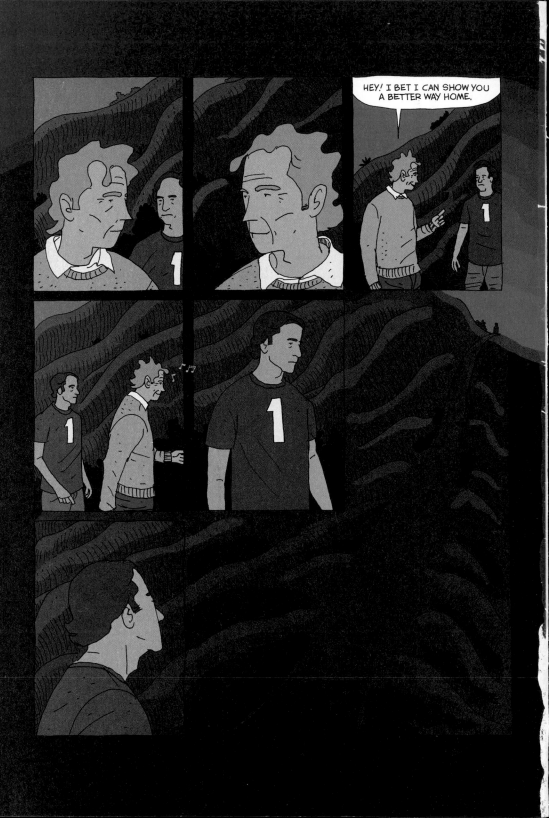